FOOLING UTOPIA

While recently I gazed with fascinated eyes at the tasteful decorations in your house, Busleyden, I wondered by what incantation you had charmed the fates so as to bring back so many ancient masters. For I think that only the hands of Daedalus could have built that famous house of yours with its artfully devised passages. The pictures there Apelles seems to have painted. The sculptures one might believe to be the work of Myron. When I looked upon the terra-cottas I thought them the product of Lysippus' art. The statues made me think of the master Praxiteles. Couplets identify every work of art, and such couplets as Vergil would have been glad to write, if he did not actually write them. Only the organ which produces varied tones by modulation is, I think, beyond the powers even of the ancients. And so your whole house is either an accomplishment of antiquity or a recent accomplishment such as to surpass antiquity. Well, may this new house be slow, may it be late, in growing old. And may the house in its old age still see its master, not even then grown old.

Thomas More to Hieronymus van Busleyden
on his splendid house in Mechelen

From *The Latin Epigrams of Thomas More*, English Translation by Leicester Bradner, University of Chicago Press, 1953.
First Published in the 1518 Basel Edition of Thomas More's *Utopia*.

CONTOUR 7

A MOVING IMAGE BIENNALE MECHELEN 2015

FOOLING UTOPIA

Preface

From its inception, CONTOUR has been committed to supporting artists' productions, ensuring high standards of curatorial practice and presentation, and showcasing stimulating, cutting-edge art made in moving image in the best possible light. This year is no exception. This, of course, would not have been possible without the dedicated artistic team who worked for the seventh edition of the Biennale; curator Nicola Setari has worked unflinchingly, with enthusiasm, care, and to the highest professional standards to put together this exhibition, the most ambitious CONTOUR to date. Special thanks must also go to Steven Op de Beeck, our committed director and Alyssa Decq, our tireless production manager, who ensured the exhibition looks as good as it does, together with the meticulous technical team, as well as Lola Daels and Laura Tack for their contribution to the production. Thanks also to Hannes Dereere, Studio Luc Derycke and Studio RGB who ensured the CONTOUR message gets out there in various shapes and forms. Video and film are among the most difficult art forms to install properly and we at CONTOUR pride ourselves on maintaining high standards of presentation. Special thanks must go to all our sponsors and partners, without whose support the scale of this exhibition would not be possible, and also to all the lenders. Last, but by no means least, warm thanks to all the artists who engaged in this project and shared with us their time, ideas, and work. Needless to say, without them there would be no CONTOUR.

Heidi De Nijn, chairman, Contour Mechelen vzw

In Search of a New Life[1]

Nicola Setari

Preamble

"Had we been master of such a servant, we would have rather lost the best city of our dominions than such a worthy councilor." Charles V upon receiving the news of Thomas More's execution in 1535

CONTOUR 7 is dedicated to Sir Thomas More, the European humanist and statesman, who died as a martyr. This focus has two motivations. The first is that his book *Utopia* transformed the literary genre of "mirrors for princes," guidebooks for rulers on how to govern properly, into a thought experiment about the ideal society. This experiment was so radical and deep that to this day it is quite difficult to decrypt the intentions of the man who conceived it and whether or not the society he imagined was actually ideal. In a way *Utopia* put an end to the genre of "mirrors for princes" because from the beginning this book questions the very possibility of good council to the powerful, including all the risks involved, as More's life would prove later on. Because of the book's ambivalence and constant playfulness and irony, while dealing with the most deadly serious matters, I believe it functions, when looked at in its integrity, as a mirror for artists. By this I mean that it is a piece of literature that can also be understood to function as a contemporary work of art, one of an exemplary kind, in particular when it comes to dealing with issues of politics. As such it perfectly fits a central concern of CONTOUR 7, which is devoted to the search for alternative ways of understanding the relationship between art and politics, in particular within the current European framework.

The second reason for this dedication is that Thomas More's life can be used as a "mirror for politicians," especially for today's politicians. I do not mean this to be the case regarding the actual content of his beliefs, but rather because of More's vast knowledge and his decision to place his conscience above everything else. The credibility and popularity of politicians have probably never been so low. In our post-ideological societies the economy has become the new god that dictates the political agenda, and it is rare to admire this or that politician for an act of conscience.[2] More instead used his humanist values as a constant reference in the policies he pursued and while he did make dramatic mistakes during his political career, such as the persecution of Protestant reformers, he also fought against the prevarications and appropriations of the English aristocracy, toward which he was always very critical.

At a deeper level, Utopia refers to the search for a better life, a search that we all share, wherever we come from and whatever we are doing. This on its own represents the best reason to dedicate CONTOUR 7 to More, the inventor of Utopia.

Two Concepts of Utopia and of History

In the opening pages of his essay *Utopistics or Historical Choices of the Twenty-first Century*,[3] the hugely referential American sociologist, Immanuel Wallerstein, writes what can be considered an attempted requiem for utopian visions:

> Utopia, as we know, is a word invented by Sir Thomas More, and it means literally "nowhere." The real problem, with all utopias of which I am aware, is not only that they have existed nowhere heretofore but that they seem to me, and to many others, dreams of heaven that could never exist on earth. Utopias have religious functions and they can also sometimes be mechanisms of political mobilization.
>
> But politically they tend to rebound. For utopias are breeders of illusions and therefore, inevitably, of disillusions. And utopias can be used, have been used, as justifications for terrible wrongs. The last thing we really need is still more utopian visions.[4]

Wallerstein proposes to replace these visions with what he calls Utopistics: "the serious assessment of historical alternatives, the exercise of our judgment as to the substantive rationality of alternative possible historical systems."[5]

The problem with Wallerstein's understanding of Utopias is that it not only fails to grasp that as works of literature and of art, they have a far greater complexity and applied intelligence in them than he gives them credit for. Perhaps more importantly, the purely rational assessment on which he claims his Utopistics to be focused will ultimately produce extremely dry and unimaginative conclusions based on a rather shallow anthropology that ignores humankind's profound need for the hope that comes with utopias. I would like to counter Wallerstein's understanding of Utopia with that of Ernst Bloch. Bloch was an unorthodox Marxist who wrote *The Spirit of Utopia* at the end of World War I. Rather than taking Utopia as a negative starting-point in the opening pages of his study, he formulated a negative diagnosis of Europe in his day and age:

> The Romanticism of the latest reaction has inherited absolutely nothing real, is neither objective nor enthusiastic nor universalistic, but simply stupid, [...] in its pathos of the "autochthonous" capable only of eliciting the decline of Western Civilization into animalistic insensibility and irreligious obliteration: faded bud, faded blossom, and for today just a civilized enervation, a large fleet, and merely the pessimistic registration of the continuing passage of history as the only goal, but for Europe only imminent, eternal death.[6]

Bloch referred to the nationalist and positivist perspectives on the socio-political realities that had gained considerable ground in European societies at the turn of the twentieth century. These views have regained a wide following at the turn of the 21st century.

The following quotation explains Bloch's positive concept of Utopia:

> May a new expanse appear, the world of the soul, the external, cosmic function
> of utopia, maintained against misery, death, the husk realm of mere physical
> nature. Only in us does this light still burn, and we are beginning a fantastic
> journey toward it, a journey toward the interpretation of our waking dream,
> toward the implementation of the central concept of utopia. To find it, to find
> the right thing, for which it is worthy to live, to be organized, and to have time:
> that is why we go, why we cut new, metaphysically constitutive paths, summon
> what is not, build into the blue, and build ourselves into the blue, and there
> seek the true, the real, where the merely factual disappears—incipit vita nova.[7]

As Bloch suggests, Utopia is the search for a new life. His book is exemplary in tracing the spirit of Utopia throughout the history of art and architecture, anchoring the role of art in society, while underscoring the constant struggle of artists to live up to their utopian visions.

For CONTOUR 7 we could not afford nor did we want to retrace the entire history of Utopia in modern art or even just in lens-based media, and instead we have decided to work with an extraordinary group of artists, who, in the majority of cases, have made new works for the exhibition expanding the reflection on and expression of Utopia in unexpected ways. We also decided to show Utopia's literary history in a library that, together with the advisors[8] to the Biennale, we chose to dub the Fooling Utopia Library.[9] At the same time, CONTOUR 7 does propose to take a historical dive and have another look at More and his age. This proposal should not be understood as an effort to provide an accurate chronology or insight into that era, a task for traditional historians and scholars of the Renaissance, of which I am neither, nor is it celebration of a historical figure. Instead it seeks to reveal the kind of links that Walter Benjamin formulated in his *On the Concept of History*:

> Historicism contents itself with establishing a causal nexus of various moments
> of history. But no state of affairs is, as a cause, already a historical one. It
> becomes this, posthumously, through eventualities which may be separated from
> it by millennia. The historian, who starts from this, ceases to permit the conse-
> quences of eventualities to run through the fingers like the beads of a rosary. He
> records the constellation in which his own epoch comes into contact with that
> of an earlier one. He thereby establishes a concept of the present as that of the
> here-and-now, in which splinters of messianic time are shot through.[10]

As Bruno Latour has pointed out in his Manifesto on Compositionism,[11] the historical epoch we find ourselves coming into contact with when trying to escape the dualisms of modernity and to recompose the divisions of the twentieth century is the sixteenth century. More and his Humanist circle, their engagement with the Latin literary tradition of *serio ludere*, serious play, revised for the problems of their time, offer an interesting context to begin to "establish a concept of the present," of the contemporary, which can be relevant for our time. More's *Utopia*, with its multiple layers of reading, interplay between fiction and facts, and game of mirrors in its narrative structure, represents a reference to the kind of politically engaged art and literature that it is worth spending time with.

The city of Mechelen bears many traces of its golden era during the 16th century, when it was the capital of the Low Countries, and therefore this city is ideally situated for this exercise in establishing a link with that epoch. The venues of CONTOUR 7 also link up other moments and contexts in the history of Mechelen, from its strongly religious heritage, the former monasteries which now house the Cultural Centre of the city and the social organization Emmaus in De Noker, to its Renaissance secular history in Hof van Busleyden and De Vlietenkelder, and finally the city's dystopian period during the Nazi occupation in World War II, which is historicized in the new museum of Kazerne Dossin. These locations as well as local legends, such as the one surrounding the monstruous water demon De Nekker, constitute the backdrop for the underlying theme of CONTOUR 7, Monsters, Martyrs and Media. A good example is *The Shores of an Island I only Skirted*, the work by Sander Breure and Witte Van Heulzen presented in Kazerne Dossin, which invites the visitor to reflect on the tragedy that occurred on the island of Utøya in Norway, where ultra-nationalist, right-wing fanatic Anders Breivik[12] killed 69 young representatives of the Labor Party, in combination with the ongoing efforts of migrants or refugees to reach the shores of safer lands. Or with the last work in the "parcours" of CONTOUR 7, *The Nekker Tree* by Angel Vergara in the garden of De Noker, where in the 16th century the Alexian order took care of the city's mentally ill. The title of the work refers to the many places in the city that are named after De Nekker, a creature known for abducting adults and children throughout Mechelen's history. Vergara's video installation integrates paradisiacal visions of the tree in the courtyard with brushstrokes that produce strange and disquieting creatures. This work captures the oscillation between visions of Utopia and of dystopia, with its monsters and martyrs, that are at the heart of CONTOUR 7.[13]

This is not the first exhibition to address Utopia as a theme. There have been many in recent years. The Whitechapel in London, for example, organized one entitled *The Spirit of Utopia*, a title borrowed from Ernst Bloch's book. Another major show was Utopia Station,[14] which was part of the 50th Venice Art Biennale in 2003. What distinguishes CONTOUR 7 is the possibility to stage part of the exhibition in the actual place where More's book found a fundamental source of inspiration and where he probably wrote a major part of it. What follows is a short account of the trip that led him there and the circumstances under which he wrote *Utopia*, which serve as a reference for CONTOUR 7.

More's Voyage to Utopia

Credit for the invention of the word "Utopia" goes to Thomas More, who introduced it in his book on *The Best State of a Commonwealth and the New Island of Utopia*, which is *Utopia*'s complete title. It was written in Latin and first published in Leuven in 1516. The book was mostly drafted during More's five-month stay in Flanders in 1515 and was finished in London upon his return.

I like to believe that it was sunny when More landed in Bruges on May 18, 1515 for his long diplomatic mission in Flanders. At the time he crossed the English Channel his life was on a threshold and European history was at a turning point. Bruges had already begun to lose much of its power because the Zwin Channel had just a few years before dried up entirely, but it was still the city an English ambassador would travel to if he needed to meet with his counterparts from the Low Countries, the capital of which was Mechelen. At the time of his landing, More, age 37, was very proficient in Latin and Greek, but had little, if any, diplomatic experience. It probably wasn't very clear to him what to expect and he certainly did not imagine he would be staying in Flanders for over five months. This mission on behalf of King Henri VIII was led by Cuthbert Tunstall, a prominent political figure of the time and later the bishop of London.

In Bruges, together with the other envoys from England they met with those of the young Prince Charles who, a few years later, would become Holy Roman Emperor at the death of his grandfather Maximilian I. The goal of the embassy was to settle the disputes that had arisen among merchants trading wool. Margaret of Austria, a famous resident of Mechelen and aunt and tutor of Prince Charles, had managed in 1507 to make a commerce treaty that was much more favorable to the Flemish cloth industry than to the English. Henri VIII did not like to respect his commitments to women, as history later would confirm, so a new balance needed to be found.

While in Bruges, More met his dear friend Erasmus, who must have insisted that as soon as he could get away from his entangled diplomatic mission, More should go to Antwerp and Mechelen, where he had better chances of satisfying his humanist appetites, thanks to his friends Peter Gillis and Hieronymus van Busleyden.

By July 21, 1515, the negotiations in Bruges had come to a stall and More and the other envoys were able to leave until further adjournment. Sure enough More followed Erasmus's instructions and first stayed with Gillis in Antwerp and later with Busleyden in Mechelen, in his magnificent palace, filled with art and antiquities. More actually dedicated several poems to Busleyden and his home,[15] and he also wrote about also in a letter to Erasmus.[16]

More was a relatively free man during this time because he had not yet joined the court of Henri VIII. Unlike many other of his contemporaries, he was reluctant to enter into the grace of the sovereign, well aware of the dangers this could lead to and, most importantly, of the restrictions on his personal freedom this would bring.

The first of *Utopia*'s two books addresses the question of whether it is opportune for a man of letters to become a king's councilor. To give a sense of the paradoxical situation More was caught in, there is a memorable passage in *Utopia* that is worth quoting. An English cardinal asks what is the main cause that makes thievery necessary, and Raphael Hythloday, the fictional Portuguese navigator who discovered the island of Utopia, replies: "Your sheep, which are usually so tame and so cheaply fed, begin now, according to report, to be so greedy and wild that they devour human beings themselves and devastate and depopulate fields, houses and towns." This is a very playful and poignant image to criticize the English aristocracy, which was transforming agricultural land into pasture to increase their profits through the wool trade.

The man writing these words, albeit putting them in the mouth of a fictional character, was the same one fighting for the English wool industry's interests in Bruges. He must have felt the tension and the moral dilemma quite deeply. The irony and satire that make *Utopia* such a complex book to grasp is also the product of this tension. More did not believe such a perfect society could be realized entirely, nor did he want it to happen as he knew it would come with its own restrictions on freedom, but he was convinced it would stand as a lasting provocation and counter-narrative to the one of conquest, conflict, and war that prevailed in European nations.

Around the time More arrived in Flanders another great humanist, Niccolò Machiavelli, was trying to give advice to kings in *The Prince*.[17] The book was the expression of the author's desperate efforts to regain the favors of the Medici family, after having suffered political humiliation in his beloved Florence and having been forced to retire to the countryside. The two eminent representatives of the Italian and English Renaissance never met, nor is there any evidence that their works inspired each other, but the parallels between their human and literary trajectories have attracted the interest of many scholars. The Machiavellian school of politics can be seen as the opposite of the Utopian school and perhaps is the one winning the battle in present-day Europe. Nevertheless, one should not forget that Machiavelli also had a very refined sense of humor. His *The Prince* is also a classical example of the genre "mirrors for princes."

More's intention was to terminate his services to the crown after his diplomatic mission to Flanders, and in fact upon his return to England, in late October, he refused the pension the king offered to him. By the end of the following year, around the time *Utopia* was in print, he was so often at court and so frequently asked to entertain and advise the sovereign that he felt like he had become his fool. He was, in fact, writing to his friends that he had to find a way to make himself less likeable to the king.

More did not embrace the radical mode of living of the Utopians, the inhabitants of his island; on the contrary, he made his political career through many compromises. Even in *Utopia*, written before he entered court, More, or, rather, his fictional character, discusses with Hythloday the costumes of this mysterious people in the New World, and they disagree on a number of important points, including the abolition of private property.

More devised Utopia in order to be able to deal with the reality that surrounded him. From the moment he returned from Flanders, he embarked on a sustained effort to improve English and European society. He accepted playing the king's fool as an advisor and, as long as this did not drive him insane or interfere with his ethics, allowing him to push social reform. Together with his friend Erasmus he embraced the idea that a certain degree of folly and satire was absolutely necessary to remain sane, especially in troubled political times. As we know, his life reached a tragic end when Henri VIII sentenced him to death for high treason. The humanist More had somehow anticipated this fate in the first book of *Utopia*, where Raphael Hythloday, the fictional navigator who discovered the island of Utopia, suggests that survival at court is only possible by compromising your own moral standards.

There is still much debate among scholars on why More decided to locate the island of Utopia in the Americas, a choice in stark contrast with the idea of the superiority of European civilizations. He was certainly fascinated by the reports on the recently discovered continent and the opportunities it offered. That he linked his narrative about the island to the travels of Amerigo Vespucci in the New World is highly significant and is reflected in several customs of his utopians. Over a decade before the appearance of More's *Utopia*, Vespucci published letters[18] in which he described the customs of the people he encountered during his voyages, portraying them as living in the state of nature, with hardly any form of civil organization. More consciously subverted Vespucci's perspective in this regard, which at the time already sounded like a legitimization of the Spanish and Portuguese appropriation of land and resources on the newly found continent.

Strikingly, when drawing a connection between these two narratives, More only pretended he wanted to make readers believe in the true existence of *Utopia*, while Vespucci, whose voyages cannot all be accounted for according to historians, wanted his readers to believe in the facts he gave on the peoples he encountered. But we know that they did not live in the conditions he described, and, more importantly, he failed completely to understand they also had advanced cultural systems.[19]

Erasmus, More and Fools

Ulrich von Hutton was one of the authors of the *Letters of Obscure Men*, a brilliant collection of satirical letters, which first appeared in 1515 (in Latin). Both More and Erasmus were familiar with them and their fictional character most likely provided a source of inspiration for the letters that accompany More's *Utopia*. They were written in support of Johann Reuchlin, a German humanist, and they mock the doctrines and modes of living of the scholastics and monks, mainly by pretending to be letters from fanatic Christian theologians arguing about whether or not all Jewish books should be burned. Reuchlin and Erasmus were strong believers in the need to study Hebrew in European universities, while the scholastics were against this and had managed to convince Emperor Maximilian I to make a decree establishing that all copies of the Torah had to be burnt. Fortunately, the decree was shortly after revoked. In 1516, Erasmus convinced Hieronymus van Busleyden to finance the first *collegium trilingue* in Leuven, where the study of Hebrew was promoted. This would be Busleyden's greatest achievement shortly before his premature death.[20] Von Hutton wrote to Erasmus in 1519 asking him to describe Thomas More, a man he greatly admired but never met. In his reply letter, Erasmus portrayed his friend with great enthusiasm, giving us details about his food habits, his love for animals, and his conviction that the same education should be accessible to men and women. Erasmus writes about More that, among other things, he enjoyed being an actor in his youth and liked the company of jesters:

> When a youth he both wrote and acted some small comedies. If a retort is made against himself, even without ground, he likes it from the pleasure he finds in witty repartees. Hence he amused himself with composing epigrams when a young man, and enjoyed Lucian above all writers. Indeed, it was he who pushed me to write the "Praise of Folly," that is to say, he made a camel frisk. [...] In human affairs there is nothing from which he does not extract enjoyment, even from things that are most serious. If he converses with the learned and judicious, he delights in their talent; if with the ignorant and foolish, he enjoys their stupidity. He is not even offended by professional jesters. With a wonderful dexterity he accommodates himself to every disposition. As a rule, in talking with women, even with his own wife, he is full of jokes and banter.

Ten years after this letter was written and while in Basel, Erasmus received from the hands of Hans Holbein (and as a gift from More) a sketch of More's family that the artist had drawn during his stay in London between 1526–1528. In this sketch, dated 1527, Holbein portrays More and his family at the apex of his political career as Lord Chancellor of England. More's father, wife, daughters, and son are all present, but there is another figure as well, Henry Patenson, More's fool.[21] Patenson, was called master Harry in the family circle. In both the sketch and the reproduced painting he is dressed in elegant attire, rather than wearing the jester's traditional dress. Many interpreters of the painting have pointed at the resemblance of More's fool with King Henry VIII, both in pose and clothing. King Harry, as his friends were allowed to call him, enrolled More among his councilors in 1516, not without difficulties, as we read in Erasmus's letter, and this opened the door to a political career that in seven years led him to become Lord Chancellor, the highest political office in England at the time. In his painting of the More household, Holbein seems to have intentionally wanted to express More's need to reverse his relationship with King Harry—a relationship that, as he probably felt, put him in the position of the fool—by making his family fool dress like the king instead.[22]

We don't know when exactly More hired Patenson to be his family's fool, but such a figure was quite common in affluent English households in the 16th century. The fool's role was to provide entertainment by making jokes and performing scenes that might provide light forms of catharsis at the end of a day's work. For a moment, the fool suspended the hierarchy of relations in a family or at a court, and he was allowed to say things that no one else was. King Henry VIII also had a jester, Will Somers, one of the few members of his court who survived various periods of Henry's tumultuous life and accompanied him to his grave as opposed to being sent to it by Henry, which, as we know, sadly occurred to More and many others of Henry's political advisors. Another example is More's enemy at the time, Thomas Cromwell, who succeeded him to the position of Lord Chancellor after having been one of his main prosecutors during his trial. Fools or jesters have existed at least since ancient Egypt and were common not just in Europe, but also among the Aztec people in the 14th to the 16th century.

There is no evidence that Patenson was with More during his first diplomatic mission to Flanders in 1515, while he did travel with him on several other occasions. In *Utopia* there are repeated references to the figure of the fool, just as in Erasmus's *In Praise of Folly*. Probably the clearest evidence of the importance of fools in *Utopia* lies in the very name of the fictional navigator that discovered it: Raphael Hythloday, which is a word game that means "peddler of nonsense." Many commentators on *Utopia* believed that Raphael was Erasmus in disguise. For a more in-depth reflection on this interpretation, see Hilde Van Gelder's essay in the catalog and her reference to the works of Chiara Fumai and A Dog Republic in CONTOUR 7.

The Biennale's motto, Fooling Utopia, aims to capture not just the ways in which More's books and other Utopias fool us as to their intentions; this motto was also chosen to express how More and along with him all socially engaged creative practices have to fool their Utopias in order to deal with the realities of the world. To fool one's own Utopia means to accept having to find points of mediation with particular, given circumstances, as well as occasionally having to play the fool in them.

More, Shakespeare and the Wretched Strangers

Thomas More:
Imagine that you see the wretched strangers,
Their babies at their backs and their poor luggage,
Plodding to th' ports and costs for transportation,
And that you sit as kings in your desires,
Authority quite silent by your brawl,
And you in ruff of your opinions clothed;
What had you got? I'll tell you: you had taught
How insolence and strong hand should prevail,
How order should be quelled; and by this pattern

Evil May Day is the name given to a riot against foreigners that took place in London in May 1517. An angry mob of over a thousand young men headed to Saint Martin's Le Grand, a neighborhood where numerous foreigners lived. There they found Thomas More, at the time deputy-sheriff of London, awaiting them. He managed to calm down the mob by delivering a speech in defense of foreigners and obedience to the rule of law. The mob was later dispersed by the soldiers of King Henry VIII and the few arrested and sentenced to death were pardoned thanks to the intervention of Queen Catherine of Aragon, also a foreigner in England. These events took place several months after More had received the first copies of his *Utopia*.

The above quotation is a poetic version of More's speech during the Evil May Day events. It is easy to associate these verses with the images of refugees "plodding to the ports" to seek asylum from wars and "ravenous fishes" in today's media. There is no getting used to these images, even if they continue to recur throughout history and at the present time on a daily basis. On the contrary, the urgency they suggest underscores that no one can ignore them anymore, no one "can sit as kings in *their* desires." But how can art make sense of these images, of the lost lives of people in search of a better life? Of people on the run who view Europe as Utopia and that we, as residents, so often despise or protect like a fortress. To still reflect on Utopia means to ponder the overlaps and intersections between these incommensurable life systems. To insist upon this reflection and relate it to the question of whom today is the martyr and whom the monster, as CONTOUR 7 attempts, is hardly a purely intellectual exercise. On the contrary, it is an effort to distill our affects and beliefs and instill some sense of hope and orientation. An art exhibition can only have humble ambitions, but through the artworks and the curatorial research it can connect to a wealth of experience and knowledge in such a way—when properly attuned to the questions everyone is asking in the present—that a real difference is made.

A last example I want to bring in is my personal discovery of the fact that William Shakespeare's authorship of his plays finds its confirmation in probably one of his least known, *Sir Thomas More*. The quoted passage is taken from this Elizabethan play, of which the credited authors are the playwrights Anthony Monday, Henry Chettle, and William Shakespeare. Scholars have identified Shakespeare's handwriting in three pages of the original manuscript by comparing them with the signature in his will. These are the only lines from any of Shakespeare's plays of which we have a trace of his writing. There is actually only one copy of the original manuscript and it can be found at the British Library in London.[24]

It is probably a result of the irony of history that the scene of the play dedicated to More's calming of the angry mob is the one that Shakespeare wrote himself. This tie between the life and fictional work of the two men is uncanny and transcends the fact that More's influence on Shakespeare is well known.[25] It speaks instead of the kind of weaving together of fact and fiction that is vital to art.

Shakespeare seems to grasp More's spirit by making him pronounce a speech, in which More basically proposes to the mob a dystopian thought experiment to dissuade them from forcing the foreigners into exile. If the mob obtains what it wants by sheer violence, it will give others the perception that they can also obtain what they want by force and this will lead to a situation where everyone is a threat to anyone. *Homo homini lupus*, man is a wolf to other men, to evoke the proverb dear to Hobbes in his *Leviathan*.

More than a century after More's *Utopia*, Hobbes used this image to explain the condition of men outside of the State. The problem is that for More this is the condition of men within the State when it is not wisely governed. More did not embrace the kind of competitive and self-interest-driven anthropology underlying the proverb, but in his *Utopia*, even "sheep feed on men," if no one controls the powerful. While the first accounts of explorers from the Americas were busy persuading Europeans of the uncivilized and cannibalistic practices of the peoples of the newly found continent and justifying the occupation of those lands, More in fact provided a social critique of how the aristocracy in England and in Europe was feeding on the poor by converting agricultural land into pasture through the practice of enclosures. He thus expressed his commitment and solidarity with the rights of the "wretched strangers," as the passage from Shakespeare's play bears witness. Both defenses of the weaker or more marginalized members of society reflect his most lasting legacy, also for our times.

A Final Note on the Vortex
(the Campaign Image of CONTOUR 7)

"Descent into the Maelstrom" is a short story by Edgar Allan Poe that takes place in Norway near the Lofoten islands, the site of one of the world's strongest maelstroms. The central moment in the story is when the fishing boat of two unfortunate brothers is being sucked into this gigantic water vortex during a storm. The older brother is completely paralyzed by the fear of death, while the younger marvels at the spectacle of the vortex and at the realization that fate has set aside a grandiose death for him. This thought makes him more attentive to what is happening around him and he realizes that chunks of wood, instead of being sucked into the maelstrom, are progressively moving outwards and away from it. So he tries to convince his older brother to jump with him, but after failing to get his attention he jumps alone clinging to one of the chunks. This saves his life, while his brother tragically drowns.

While imagining CONTOUR 7, with its monsters, martyrs, fools and Utopias all caught in the vortex of media, this story of Poe gave me hope. Our gaze represents a crucial weapon when it comes to dealing with the vicissitudes of life. Depending on what we fix it on, it will help us find our way through the vortex.

CONTOUR 7 is located at the crossroads where life, history, and fiction collide, with the intensity necessary to bring about a break-through in the real world.

Notes

1 I owe my first real encounter with Utopia to a special issue of *Janus Magazine* for the exhibition *Utopia Station* at the 50th Venice Art Biennale in 2003. The title of that issue was "In Search of Utopia" and it was borrowed from an artwork by Jan Fabre. "Thinking Models" for the monumental sculpture that Fabre made for the 2003 edition of Beaufort are presented in CONTOUR 7, as well as a film by him, in which he pays homage to Thomas More. The sculpture features Fabre riding a gigantic turtle into the sea. The title of my contribution for the special issue of *Janus* was *Utopia and Irony*.

My special thanks for reading and commenting on this essay and many others I have written goes to Charlotte Bonduel, my wife. We first got together in that very hot summer in Venice.

2 As I write these words Angela Merkel, whose credibility was below zero in recent months because of her intransigence vis-à-vis Greece's risk of default and ongoing social crisis, has apparently declared that Germany will put no limits to the number of political refugees it will welcome. One wonders if this could be a sign of a change of the tide.

3 I. Wallerstein, *Utopics or Historical Choices of the Twenty-first Century*, The New Press, New York, 1998.

4 Ibidem, Ivi 1.

5 Ibidem.

6 E. Bloch, *The Spirit of Utopia*, Stanford University Press, Stanford, 2000, 2.

7 Ibidem, Ivi 3.

8 Chus Martìnez, W. J. T. Mitchell, and Hilde Van Gelder served as advisors for CONTOUR 7, and I am most grateful for their ideas and work for the Biennale. I would also like to thank Steven Op de Beeck, the director of Contour, and the amazing team that has made the biennale possible.

9 The reason for this name will become more clear in the course of my argument, but for now it is sufficient to point out that it tries to convey the sense that Utopias always fool us as to their true intentions.

10 W. Benjamin, "On the Concept of History," in *Selected Writings* vol. 4, edited by Howard Eiland and Michael W. Jennings, Harvard University Press, Boston, 2006, 397.

11 B. Latour, "An Attempt at a Compositionist Manifesto," in *New Literary History*, vol. 41, nr. 3, Summer 2010.

12 In a YouTube video posted six hours before his attack, which also involved government buildings in Oslo, he made a call to embrace "martyrdom."

13 I will not refer to other works in the exhibition in the course of this essay, since for each there is a separate text presenting it in the catalog.

14 The catalog of this exhibition featured a long conversation between the curators and Immanuel Wallerstein, who just a few years earlier had published his *Utopistics*.

15 One of which appears in this catalog.

16 See the timeline of the conception and production of *Utopia* later in this catalog.

17 N. Machiavelli, *The Prince* (1513–1532), translated by Luigi Ricci, Oxford University Press, London, 1921.

18 A. Vespucci, *Mundus Novus* (1503), translated by George Tyler Northup, Princeton University Press, 1916; and A. Vespucci, *Letter to Soderini* (1504).

19 The Mexican artist Maria Thereza Alves pointed out to me in an email correspondence, which took place while I was writing this text, that More's *Utopia* expresses ideas that were later used to justify the colonization of land of indigenous peoples in the Americas. According to this perspective, More's view of the non-Utopian populations in the Americas stressed their inferiority compared to those of European nations. She also referred to the recent PhD dissertation "Unsettling Hope: Settler Colonialism and Utopianism" by Karl Joseph Hardy, which puts forward these arguments in a very strong and persuasive manner. Personally, I disagree with them on the grounds that the book cannot be reduced to being a conceptual toolbox for settler colonialism and that it contains many passages, in which More stresses the high degree of civilization in the Americas and is mainly concerned with using this anti-Eurocentric perspective to criticize the Europe of his age. Most importantly, there is no incontrovertible evidence in the book that the Utopians originated from Europe. Here is a link to the dissertation: https://qspace.library. queensu.ca/bitstream/1974/13154/1/Hardy_Karl_J_06095600_PhD.pdf

20 For more information about Busleyden, see
    H. De Vocht, *Jerome de Busleyden: founder of
    the Louvain, collegium trilingue: his life and
    writings*, Brepols, Turnhout, 1950.

21 The original painting seems to be lost, but the
    sketch still exists. More played a decisive role in
    securing commissions for Holbein in the circle
    of his friends during his first stay in London.
    Holbein had been recommended to More by his
    good friend Erasmus, who had met Holbein in
    Basel in 1518 and secured woodcuts by him and
    his brother for the third edition of Utopia that
    appeared that year.

22 For more about Patenson and his relationship
    to More's family, see: N. Hall, "Henry Patenson—
    Thomas More's Fool," in *Moreana*, v. 27,
    101–102, May 1990, 75–86.

23 W. Shakespeare, *Sir Thomas More*, edited by
    John Jowett, Methuen Drama, A and C Black
    Publishers LTD, London, 2011.

24 In Protestant England to conceive such a play
    was less than obvious, as demonstrated by the
    heavy hand of the official censurer at the time,
    the master of the revels, who deleted parts of
    the play and re-wrote others: a process that can
    be observed on the original manuscript.

25 Shakespeare's play *Richard III* is indebted to
    More's biography of the last king of the House
    of York. More wrote it to provide an example
    of a tyrannical sovereign whose footsteps King
    Henry VIII should strive to not follow.

Conversation between Chus Martìnez, W. J. T. Mitchell, Nicola Setari and Hilde Van Gelder

03.06.2015 – Paris

NICOLA SETARI (NS) "Fooling Utopia" is the motto of CONTOUR 7. I would like our conversation to further reflect on this motto as it invites us to think about the relationship between foolishness, madness and utopia. I also shared with you via email in advance of our conversation this work by Gilberto Zorio that he made in 1971, more than forty years ago. The title is "E' utopia, la realtà, è rivelazione." Reality is utopia, is revelation. I was curious about your own comments on the work, how it inspires you, if it does.

W. J. T. MITCHELL (WJTM) I immediately turned it into a Hegelian series of terms: the thesis is utopia, the antithesis is reality and the moment of their encounter is revelatìon.
I could unfold the logic behind that, but the idea of revelation is something new coming into the world, a new idea has provoked a transformation of reality and become a way to construe it. Or, since I think utopia always implies its opposite to begin with and that opposite is not so much reality as it is dystopia. You can see already in More's *Utopia* that within Utopia there is this dark implication that if we got the utopia that More wants, it wouldn't be all that we hope for. We know every dystopia starts as a utopia. So *1984* by George Orwell is the realization of this truth. It is what made Orwell so unpopular on the left, because he associated

it with English socialism; he said this is a slander on English socialism, we didn't intend a police state, a kind of tyranny of the single party. So utopia and dystopia both imply each other, you can't have one without the other. They confront a reality, which is always a mixture. And the revelation is, well, maybe there could be a change.

NS I like the Hegelian reading, I think Zorio would like it as well.

WJTM Particularly, such revelation is not a synthesis of reality and utopia, it's a transformation, itself—a kind of non-reality, revelation occurs, something is unveiled, something you didn't see before. I have a Blakean reading of Hegel which is I think correct—most Hegelians I know tell me it's actually the correct reading, that synthesis is not the end. Synthesis is the moment of production of a new antithesis. So contrariety rules all the way, it never resolves.

Another connection I saw was actually with George Bernard Shaw, who has a wonderful saying: "reasonable men and women see the world as it is and accept it; they are realists. Unreasonable men and women look at the world and wish it were something different. Therefore, all progress depends on unreasonable people." Unreasonable people, fools, they dare to think of alternatives, revelations.

NS   Hilde, what are your thoughts?

HILDE VAN GELDER (HVG)   I brought
with me this very little booklet,
which includes two radio confer-
ences expressed by Michel Foucault
in December 1966. The first one is
called "Le corps utopique"; the second
one—better known—is "les heter-
opies."[1] Foucault argues that human
bodies need utopias. Utopias are
projections. It's a self-evident argument, but one necessary to repeat as it
allows us to understand that there is
an intricate connection between utopia
and reality. As a strategy of survival,
we make projections of a better or a
worse world, and somehow that helps
us to see ourselves through reality.
Utopias allow us to accept our own
bodily condition.

NS   So the body needs utopia.

HVG   The body needs utopia; it's
as simple as that. In this way, we
can accept our imperfections and
our inherently mortal condition
here in the world.

NS   But what do you think about
the fact that Zorio made a work with
a different inflection of the word
utopia compared to the one that
dominated in the late sixties and early
seventies? The notion of revelation
seems to me to be very disconnected
from the notion of utopia; they come
from very different contexts.

HVG   Foucault, once again, is useful
here. He says that it is a kind of
revelation to realize that utopias are
born from the body and that they
are dangerous because they can turn
against our bodies. His revelation is
that utopias may be auto-destructive

to ourselves. If we rely too much on
utopias they may become dangerous,
since then we tend to forget that they
are but projections.

WJTM   Almost like the utopia—
dystopia dialectic.

HVG   Yes. So, as you say, Nicola, what
we need to do is to fool the utopias.

NS   Fooling utopia can be read
both ways. The fact that we need
to fool our utopias is that we need
to embrace them and at the same
time fool them in our mediation with
reality. But *Utopia* itself as a book,
as a thought experiment, is fooling
us all the time. More's *Utopia* is
constructed to fool us by embodying
this dialectic between utopia and dystopia, as opposed to just celebrating
a utopian scenario or thinking.
    Chus?

CHUS MARTÌNEZ (CM)   Probably I don't
believe Foucault, probably I'm a
person in disbelief of everything
he writes—I enjoy it, but I disbelieve
him. I do think that utopias are really
not what the body needs. Actually
what the body needs is [something
that is] finding a language, but it took
more than a hundred years. The last
one hundred years we have been
learning what the body needs and
how to express exactly what the body
needs. For me, utopia is a dream of
reason, and reason in a very classical
way of understanding it, but in a hurry,
because at the end of the day it is a
very normative reason or logos in a
hurry. And it has all these theatrical
moments that we love, and probably
there I could agree with Foucault that
we need that theater. But then, there
is a problem with any force that tries

to summarize or program our state.
And all the forces that try to do it
are slow forces, so utopia is for me
something very fast. Something that
you can do fast and could repeat, and
you could also communicate because
you could just share it, and we could
just actually share similar utopias or
even the same utopia. So it travels
fast, in our minds, in our dreams, so it
produces an image of it, but what
really interests me is what is in front
of this fastness, that you could not
even name, that cannot be summa-
rized or choreographed in the same
way. For example, I've been spending
some months reading something that
I thought, in my life, I would never
read or even be interested in. Which
are summaries, scientific summaries,
of people that claim that they found
something in plants that they could
call intelligence or memory. By reading
these articles, which are first of all
incomprehensible for me, but also a
bore, I am obliging myself to put me
into a logic of those that are studying
plants in a way that has never been
studied before. It all started in the
sixties and there is all kinds of people
studying drugs, and how plants are
chemical plants in a sense and how
plants are biochemically telling us
about substances that could affect
our mind and those kinds of dream-
ing and taking you wherever, going
to paradise and things like that. This is
really interesting because they are
interested in finding out something—
the something that I want to find out
is how a plant, in a mindless way,
produces intelligence. Intelligence that
is not centralized, that has no centre.
Apparently, Darwin, at the end of his
life, was obsessed with that. The fact
that he figured out, having dealt all his
life with animals, he kind of missed the

"big shot" of the plant, so to speak…
There is a beautiful book he wrote at
the end of his life, saying "what if what
we really need to look at are the rules
of all these plants, that are covering
the planet." It is a beautiful letter
and that is the last text that he wrote.
Then, what these guys are doing is, trying to figure out what is at stake in this
thing, but they have no language for
it. Since they have no language for it,
for the mindlessness of the intelligence
of plants, they borrow, creating a huge
scandal because they borrow language.
So they say "plants do have memory."
There is a paper by Stephan Mancuso
stating that he did an experiment for
ten years to prove that certain plants
remember things, and remember it
for months, 28–29 days, and an insect
apparently forget this overnight. So he
says: "The plant remembers." It took
him five years to publish the article
because they say "the data are correct,
but we don't want to publish anything
with this language, we refuse to,
stating that there is memory in plants
because there are no neurons, and
if there are no neurons, there is no
memory. So his answer was changing
the name of his lab in Florence to
The Neurobiology of Plants. Then he
suffocated the whole scientific community with this kind of non-revelation.
On the one hand it is a revelation,
he discovers something that we need
to prove what it means, but on the
other hand nobody wanted it. What
I'm saying is that all this going along,
going visceral, into the mindlessness of
things—more than the utopia picture, so to speak. But the question is
language, and probably what I would
learn from utopias that there are
certain fictions that are very close to
reality, so close that it is difficult to tell
the one from the other. Probably the

work of Zorio is producing a rhythm between those two moments and I think that is beautiful. But then the fiction is the white cube, the white cube is already a fiction and then you have the light in the white cube, illuminated by a fictional light which is the blue light, which is the light of artificiality somehow, it is not the light of the sun, it is not the yellow light, it is not the light of life, it is also another artifice. So he is superimposing these two artificial languages which are great. The question is also how to understand what Foucault is saying when he is saying if utopia is the language of the body, what the body wants, and how can the body want something that we are ready to take and to actually express in language and in images and in experiences, that have not taken any programmatic form, or any nostalgic form, or any scenic form.

NS   That have not been commoditized.

CM   Yes, I think it would be interesting how to mix up this language of naming futures or participating in futures which are humanly produced. Could we share with all these different systems of thinking which are not so centralized? How to decentralize utopia, how to take utopia out of the mind…

How to make the utopia, the utopia of a plant or how to let it break into different intelligence.

HVG   Did you read just this week in the newspaper that they also have some sort of proof that stones "live." This has been another hypothesis for a long time.

WJTM   Yes, I was thinking even metals have memory.

CM   These are metaphors, but the funny thing is that, in this congress, of which I have the report, they start to throw weapons at each other at the end because they say "stop with metaphorical language."

WJTM   Good luck with that. They have been saying that for a long time and it never works.

CM   I know, but it is beautiful how they discuss it, because they claim that there is information that can be proof and systems. In stones it is probably different but there is something as well. The kind of going out of our mind to be seen from the mind of the stone or the plant or the animal or the dog—without mysticism is an interesting exercise which probably is going to take us—I don't know—three or four hundred years.

NS   Clearly you're guiding us to understanding a non-anthropocentric utopia. The utopia of plants would probably be the disappearance of the human species.

CM   Not necessarily. Utopia is rooted in a very specific understanding of how the mind rules. And that is what I don't—of course I relate to it, I love it, I learn from it, I read it, but I don't think that there is any future in that thinking anymore. But of course, it is the chair we are sitting in, it has been our training room for political thinking, for social articulation, but it is also, today, causing us many troubles, and it is difficult to get out of this thinking because we lack languages.

HVG   You mean the fact that it puts humans in the centre of the world or…?

CM   No, not only, I think. Take the plant as an example of a co-human. What I am saying is that in every sample of life, whether you are the director of a department or the housewife of your house, you try to impose a programme. Another guy that I really like, Tim Ingold, in *Lines: A Brief History* tried to make an exercise that tries to take you along without a programme into reality, trying to be unreasonable about reality, but without reasoning in—in and all-encompassing. These exercises that we have been reading through people that are really radical anthropologists, Bateson as well in certain of his writings and so on, would be interesting to take into account in parallel with this thinking that has been forming our life, that has been forming our intellectual life and in countries like in mine, to take it absolutely to a very concrete example, they cause more problems than solutions. They are—the utopian thinkers—collapsing any possibility of future because they are completely unable to think outside this frame. So, how can we train ourselves in a different political, social language that acknowledges what we learn into that kind of lack of utopia, but also acknowledges the impossibility that we have, yet, to come with different mind systems.

NS   You are liquidating utopia in a way, it would seem like your starting statement went in that direction.

CM   Yes, it is. But as every dead end is like a book you have in the library and you don't read for many years, one day you read it and you think it is amazing. So it depends, it also needs to be forgotten…

WJTM   It needs to be re-read.

CM   … just to formulate another, I call it innocence. We need to become innocent towards certain things in order to be able to read them again.

WJTM   I think it makes a lot of difference whether you talk about this in terms of reason and the unreasonable, as opposed to rationality and irrationality. I'm thinking strictly of Shaw's opposition between the unreasonable person. The best example of the unreasonable person is actually the purely reasonable; I think that is the message of the critique of pure reason, as opposed to a practical reason. Practical reason, which is the guide for reasonable people, who act in accordance with the way things are. They accept reality, they don't think it can be fundamentally changed, no individual could do it, things will happen. As Henry Ford said, "history is just one damn thing after another, so get used to it." That is being reasonable, that is being an American pragmatist.

NS   As literal as it gets.

WJTM   But pure reason is equivalent to a kind of madness. That's when you refuse to accept empirical reality. You construct a world, an ideal world out of symbols, that doesn't exist, but you insist on it just the same. That is why, and you are bringing me back to More's *Utopia*—I haven't read this since I was in graduate school—but now I am working on madness. And everything I highlighted is when More begins to merge with Plato, and the Phaedrus, and think about the madness as the motive power of human change and progress, or even endurance. Plato says, he's arguing with Aesop(*us*), who said: "Friendship is best, love is bad, because love leads to madness." It is irrational. Plato argues that the human species would die out, if it weren't mad, if it didn't go mad with love. From the reasonable standpoint, why would you ever get married? Reasonable people would understand, this is sex maybe? For pleasure? But there is this added thing: we reproduce. So human endurance itself depends upon us being fools.

NS   Which Erasmus also picks up in *Praise of the Folly*.

WJTM   Yes. Thinking of folly, not as clowning so much as humour, but folly as derangement, as inspiration. This is another meaning of revelation, I think, that utopia plus reality, then something that won't allow you to accept things the way they are, or that says "I'm going to act in defiance of what I know is reasonable."

CM   It is quite funny, when I opened the e-mail and you said revelations are a little bit of a problem, and then I opened the e-mail and I saw the same as this plant scientist. I'm working at the university, imagine that I don't talk about innovation anymore, and I insist on revelation. So if I don't innovate, we have revelations. It is the same, it is kind of the same, but it would just make them mad, they would not accept that such a language—and it could introduce through innovation—try to produce revelations. It is what they want, they want to know thinking, or that is what they wish for, as a revelatory force, as an image printed from the material that we depart from, but it would be completely different. That is what the industry tells us we should think about, but the industry knows that this is only upgrading. What they meant was a less prominent bottom of a soft surface, they are not making revelations.

HVG   Is that then where you see art position itself, as a sort of revelatory force?

CM   Not in the metaphysical, classical way, but I think probably, art today is doing two really interesting things. One is absorbing, going in, soaking in completely. If you look at certain images of corporate life and how images were produced fifteen years ago and how artists are making them again. They just close the gap, they are merging, and they are really making it more obvious, certain things, by doing this process of just soaking in, like a sponge, going back to exactly the same liquid, trying to do it with exactly the same elements. It is like adding spices. And in that sense it is hugely conservative, and beautifully preservative of what we already had, but on the other hand it is highly stupid, a stupid or a fool(*ish*) force, trying to produce revelations.

NS   I want to connect a couple of things and then Hilde, I don't know if you want to respond? In my email I also referred to Marx and the political thinking and theory of the nineteenth century, that is built up, developed somehow on utopia in a negative understanding. It is probably Marx who is responsible for that, more than anybody else, and then you have very sporadic returns to utopia, Bloch's, the spirit of utopia is probably the example in which some kind of utopian thinking is re-incorporated into marxist thinking. Mainly in an attempt to read the history of art and architecture as a long trajectory of utopian expression. Therefore no longer as a social expression but as a form, a spirit guiding art and guiding human endeavour to express some kind of revelation. Bloch was very much concerned with the lack of space for revelation and hope within the purely Marxist horizon. He understands utopia as the disruptive moment in which creativity and art introduce some kind of revelation about the human experience, as opposed to politics where instead rationality and organization seem to be the priority.

For me it is extremely symptomatic of the desire of otherness that More embeds the narrative of *Utopia* within the discovery of the New World. Utopia is literally a construct of an ideal place that he wants people to actually believe exists and it exists in the New World. Amerigo Vespucci had published in 1507 his letters from the new world which were like blockbuster literature and describing the customs and the behavior of the people. Something like a first hand ethnographic report of the people living in the New World. They were portrayed as the most uncivilized and barbaric population possibly imaginable with very few qualities. One of the few that was recognised by Vespucci was the fact that there was no private property, that these pepole lived in complete sharing of everything. So More picks up on this idea and then plants—to use a metaphor—he plants his island in the midst of this completely barbaric landscape and proposes a civilization that is constructed as you say, on very rational guidelines, but where the fools are constantly acknowledged as vital figures of the social body, they are far from rejected.

I think the rereading of *Utopia* pushes you very far away from the modern understanding of utopia, the 19th–20th century one. And that's where perhaps a rereading of a closed book, an ended story can actually add something, then the question is what would be a corresponding kind of utopian thinking today.

WJTM   As a child of the 1960s, I always associated utopia with the commune movement and the abolition of private property. It was not just a rational organisation of society but also an emotional and spiritual reorganisation that often had to do with new age religion, and a re-alignment of the human relationship to nature, including the vegetated universe. Of course the great challenge was that most of the people who entered into American communes in the 60s were English majors, or artists, or poets and musicians who suddenly discovered that, to make their utopian commune sustainable, they had to live on the land. They had to learn how to deal with plants, how to grow things, and they knew nothing about it. So it was a re-education from the ground up in subsistence farming, involving people from cities who had been completed detached from that tradition. They had to learn how you operate machinery, how you repair a tractor or a car. My generation tried to realize utopia overnight, simply by leaving the city, or finding an enclave in the city that you could rope off and turn into an ideal community. It was a noble, idealistic form of utopian folly, and it mostly failed, though the idea itself never completely disappears, as we can see from

the Occupy Movement of 2011–12,
a utopian experiment in primitive
democracy located in public spaces like
Zucotti Park and Tahrir Square.

HVG   I would like to link that to the
project of decolonization. The 60s
was the first big wave of decolonizing
nations, sometimes almost even entire
continents. Nowadays, the conversation has shifted towards what one
could identify as a second wave of
decolonization, this time of nature.
As we have to radically rethink
our relationship to nature, there's
probably something to be taken from
reconsidering these two movements.

WJTM   Pantisocracy, "the British
Romantics' utopia" envisioned by
Samuel Taylor Coleridge, was to
be built on the Susquehanna River.
It had a Unitarian religious framework, a synthesis of all religions.
But the project fell apart when they
realized they couldn't imagine their
pantisocracy without servants.

As with More's *Utopia*, someone
has to do the unpleasant work, so
slavery turns out to be absolutely
essential to the functioning of his
utopia. This was the great shock
to the American communes. When
people found out: we're not gonna sit
around reading in libraries and writing novels anymore, which is what
we were doing in graduate school.
We're going to have to get our hands
dirty repairing tractors. We're going
to get grease all over our bodies.

This makes me think of *The
Futurological Congress,* the great
utopian novel by Stanislaw Lem,
which has now been made into a film
called *The Congress.* I think quite a
mediocre film but *The Futurological
Congress* is a brilliant utopia/dystopia

because it's about how you could fool
yourelf with drugs into thinking we
now live in the ideal world. To me it
somehow captures the folly of utopia;
the kind of dialectial framework that it
always implies. Lem's "pharmatopia"
of happy drug addiction conceals a
reality of terrible suffering that can be
revealed (speaking of revelation) by
taking another drug that counteracts
the narcotics that produce happiness.

CM   The Utopia library in
CONTOUR 7 should include
a writing workshop. I have this idea
of doing what Siemens did in the 50s
and 60s, which was going to offices
and then dedicating one hour a day
or some time a day to collect or
write together in the working space,
because that's what people were
doing, they just read e-mails and
write another e-mail and every three
e-mails you send is to your wife or
to a friend, or to whatever, so just
collecting this and then doing it with
authors. Like, I'm completely into,
I'm of course married to a writer but
I was the other day discussing with
Tom […] because I am into this […]
idea of going with the flow, producing
an anthropology of what decurrent
things, not trying to affect it, just
trying to embrace it. So instead of
"students don't read" (angry tone),
saying: "they don't read" (normal
tone). So we're happy about that
fact, it means that I need to change
my behavior, because why would
I recommend books to people when
they do not read so I have to do
something else. And this investigation
of "do something else" is becoming
interesting. So Tom […] just did this
beautiful book on an anthropologist
that goes into a company trying to
figure out what's going on and just

observing the whole company under an anthropological point of view, it's a beautiful novel. But you could have this kind of writers in discovering this and then people are interested. It's very difficult to impose exercises.

Everyone is telling you that they are interested in coup glasses and they just want you to go into their interests. So don't fight it, just […] these communities and try to just […]

HVG   Yes, that could surely be done, I see many ways how it could be done, concretely.

NS   I think this pushes us in terms of our agenda into the lunch conversation, because part of what I wanted to discuss during lunch more off the record were more concrete things, like the Salon like the library, so I think this is less for the record, although it is interesting that we have a moment on the record, like the meta…

CM   I think it is fundamental.

NS   What do you think about the idea to present the first edition of the book in the exhibition? I am totally fascinated by the circumstances that led to the drafting and publishing of the book and I would like this story to be somehow told.

HVG   I think you have a methodology issue there that is fundamental and it's also how you have approached CONTOUR because the book is some sort of a result of fictional conversation between friends, there is this whole idea of friendship, of thinking together of collaborative research. And what you do here and now also, you brought together your friends, you're engaging a discussion and

a conversation. and maybe that can also be implemented somehow in CONTOUR, that you organise conversations between people and that's were the book will come alive.

NS   So in a way, using Utopia and More's *Utopia* as a pretext to reflect on the conditons of producing culture.

WJTM   And I have another text for your library. Do you have Samuel Johnsons' Rasselas?

WJTM   *Rasselas: The History of the Prince of Abyssinia* (Abyssinia being one of the legendary locations of the Garden of Eden) is a utopian novel set in a place called The Happy Valley. Samuel Johnson, AKA "Doctor Johnson," known as the greatest conversationalist of the 18th century, wrote the novel in one week to raise money for his mother's funeral expenses. The novel belongs to a very special genre called, the apologue—a dialogue or conversation on philosophical subjects, very much like the one we are having here.

CM   That's a really great term!

WJTM   So it's a dialogue among friends about deep philosophical ideas. It was a very important genre in the 18th century, Diderot wrote *The Letters to The Blind* as part of this genre. It can take the form of letters, but also of a conversation, face to face.

Rasselas is a face to face conversation. It's about the happy valley, and the inhabitants of the happy valley and why everything is fine there. Of course it immediately gets into Folly, and the inability of human beings to endure or sustain happiness. Its location in Abyssinia links it with the Garden of

Eden, which by the way is the vege-
tative/vegetarian utopia. There is no
death of animals, the lion and lamb
co-exist peacefully and Adam and
Eve conduct "sweet gardening labor."
Milton refers to this Edenic utopia several times as a "plantation," and there
is a strong implication that he has in
mind a kind of colonial plantation, in
which God's angels will be overseers,
and the human race will do the work.

CM   It's very beautiful, Johnson
also wrote a book called *The Vanity
of Human Wishes*.

NS   So maybe we need to have
doctor Johnson.

WJTM   I think Dr. Johnsons's voice
should be heard, his conversations
with his biographer Boswell were
legendary. They exemplify what Jurgen
Habermas regards as the beginning of
the English public sphere, the "com-
mons" where private citizens gather to
debate freely on the issues of the day.
They were located in coffee houses, in
which (in Habermas's view) a kind of
"real utopia" of freedom and civility
could be acted out.

CM   Yes, put just some wine and
it would also be the Spanish model.

HVG   Well we can have beer
in Mechelen.

2nd half
(without Chus Martìnez)

NS   *Utopia* belongs to the literary
genre of satire. We started to address
the question of contemporary satire
via email a some time ago, I think
we should pick up our conversation
from there.

WJTM   One thing about satire is
that the utopian impulse partly has
common origin in the area of the joke.
Freud reminds us that jokes originate
in grievances, complaints, absurd-
ities, misunderstandings, and folly.
If dreams are (for Freud) projections
of wish fulfillment and jokes are
expressions of pain, disappointment,
and grievance, then Utopia is somewhere between the dream and the joke
in my view. Satire (the word stems
from the Greek "satyr plays," which
were excercises in low folly, drunken-
ness, and crazy bestial sex) is a genre
that starts as a negative practice of
caricature and polemical attack on
folly and vice. It aims to rid the world
of the stupid and the foolish, on the
one hand, and the evil, vicious, and
corrupt on the other. So both of those
tagets—stupidity and evil—are in
the crosshairs. But then satire has a
tendency to go to an extreme where
it turns into fantasy. The grotesquery
of the fools and villains becomes so
monstrous that you enter a world
that's completely lost touch with
either the ideal or the possibly realistic
reform. It becomes a fantasy world.
Jonathan Swift is the great master of
this segue from satire to fantasy. Swift
may be ridiculing actual English politics, but how can he do it? He has to
invent two islands divided by religions,
the Bigendians (who crack their eggs
at the big end) and the Littleendians
(who crack them at the small end)
and who are willing engage in holy
war to settle their differences. Swift
was thinking, of course, of the ongoing fight between Catholicism and
Protestantism over the urgent question
of whether a piece of ordinary bread
is to be seen as a symbolic reminder
or a magically transformed piece of
God's body. Satire shifts the question

into a world where the absurdity of the whole dispute can be made clear. Satire, like utopia, always holds up a mirror to the real world we inhabit, but defamiliarizes it, makes it exotic, strange, or fantastic, so that we can look our own world with fresh eyes—with a sense of revelation, to come back to our beginning.

Or the academy itself, represented in Swift's island of Laputa, is an island floating in the sky, detached from the real world. It's a utopia of absent-minded professors, especially philosophers, where nobody can remember anything of practical importance, so they have flappers to remind them of what they said 5 minutes ago. They speculate constantly, producing new theories every five minutes. So satire crosses over quite readily from a kind of attack on real conditions, real vilains, real fools, into the projection of monsters or allegorically named fantastic creatures. The last book of *Gulliver's Travels*, and maybe this should be on your shelf as well, *The Voyage to the Houyhnhnm's*, is the utopia of horses. If you're gonna have a utopia of dogs, then why not horses? The horse is a much more noble creature and the Houyhnhnm's treat Gulliver as a vicious fool because he's just a human being, and therefore incapable of reasoning and living in harmony with his fellows. (The Houyhnhms regard human beings as a primitive species that they call the "Yahoos," who are mainly characterized by their dangerous forms of folly, such as greed, violence, and war). The Houyhnhnms, by contrast, have figured all this out.

So utopia always leads to a dialectical genre that can't be pinned down to either ridicule or polemic but also tend to have a component of fantasy, a projection of possible futures or alternate histories. That's why the island is often the location, a fictional heterotopia (to echo Foucault's term) that is "outside" the world of normal reality. *The Island in the Moon*, William Blake's satirical play, is a spoof on the Lunar Society located in Birmingham, England in the 18th century. It was a place where Enlightenment scientists such as Joseph Priestley (who discovered oxygen) and Erasmus Darwin (author of *The Loves of Plants*) would gather to discuss new inventions and technologies. Blake, of course, turns them into a society of lunatics, which somewhat loses its sting when you learn that this was a term they cheerfully applied to themselves. So satire is a very flexible genre. It's not some kind of well-defined thing that sticks to a single set of conventions: it can veer into low comedy at one extreme, seriously philosophical dialogue (the apologue) at another, and merge with fantasy, allegory, and even tragedy. The best ones are, I think, often resourceful in using these contrary, multifarious energies.

NS   Thank you. Hilde?

HVG   Yes, little margin little notes, since you were speaking of *Gulliver's Travels*, in his [...] Utopia, that Foucault calls the oldest and the most important roman *The Utopia of the Giants*, for him that's the most revealing, so probably we can...

WJTM   How is it called?

HVG   He's not specifying, it's just: *La vieille utopie des géants*, that you find in so many legends in Europe, Africa, everywhere.

WJTM   In the Bible too. There were giants on the Earth in those days, and people lived for a thousand years.

HVG   Another important author to be mentioned in relation to satire is Erasmus' and More's own source, Lucian.

NS   He is definitely very prominent. Lucian is central, their obsession with Lucian and his pseudo-historiography is extremely fascinating and he's the first science fiction writer, he's the first guy to articulate a travel to the sun, to the moon. So definitely he's central, yes. And he's also the eminent figure of the tradition of serious play. Both Erasmus and More belong to this tradition. He was the first to write an encomium of a fly, *In Praise of the Fly*. And from there In Praise of Folly, by Erasmus.

HVG   Yes, I really liked this text by Hans Belting on Hieronymus Bosch's *Garden of Earthly Delights*. In an extremely interesting argumentation he develops on Lucian, comparing his work *True Histories* to More's *Utopia*, as both are "fictitious travel reports."[2] To Belting, both use the same satirical strategies, where actually facts are turned into fictions and fictions in their turn are turned again into facts. In More's *Utopia*, "fiction liberates argument by disguising it," Belting argues. More ends up acknowledging that Utopia "exists" but at the same time he readily denies it. Meanings are generated in the sweep of paradoxes around this enigma. In a similar way, there is a lot to be taken today from the visual arts, especially video, to actually generate that shift between fact and fiction.

WJTM   Which is the paradox of an image as such.

HVG   And satire was a strategy of protection of course.

NS   One of the reasons for putting the attention on More is the paradox of his life in relationship to Utopia, his human trajectory kind of speaks of a contradiction with many of the things that he articulated in *Utopia*. But he never disavowed Utopia. It was not like at some point he said: "this book is no longer in line with my feelings and thoughts." The paradox is in the way in which his existence was caught in a contradiction with the book for some of the positions he later took in his life. But also, one of the things that is clear is that his conflict with Henry VIII was mainly centered around More's defence of the separation of kingdom and Church, which Henry VIII later in his life saw as an obstacle as he became more and more influenced by the ideas of the Reformation. The monsters and martyrs theme of CONTOUR 7 stems from More's own life, caught as it was between the monstrous persecution of the reformers and the safeguard of his conscience to the point of becoming a martyr himself.

WJTM   Yes, I think it is essential not only to emphasize *Utopia* as a text but More's life and his existential proximity to insanity. At some point the narrator Hythloday clearly says that it is better to stay away as much as possible from power, which has a tendency to drive one mad.

NS   Yes, he says, "to not become insane." There is this really incredible moment in the text in which More uses an example taken from theater to prove the point. Plautus's theater, Plautus is the Latin author who wrote comedies deeply imbued in satire. There's a moment in which in the dialogue More says: if you are dealing with the sovereign and you break bad news to him all the time, it's like performing in Plautus's comedy and bringing Seneca in, who kills all the fun.

And then Hythloday answers: but if you don't interrupt the fun then you become insane like the people that are playing in the play. So if you don't play the Seneca of the situation, then you just get absorbed into the game.

WJTM Time for a reality check. This is one of my madness projects that has taken me into the question of sovereign madness and the theory of sovereignty. I think of Derrida's book on the sovereign as a beast of prey, and the whole Carl Schmitt-Agamben discussion on the sovereign and the state of exception. The fundamental definition of the sovereign is "he who decides on the exception." This was George W. Bush's definition: he called himself "the decider." But what the sovereign decides upon is the exception, which is the moment when the law is suspended. So sovereign is both above and below the law, it is the law of the sovereign that he can and sometimes must break the law. So in relation to something like normativity and normality, the sovereign position is technically a position of abnormality and madness. The sovereign is the one who can say "forget about normality; these are not normal times and it's my job to acknowledge that and to institute a new rule beyond norms. So of course, this shows itself in all kinds of figures. Especially in Shakespeare, think about the mad kings, and the relation of the fool to the mad king in Lear. The fool keeps telling Lear the truth,

and Lear keeps saying "careful, don't go too far, you're in for a whipping," and the fool makes a joke of that, but keeps reminding him: "Hey you're the one who's decided to split up your kingdom, who didn't listen to the one daughter who actually loves you. This is all your fault because you're crazy." Or in Hamlet: we are confronted with an undecidable puzzle. Was Hamlet merely playing the fool or is he really crazy? Blake's figure of madness was Nebuchadnezzar, the Biblical mad king, who turns into a beast (a wolf actually, kind of a werewolf). Have you seen the Blake print of Nebuchadnezzar?

NS Didn't you publish it somewhere? I think I've seen it, probably in your lecture on madness.

WJTM Yes, Blake takes the Biblical figure quite literally. When Nebuchadnezzar goes mad he goes around crawling on all fours and becomes a kind of werewolf, with claws and fangs. But he's also the law giver, the absolute monarch who is above the law, so it's a very important part of the theory of sovereignty, that the sovergein is uniquely vulnerable to madness. This isn't just a psychological so much as it's a structural effect of having absolute power over life and death, a position in which it is very easy to become mad. Perhaps this is why utopia, as the vision of the perfected state, is also so closely allied with human folly.

Notes
1   Daniel Defert (ed.), *Foucault. Le corps utopique, les héterotopies* (Paris: Lignes, 2009).
2   Hans Belting, *Hieronymus Bosch. Garden of Earthly Delights* (Munich: Prestel, 2005), p. 109.

Lessons from Moria

Hilde Van Gelder

"Revolution is going to come down the line from the ship, you know—like rats."[1]

On June 9, 2015, the UN High Commissioner for Refugees (UNHCR) and the International Organization for Migration (IOM) announced that since the year's beginning one hundred thousand refugees and migrants had managed to reach Europe.[2] Both organizations reported a significant rise in boat traffic in the Aegean Sea, to the islands of Lesbos and Kos in particular—which are located only a few nautical miles from the Turkish coast. Since then the influx has gone up dramatically. In July alone as many as 50,000 refugees arrived on the Greek islands.[3] About half of them arrived on Lesbos, where there is only one refugee center. It actually was a closed-down facility for asylum seekers who had exhausted all legal procedures, situated near the village of Moria. If the center has an official capacity of 410 people, right now it provides shelter to some one thousand people. The overpopulation at Moria, as the site is commonly called, has meanwhile given rise to utter chaos and squalid conditions: overflowing men's toilets, piles of rubbish, and a proliferation of makeshift camps elsewhere on the island.[4] Recently, Doctors Without Borders dispatched a relief aid team to Lesbos.[5]

For all of us who regularly watch or check the news it is impossible to ignore: the shocking images of groups of exhausted people sleeping in the parks and backyards of "tourist resorts," as these paradisiacal islands were generally referred to until very recently. In the most eye-catching media reports, one will see Western tourists walk, bike, or ride past the long lines of have-nots forced to camp out in the streets.[6] With dignity these tourists try to keep up their temporary status as sponsor of the idyllic island economy The surly gaze on many of their faces also betrays their discomfort, however. The contrast between the two categories of "visitors" is conspicuous indeed. Many of the "legally" flown-in tourists will have been enticed by appealing ad slogans, tempting them to go on "a magical Odyssey."[7] Conversely, the recent press photos taken on the islands show images of their fellow human beings who literally washed ashore; most of them are of Asian or African origin, and their faces betray the pain of their hellish journey into the EU.

Living Like a Dog

The stories on everyday life in Greece that reach us today are distressing. Many among the population are starving.[8] The stray dogs, which were until recently a common element of street life, are gone. What happened to them? It is subject to wild speculations, the more so because their cadavers are rarely recovered. Some news sources put the blame on the new migrants, who would be so starved that they even have no scruples anymore about stealing someone's pet.[9] As rumors have it, they ritually slaughter the animals and subsequently store them, cut up into pieces, in freezers for consumption. Recent scholarship questions such rumors, however, in the absence of hard evidence for such practice.[10] Another conspiracy theory claims that the street dogs' systematic disappearance is the result of an undercover operation organized by proponents of Golden Dawn, Greece's fascist political party. This would be an effective way for this party to pit the local population against the numerous migrants. Whatever the truth in this matter, the figure of the dog features as an interesting symbolic mediator in today's Greek society. Its disappearance is seen as a bad omen. Serving as an opportunity for native factions to vent their anger, the alleged eating of dog meat by newcomers is also a way to stigmatize them.

For thousands of years there has been a special, close bond between mankind and dogs of course.[11] Having such alarming reports circulate within a community should therefore be seen as a cry for help as well: this community wants to express that it has fallen prey to what in the cultural-sociological literature is called "moral panic."[12] If people in a community renounce their most trusted animal, as the underlying logic has it, they will eventually renounce each other as well.[13] In an attempt to keep further social destabilization at bay, the community will draw a line between those who are "civilized"—and therefore do not eat dogs—and the "wild" others.[14] Eating dogs has long been common in certain parts of China, and this is an issue that is also hotly debated today.[15] However, *Father and Sons* (2014), a moving film by Chinese filmmaker Wang Bing, presents a very different image of the man-dog relationship in his native country. This movie zooms in on the life of Cai Shunhua, a former farmer. With his two sons he lives in a tiny, windowless room measuring only four square meters. This "box" was made available to them by the owner of the stonecutting factory in Fuming, where the father works as laborer. Generously the man and his sons share their modest dwelling with three dogs, a bitch and two pups. There is a little basket for the animals in the middle of the room, next to the only bed. The mother dog and the two pups thus serve as a metaphorical mirror for the dead-end "dog's life" led by the father and his sons.[16]

The little action in the film is largely confined to the bed, in which the two young teenagers barely fit. They sit there watching TV or tapping on their cell phones, the only forms of luxury at their disposal. At night the father leaves for his night shift (after sleeping in the bed during daytime), and when he turns off the light for his kids, their cell phones light up in the dark. The scene actually reminds one of Andersen's fairytale *The little matchstick girl*. The ramshackle room in which these boys spend most of their time is like a platform for diverting their thoughts, their cell phones serving as virtual escape capsules.

In a radio conference held on 21 December 1966, Michel Foucault in fact introduced the large, parental bed in which children like to "swim between the blankets" as a special place: it is where they discover "the ocean."[17] He refers to this bed as a "heterotopia," understood as a real place which, for instance during kids' play, can be transformed into a *"radically* other site"—a *"counter*-place" (24). A heterotopia differs from all other places because it "juxtaposes different spaces, which normally would have to be incompatible" (28–29). In these alternative sites, reality and fiction come together. As such these spaces do not always have to be sites of fun or joy; a cemetery, for instance, is a heterotopia as well. Sad or joyful, the stimuli we experience in heterotopias contribute to "activating" our imagination, as Allan Sekula has claimed as well.[18]

If the utopia—literally a "no-place"—presents us with an unrealizable dream by definition, the heterotopia stirs us to action in the here and now, allowing us to throw a different light on the setting in which we find ourselves. Thus it has the potential to "mislead" utopia, as it were. Through heterotopias we may guide our thoughts beyond escapism and vague illusions, which frequently cause the demise of utopian thought. As a joyful image, Foucault's heterotopia of the "oceanic" parental bed of course largely shatters to pieces when applied to the dilapidated home of the teenage boys, Cai Yonggao and Cai Yongjin, in Wang Bing's movie. Their home feels like a "prison," which to Sekula is "the saddest of all heterotopias" (117). The sharp contrast between this ultra-miserable "cage" and the virtual dream world of cell phone electronics inevitably reminds one of a long list of failing social utopias from the past century. Still, Wang Bing is not out to condemn. His movie makes clear that despite the odds the boys care well for their pets. They are committed to walking their dogs and indoors they quietly respect and acknowledge their presence in their basket.

Contrary to the myth of his fellow countrymen as barbarian lovers of dog's meat, Wang Bing thus shows us a sprinkle of hope. No matter how hopeless their situation may be, the loyal comradeship between the boys and their dogs suggests that they will retain their dignity. Dogs also feature positively in quite another cultural text: *The Praise of Folly* (1511) by Erasmus of Rotterdam. In this work, this author extensively praises the most devoted among animals. As he writes in section 44: "What is more fawning than a dog? And yet what is more faithful?"[19] A dog, according to Erasmus, is living proof that "bad faith" and "adulation" do not always necessarily make a pair (62). The dog flatters those he loves, yet he is also truly faithful to them. In essence dogs testify to a positive form of flattery that, Erasmus says, deludes men in a commendable way. This type of flattery we may view as a "virtue" because it "proceeds from a certain kindness and candor of mind" (62), a well-meant and innocent intention. This goddess "Flattery" (61), in the Latin original also named "Assentatio," who serves the goddess Folly ("Stultitia" or "Moria" (10)), "raises the dejected spirit, it soothes those who are grieving, freshens the faint, quickens the dull, eases the suffering, mollifies the fierce, joins loves together and keeps them so joined" (62).

This is why Moria, who as "that true disposer of good things" acts as narrator in *The Praise of Folly* (10), counts dogs, extensively praising them, among the biggest fools in the world. They are always joyful and without reproach when they see their boss, even after having been apart for five minutes only. Because a dog "acts to make every man more pleasing and more dear to himself," thus stimulating more "Self-love" or "Philautia," as Moria decides, a dog's mode of flattery is cause to "the main point of happiness" (61–62). There is no larger symbol of goodness than the dog and this noble animal has of course featured in this role throughout the Western artistic and pictorial tradition. There is good chance that at one point Cai Yonggao and Cai Yongjin, like today's many refugees, will embark, in search for a better life elsewhere, faraway. Given their family background, it is hardly to be expected that during that passage the boys will eat the dogs that cross their way. Wang Bing's film, in other words, subtly shows us how we should be cautious to trust rumors and tall stories.

The artists' collective A Dog Republic also capitalizes on this within CONTOUR 7. Through so-called "barking conversations" between human beings, they stimulate us to reflect on both the discourse we develop and the underlying premises we rely on.[20] The creative force emanating from seemingly absurd barking conversations is enormous. In the imaginary "republic of Dogland," one can experiment in a humorist fashion with inventing forms of community where good faith, trust and flattery go hand in hand in more sustainable ways.[21] The explicit reference included in the collective's "First manifesto" to a "constitution" and "democratically approved" decisions is well taken in the light of today's challenges to social cohesion.

Europe between Grand Vision and Monstrous Creation

Until recently, both European politicians and the media had paid little attention to the issue of migration. This striking silence has contrasted sharply, in the past decade, with the extensive attention for this issue in the world of visual art—in particular in the socially committed photography and video scene. For example, in the spring of 2006—the "year of the Fire Dog"—Herman Asselberghs completed his gripping video essay *Capsular*.[22] For this project, he took the ferry across the Strait of Gibraltar to go to Ceuta, a Spanish enclave on the coast of North Africa. His trip was triggered by a news event in the fall of 2005: African migrants sought access to the enclave by crossing the barbed wire fence, which then had a height of three meters. In response, the Spanish government, with support from the European Union, almost immediately decided to increase the fence's height to six meters. The aim of Asselberghs' trip was to come to terms with the remarkably vague media reporting on this event. He wanted "to see with his own eyes how the reality differs from the media images."[23]

It resulted in shocking recordings, made under difficult circumstances. For instance, Asselberghs had to hide his camera when filming the first iron curtain on European soil since the collapse of the Berlin Wall. He also had to hide in the shrubs to record shooting exercises by border patrol officers from a safe distance. On the desperate people who died near the fence or in the nearby coastal waters, the voiceover of *Capsular* has this to say: "[k]eeping these people off screen as much as possible seems part of a policy to render their lives present as a threat."[24]

On the fully glass-covered ferryboat from and to Algeciras, where filming was also prohibited, Asselberghs, with a hidden camera, scanned the horizon in vain for signs of trafficking of migrants. At first sight, then, *Capsular*, which is perhaps best described as a counter-documentary, shows nothing spectacular at all. The work merely registers a specific reality, but this aspect precisely defines its unsettling effect on viewers. What we see is a procession of successive capsule-like environments: from a highly secured port terminal and a ferryboat, closed-off like an aquarium, to a heavily guarded fence-annex-barbed-wire structure surrounded by overseas coastal territory. Next, there is the journey back on the covered capsule boat to the heavily guarded fortress that is the European continent. In between there is an extensive water surface—as a seemingly meaningless intermediate zone.

In his 2006 documentary, Herman Asselberghs shared his doubts with the viewer as follows: "You find it difficult to decide whether this enclave is pioneering terrain for a vanguard carrying out a mission in enemy territory, or just a ridiculous patch of land about to be pushed off the African continent" (17). Today, precisely on what should have been the festive thirtieth anniversary of the signing of the preliminary Schengen treaties, Hungary is rapidly erecting a fence with a height of four meters along its 175-kilometer border with Serbia, on the outer edge of the EU. For the first time, France and Austria have temporarily closed border-crossing points with Italy. Unmistakably this European contortedness uncovers the shady side of the hope for stable prosperity, human rights, solidarity, and justice, which has characterized the European project since the 1950s.

A decade ago, artworks such as *Capsular* revealed to us already that the EU border is no longer found on the outer boundary of its territory. The EU border is mobile and has been moved to places where "confinement" of "undesirable people" is needed (18), such as transit zones in airports. In this respect, Eyal Weizman argues that today we find ourselves worldwide in a "dynamic morphology of [...] spaces," which "resembles an incessant sea dotted with multiplying archipelagos of externally alienated and internally homogeneous ethno-national enclaves under a blanket of aerial surveillance."[25] But the homogeneous character of those national enclaves is also under pressure today, which leads to shockingly conservative responses in some EU countries. "The boat is full," as the spokesperson of the Hungarian government, Zoltán Kovács, put it bluntly when announcing that his country was unilaterally suspending the EU political asylum legislation indeterminately.[26] Several Facebook comments, as reported by *The Guardian*, suggested that the EU was now revealing itself to be a veritable "monster."[27] The Union is swiftly evolving into a hermetically sealed "gated community."[28]

Despite the many emotional calls for (a redistributive) solidarity, the barriers to developing sustainable forms of peaceful coexistence between the old and new Europeans seem enormous.[29] Paradoxically, a sign of change is coming precisely from Moria. Gradually, and partly owing to the mounting humanitarian aid, this place is being transformed from a "closed prison" into a more humane shelter for the many desperate refugees washing ashore in their frequently overloaded inflatable dinghies.[30] For the time being, Moria is and will continue to be a deeply regrettable heterotopia. But a name is an omen. It is outright *unheimlich* to have to observe that a "*radically* other site," a "*counter*-place" for failing asylum and migration politics in Greece, is evolving in the village of this illustrious name.[31] It seems as if the goddess Moria herself urges the world to take seriously the "folly" of those who put their own lives on the line, as well as those—all too often—of their children.

It was again Michel Foucault who explained why the figure of "the Madman, the Fool, or the Simpleton"—thereby explicitly paying homage to Erasmus—is the one who "reminds each man of his truth."[32] This applies in particular to the figure of the sailing fool. By signing up on a ship, every sailor accepts his being believed dead already: he has a much larger chance, after all, of dying prematurely. Still he will go aboard good-humoredly. It is that disarming smile of the fool that we empathize with because it tells us the one big truth, says Foucault, namely that of "the nothingness of existence" (13). This truth presents itself to us more strongly in times of growing collective "madness," when a society realizes that the "final catastrophe" is always near (14). At the same time, Foucault argues, it is also the fear for that growing "insanity" that causes representatives of a community to call for "a common odyssey (Van Oestvoren's *Blauwe Schute*, Brant's *Narrenschiff*)" (12).

It is an unwelcome development when EU citizens and their policymakers, in their fervent attempts to further fashion their collective odyssey, would close their eyes for something they do not even wish for their dogs: ending up in a "camp from hell."[33] According to populist discourse, IS fighters have found and are finding an easy way into the EU by inserting themselves into the refugee circuit.[34] Such fear reflexes, which merely focus on the potential threat of these "seafaring fools" in unstable jolly-boats, distract the attention from the misery in which many end up once they have arrived in the EU. In fact, according to reports of the Dutch Refugee Foundation (Nederlandse Stichting Vluchteling), the living conditions of the new immigrants on Lesbos are "worse than in the African refugee camps."[35] How would it be possible, then, for refugees to have freezers filled with dog's meat? In the "new jungle," a chaotic camp of some 3000 people near Calais, the slight minority of women present do not even dare to use the sanitary facilities without surveillance. The popular press concludes that the zone is a "Medusa's raft," on which a group of living believed to be dead tries hard not "to capsize."[36] This horrific scene takes place at a stone's throw from the Chunnel, in the heart of Western Europe, in a country that prides itself of being no failed state. Amnesty International calls on France and Great Britain to adopt a radically different approach, one that should also offer these people protection at last.[37]

Ship of Fools:
Incubator for Metamorphoses

In the *Moria*, as *Praise of Folly* is often called as well, the goddess Folly regularly serves as the author's alter ego, the preeminent "wise fool."[38] Who understood better that the *"fool is clairvoyant"* than Erasmus?[39] These "clairvoyant fools" travel to "Europe" because they fully trust how this society organizes itself. The EU needs to assume their willingness of commitment to unshakeable European ideals, as articulated in its constitutional principles that require compliance.[40] The EU will then be capable—befitting a "wise fool"—of generously showing its alter ego as "the true disposer of good things," while also feeling "flattered" in fulfilling its exemplary role.[41]

With an eye to the realistic conceptualization of such an enormous social challenge, the famous book *Utopia* (1516) by Thomas More, which is center-stage within CONTOUR 7, still offers us ample inspiration. In a highly ingenious way, the text relies on a subtle mechanism of irony that allows us to contemplate the relation between ourselves and the other. As known, at the end of the first part, More situates this ideal society on a fictitious island. The reader only learns how things operate in Utopia via the story of a discoverer, who once visited the island after having sailed "like the expert and prudent prince Ulysses:" Raphael Hythloday.[42] Hythloday proves to be much more than a simple "mariner:" together with Amerigo Vespucci he visited all corners of the world.

Hans Belting convinces his readers that Raphael Hythloday can be viewed as a fictional doppelgänger of More's close friend Erasmus, who himself actually dedicated his *Moria* to Thomas More.[43] *Utopia* teaches us to see the other, also in his guise of fool or idiot, as a mirror of ourselves—as a metamorphosis. In her artistic work, Chiara Fumai precisely explores this idea in the context of CONTOUR 7. During her performances she is known to put herself in the shoes of other persons, such as the illiterate cleaning woman from Napoli Eusapia Palladino (1854–1918), who had spiritualist gifts and who counted Tsar Nicolas II of Russia and Nobel Prize winners Pierre and Marie Curie among her fervent supporters.[44] In this guise, Fumai confronts us with how even the most learned people on earth can draw inspiration from apparent folly. For example, she offers us insight into what life may look like for someone else while at the same time satirically updating the allegory of the *"fol sage,"* who exposes us to new values from the fool's point of view.[45]

Michel Foucault already warned us that the rise of "madness" in a society often involves a hardly visible, secretive process—a "secret invasion."[46] Take the example of Lampedusa. Only ten years ago it was rare for tourists on this "most beautiful island in the world" to be directly confronted on the beach by people literally washing ashore.[47] For the third panel of his long-term project *The Analogue Island Bureau*, entitled *Displacement Island* (2006), Marco Poloni decided to comb the beaches of Lampedusa in clear daylight. He found, for instance, clothes, shoes, and a pack of cigarettes with exclusively Arabic text, and he photographed these items. He also made striking pictures at dusk, when the setting sun casts moving shadows across the beach and beachgoers return home—the picture only showing their back. No one is turning and watching back anymore: they have literally turned their back on the nightly trafficking.

Poloni also discovered a well-guarded depot surrounded by iron bars and filled with confiscated wooden fishing boats from North Africa— recognizable by their Arabic inscriptions and their prototypical blue painted hull and deck. He integrated two color shots of this graveyard of boats in his series, which all together consists of 69 photos in various formats. In an alienating manner the look of such ramshackle boats evokes allegoric references to the medieval ships of fools, which were known to have "social driftwood" aboard as well.[48] Such ships were doomed to end in disaster, according to popular morality, and therefore they were systematically jeered at and made fun of. No wonder, then, that the infamous guild of the Blue Barge (*gilde van de Blauwe Schuit*), during droll, festive performances allowed everyone to act for one night (on Shrove Tuesday) as a seafaring fool who does not meet "the norms bourgeois society tries to set for society as a whole" (186).

At least since the sixteenth century, as Michel Foucault has indicated, the boat has figured as a major vehicle of imagination in our culture.[49] A boat embodies many paradoxes: it is used by those who want to protect us, as well as by those who want to attack us. Boats help us see not only that there are two sides to every story, but also that the assessment of what is good and bad involves shifting notions. In another lengthy homage to Erasmus, who knew better than anyone how "all things have two faces," Foucault claims that in "things as such" we can discover the reversal of meaning.[50] Moria on Lesbos has clearly taken on that role. This same is true of Lampedusa, which, for Marco Poloni, is "a kind of heterotopic space."[51] Being an "island," Jörg Bader argues, it forms an "allegory for a globalised world that cuts the rich off from the poor."[52]

As it happens, the gap between rich and poor is also one of the central themes of More's nearly five-centuries-old *Utopia*, and it is again clear why it serves as motto of CONTOUR 7. But there is a major difference as well. After all, the ship used by Raphael Hythloday has "already sailed" to the island.[53] We therefore wouldn't even know where to sign up if we wanted to travel to Utopia. This is why such a journey is possible only "in our thoughts" (111–12). Against the danger of getting bogged down in unfeasible utopias that occupy themselves with only a "ship of the imagination (111)," Michel Foucault calls upon us, with Erasmian humor, to dedicate ourselves as much as possible to the lessons to be taken from real ships, trying to find a safe haven in the islands of the here and now, via a new *science*: heterotopology.[54]

Lesbos and Lampedusa, where these kinds of ships are regularly coming ashore, are such heterotopian islands that they are easy to locate. Quite concretely they underscore how crucial it is to find our dog-like interconnectedness again within the divided human family. They serve us as a warning against the nightmare of an encapsulated, militarized EU as the only alternative for an outside world ruined by conflict and marked by merely virtual escape capsules. They stimulate us to generously make place aboard our overcrowded ship and together cry out merrily the words etched by Albrecht Dürer into the frontispieces he made for Sebastian Brant's milestone book *Das Narrenschiff* from 1494: "To Narragonia, let us all rejoice"![55] May the collective "narragonic" courage in Europe quickly gain the upper hand. Potentially, after all, we will all find ourselves in the same boat.

Notes

1 Allan Sekula, public conversation with Jürgen Bock, Rennes, La Criée, 7 April 2012, unpublished audio-recording. Thanks to Mieke Bleyen, Ton Brouwers, Adriaan Gonnissen, Steven Op de Beeck, Nicola Setari, Stefanos Svanias, Pieter Van Reybrouck, and Jeroen Verbeeck. All translations of quotes cited are by Ton Brouwers or the author (retaining the original emphasis).

2 Cf. http://www.unhcr.org/557703c06.html en http://www.iom.int/news/number-migrants-landing-europe-2015-passes-100000 en http://www.theguardian.com/world/2015/jul/09/greek-crisis-un-refugee-agency-struggle-cope-banks-fail (14 August 2015).

3 Cf. http://www.unhcr.org/55c4d1fc2.html (14 August 2015).

4 Cf. http://www.dailymail.co.uk/news/article-3169178/Greek-islands-Lesbos-Kos-host-thousands-migrants-shocking-conditions.html (14 August 2015).

5 Cf. http://www.msf-azg.be/nl/pers/duizenden-migranten-en-asielzoekers-verblijven-in-barre-omstandigheden-op-griekse-eilanden (14 August 2015).

6 Cf. http://www.dailymail.co.uk/news/article-3099736/Holidaymakers-misery-boat-people-Syria-Afghanistan-seeking-asylum-set-migrant-camp-turn-popular-Greek-island-Kos-disgusting-hellhole.html (14 August 2015).

7 Email-advertisement of voyageprive.com, sent to the author on 11 June 2015.

8 Bruno Tersago, *Groeten uit Griekenland* (Berchem: Epo, 2015), 16–18.

9 http://www.keeptalkinggreece.com/2011/01/06/greek-newspaper-athens-impoverished-eat-pets/ (14 August 2015).

10 Orit Hirsch, "'If You Eat Dogs, You'll Eat People.' Otherising on a Greek Island in Economic Crisis," in Andrea Boscoboinik and Hana Horáková (eds.), *The Anthropology of Fear. Cultures Beyond Emotions* (Berlin: LIT Verlag, 2014), 69–84.

11 Cf. David Grimm, "Dawn of the Dog," *Science*, 348.6232 (17 April 2015): 274–279; Miho Nagasawa, Shouhei Mitsui, Ohtani Shiori, Nobuyo Ohtani; Mitsuaki Ohta, et al., "Oxytocin-gaze positive loop and the coevolution of human-dog bonds," *Science*, 348.6232 (17 April 2015): 336–340.

12 Cf. Stanley Cohen, *Folk Devils and Moral Panics* (London: MacGibbon & Kee, 1972).

13 Cf. W.J.T. Mitchell, "The Future of the Image: Rancière's Road Not Taken," *Culture, Theory and Critique*, 50 (2–3), 136.

14 Hirsch, "If You Eat Dogs," 12.

15 http://www.nytimes.com/2015/06/24/world/asia/dog-eaters-in-yulin-china-unbowed-by-global-derision.html?_r=0 (14 August 2015).

16 Cf. Jeanne Boden, "Escaping the room.
A Post-socialist reading of Wang Bing's *Father
& Sons,*" *Journal of Contemporary Chinese Art*
(to be published in the fall of 2015).

17 Michel Foucault, "Les hétérotopies,"
in Daniel Defert (ed.), *Foucault. Le corps utopique,
les héterotopies* (Paris: Lignes, 2009), 24.

18 Allan Sekula, *Fish Story*
(Düsseldorf, Richter Verlag: 1995), 116.

19 Desiderius Erasmus, *The Praise of Folly,*
transl. Hoyt Hopewell Hudson (Princeton and
Oxford: Princeton University Press, 2015), 62.

20 Participation is possible via www.contour7.be/
barking (14 August 2015).

21 First manifesto of A Dog Republic (2012),
reproduced as "A Revolution A Day 01/78,"
De Standaard, 23 June 2015, 3.

22 Herman Asselberghs, "Capsular," *AS,* 179
(2007): 14.

23 Herman Asselberghs, quotation from conversations
with Mieke Bleyen and Hilde Van Gelder,
in Hilde Van Gelder (ed.), *Bruegel Revisited*
(Bruges: Stichting Kunstboek, 2006), 31.

24 Asselberghs, "Capsular," 16.

25 T.J. Demos, Mark Godfrey, Ayesha Hameed, Eyal
Weizman, "Rights of Passage: Migration," *Tate Etc.*
19 (Summer 2010): n.p. To be consulted via:
http://www.tate.org.uk/context-comment/articles/
rights-passage (14 August 2015).

26 Cf. http://diepresse.com/home/politik/
aussenpolitik/4761198/Boot-ist-voll_Ungarn-
nimmt-keine-Fluchtlinge-zuruck (14 August 2015).

27 Cf. http://www.theguardian.com/world/2015/
jun/24/the-boat-is-full-hungary-suspends-eu-
asylum-rule-blaming-influx-of-migrants (14 August
2015).

28 Henk Van Houtum and Roos Pijpers,
"The European Union as a Gated Community:
The Two-Faced Border and Immigration Regime of
the EU," *Antipode,* 39:2 (March 2007): 291–309.

29 Cf. the Italian prime-minister Matteo Renzi: http://
www.theguardian.com/commentisfree/2015/
jun/23/mediterranean-migrant-crisis-not-italy-but-
europe?CMP=share_btn_fb (14 August 2015).

30 Cf. http://alfardmenninga.nl/2015/07/23/lesbos-
verstoppertje-spelen-met-ngos/(14 August 2015).

31 Although in contemporary Greek one uses
the word *trela* for folly, most Greeks will still
understand the ancient Greek connotation of
the term *moria.*

32 Michel Foucault, *Madness and Civilization.
A History of Insanity in the Age of Reason,* transl.
R. Howard (London, New York: Routledge,
2001), 11.

33 X., "Bootvluchtelingen op Lesbos zitten in 'camp
from hell,'" *De Standaard* (2 July 2015), 18–19.

34 Cf. http://newsmonkey.be/article/30562 and
http://nieuwsbytes.com/isis-al-4000-van-onze-
strijders-vermomd-als-vluchtelingen-in-europa/
(14 August 2015).

35 Cf. https://www.vluchteling.nl/nl/Nieuws-
Overzicht/Reisverslag-Lesbos.aspx#
(14 August 2015).

36 Pauline Lallement, "Migrants à l'assaut
d'un autre monde," *Paris Match,* 3449
(25 June – 1 July 2015), 54.

37 Cf. http://www.amnesty.fr/Nos-campagnes/
SOS-Europe/Actualites/Calais-Et-si-respectait-
enfin-les-droits-de-ces-personnes-15792?utm_
source=emailing-action&utm_medium=email&utm_
campaign=2015-08-INFO-CALAIS?utm_
source=emailing-action&utm_medium=email&utm_
campaign=2015-08-INFO-CALAIS
(14 August 2015).

38 Erasmus, *The Praise of Folly,* 48.

39 Exceptionally, the author translates from
the Dutch version of Erasmus' book: Desiderius
Erasmus, *Lof der Zotheid,* transl. Henk van der
Werf (Zoetermeer: Free Musketeers, 2013), 56.

40 Inspiring ideas were recently gathered
in *Europe: Closed Doors or Open Arms?,* Eunic
Yearbook 2014/2015 (Göttingen: Steidl, 2015).

41 Hans Trapman, *Wijze dwaasheid.
Vijfhonderd jaar* Lof der Zotheid *in Nederland*
(Amsterdam: Balans, 2011).

42 Thomas More, *Utopia,* transl. Ralph Robinson
(London: Wordsworth, 1997), 24–25.

43 Hans Belting, *Hieronymus Bosch. Garden of Earthly
Delights* (Munich: Prestel, 2005), 109 and 113.

44 Urbano Ragazzi, "'With Love from $inister': Chiara
Fumai", *Dust Magazine* (8 December 2013),
to be consulted via http://dustmagazine.com/
blog/?p=10955 (14 August 2015).

45 Johan Verberckmoes, *Schertsen, schimpen en
schateren. Geschiedenis van het lachen in de
Zuidelijke Nederlanden, zestiende en zeventiende
eeuw* (Nijmegen: Sun, 1998), 33.

46 Foucault, *Madness and Civilization,* 14.

47 Cf. Pieter Geenen's video work *Nocturne* (2006),
in which the viewer gets to read the words "la più
bella isola del mondo" after the indication of the
location where the work was filmed: Lampedusa.
In an explanatory text, the artist claims that he
was struck by the pervasive presence of this slogan
on the island, in particular in boat rental places
for tourists. Cf. http://www.silenceisgolden.be/
nocturne.html (14 August 2015).

48 Herman Pleij, *Het gilde van de Blauwe Schuit.
Literatuur, volksfeest en burgermoraal
in de late middeleeuwen* (Amsterdam: Meulenhoff,
1979), 182.

49 Foucault, "Les hétérotopies," 36.

50 Michel Foucault, *Histoire de la folie à l'âge classique*
(Paris: Gallimard, 1972), 42. This part of the first
chapter, entitled "Stultifera navis," was not included
in the English translation.

51 Marco Poloni, *Displacement Island* (Genève: Centre
de la photographie, 2013), n.p.

52 Joerg Bader, "Drifting towards the vertical beach.
About Marco Poloni's Work *Displacement
Island,*" separate text inserted in Poloni,
Displacement Island, 6.

53 Belting, *Hieronymus Bosch,* 111.

54 Foucault, "Les hétérotopies," 25.

55 Sebastian Brant, *Das Narrenschiff,* facsimile edition
(Budel: Damon, 2007), opening page.

The Monster and *l'Appareil Digestif*

Chus Martìnez

The Happy Swamp

In thinking about Utopia, one imagines radical transformation. The imagination of "transformation," however, is a tricky one. From religion to Modernity, the force that manages radical change is one that comes upon us, from the outside. The light, the machine, nature—all are energies that would shape life in a new way, unprecedented, providing human beings the opportunity during their lifetime to feel goodness, to realize the perfect conditions of dreams. In Utopias, the possibility of experiencing a radical-change-for-the-better is as important as goodness itself, if not more so. It is the possibility of night followed by day, by light, by a life that harmonizes and balances all that before was tension, and endless effort, unfairness. Consciousness and memory, therefore, are key to the recognition that Utopia got realized—that a new world free of the old one did emerge in front of our very eyes.

Utopias have to do with travel, of course, with migratory thinking, with the expeditionary mind. They heavily rely on the witness, who—based on her or his memories—should be able to say if the new place is paradise or rather just as bad as home. I often think about second- and third-generation "paradisers" or "utopians." The second generation of children born in utopian conditions still have access to the "otherness" thanks to the recollections of their parents. I imagine them saying how good things are, when compared with how bad they used to be. For the third generation, however, Utopia will merely be "home," the status quo, and they may start to rebel against it just because life is defined by dynamics and the absence thereof may feel oppressive. In a sense, my problem with Utopias is that they betray a fear for what is exterior, and they will therefore be unable to outlast the human mind's constant changes of will. They rely on intentionality and will, as well as on consciousness and memory, stressing the privileged position of the human figure and the dream of making peace with its enemies. Utopias, in one word, are anthropocentric.

Drugs Function Like Utopias

Like Utopias, drugs alter our state of mind and make us co-authors of new personal and collective image albums—images produced by our senses in collaboration with these substances. Drugs demand from us that we become witnesses, that we report from the angle of this oscillation of the before-and-after of the self. Both drugs and Utopias rely on an idea of the "natural" self; they conceive of the body as the place to which this self needs to "return," creating the social and collective conditions by rules—Utopias—or by altering our experience of the real in such a way that it becomes clear our body is not enough to cope with the many possibilities our mind is opening up to us. Both modes of thinking about what we are missing start from a notion of coherence: the belief that we, humans, need to immerse ourselves in a system of thoughts or a system of experiences that will then determine a new self. A new self that actually refers to the old self, or rather, more correctly, the original self. An original self that is "much more in touch" with what really matters and that better understands not only what is ahead, but also the possibilities of humans to become "closer" to or even get really "near" to things, animals, senses, rocks, law, equality… This wave of nearness is the expression of the human will, a will defined by awareness, alertness, clairvoyance, light… All our modern and almost modern logics of thinking revolve around light—a light that allows us to make distinctions and therefore helps us to find a balance, to seek equality. It is a radiating light that enjoys its own extravaganza and mesmerizes the body and its senses. To this day, radiance and luminosity are the key concepts that ensure the eloquence of our relation with the future. Screens are important not only because they allow us to see pictures, but also because in making us see images they illuminate us. We know all this. Light is more powerful than any other element—than any other of the thousand natures we have invented for the social or for the mind to seek refuge in. But where is the monster in all this?

The Monsters Are the Eyes of the Screens

Thinking is never entirely abstract. It is always embodied. It somehow has a direction. Children tend to draw a head and lines or rays of light coming out of it to depict the mind at work. We somehow imagine thinking as happening inside a head and reaching out to another head. On the other hand, light is culturally expressed as coming from or being outside of us, illuminating us, making us see, or taking us along on its waves. From crystals to drugs, and from screens to Utopias— all that radiates does so upon us.

And so I imagine the monster as the light itself looking at us. Or, in other words, I imagine the monster to be a force following a logic that differs from the logic of the classical view: the body as having a self, a humanistic self, or a natural self or even a liberal self. All of this does not go together with the notion of the human as having a mind from where thought is happening and where a rather coherent idea of identity can be placed as "monster." Do not think of the monster as an anomaly or a de-formation of this idea of the human; try, as long as you can, to think about the monster as the light that comes out of your phone, or your iPad, or your computer—the light illuminating you, seeing you.

The Light Is a Vitamin

Our mothers used to say this: sun is vitamines to you. They repeated what doctors started to know already at the beginning of the last century but which became popularly known much later. The history of vitamins is as complex as the history of Utopias and the development of drugs. For centuries, alchemists and doctors have known that human beings failed to have "elements" that have an incredible effect on their body and restore its balance, the health it lost. Different to drugs, vitamins do nothing; they do not influence or "expand" our senses; they merely sustain life, so to speak. It took centuries to refine the instruments and the thinking to understand that they are not magic properties but elements that can be isolated and, once isolated, can be recombined and absorbed again by our body. What surprised me the most about vitamins is not their complex history and the fascination about bio-chemicals that we all share somehow, but the fact that humans are the only animals unable to produce the vitamins they need. There is an interesting parallel here: in contrast to thinking, which is supposed to be an inside force of our mind, vitamins are exterior to us—like the light shining upon us.

The history of this external element essential to our life has my interest for many reasons. If few women played a pivotal role in the development of vitamins, as scientists and nutritionists active in laboratory research, women were crucial to the socialization of this research, to its integration in society at large. In the 1920s and 1930s, research began to focus on trying to understand the human metabolism. The isolation of vitamins started in the second half of the 19th century, and during the 1920s multiple experiments proved the role of vitamin A and D, while further studies isolated vitamins C and K (a powerful anti-hemorrhage). Gradually, the interest in dieting began to take another form, while food was not only a question of access, class, or tradition, but a question of health and a new form of self-control. Especially relevant for our context is the work and research of Catherine Kousmine (1904–1992). Kousmine was a Russian émigré who studied in Lausanne and developed a theory and a praxis on the cure of cancer based on food, or, rather, on dieting. Her first diet protocol, described in a case study in 1949, centered on the improvement and cure of a patient suffering from intestinal cancer and was highly influenced by the research of another woman, Johanna Budwig. All through the 1940s, Budwig, a German biochemist, had developed a study of fatty acids and their influence in cancer cure. In 1952 Budwig published her first diet protocol in which she basically highlighted the virtues of flaxseed oil mixed with low fat cheese and meals high in fruits, vegetables, and fiber, as well as the importance of avoiding sugar, animal fat, salad oil, meats, butter, and especially margarine. Even if Kosmine followed the discoveries and the precepts of Budwig's diet, she was also a pioneer in a new understanding of the properties of raw food for our health. She put a special emphasis on cold-pressed oils. During WWII oils were pressed under heat, from 160 to 200 degrees centigrade. The reason was simple, this technique allowed one to extract up to 70% of the grain's fat. The resulting liquid is a dark and strong smelling liquid that needs to be processed and refined, and this refining involves mixing the oil with hexane (a dissolvent), only to separate them again later. This oil lasts forever; it is "dead," as Kousmine put it. Cold pressed oils, on the contrary, are alive; they are obtained by simple physical processes, such as filtering and decanting, but they react to light, becoming rancid, and they need refrigeration once the bottle containing them is opened. Her texts are intensely eloquent in explaining how simple food has been transformed by the industrial processes and how the loss of fatty acids, also called vitamin F, plays a fundamental role in how our cell membranes are protected from external attacks, as, for example, in an immunodeficient condition.

There is no hard evidence, of course, that cancer is cured by following diets as rigorous as the Kousmine method. Nor is it my point here to explain these methods. The interesting aspect is the parallel development, as of the early 20th century, of both dieting and drug understanding and use. The common denominator is clear: the way they affect our metabolic system.

The growing interest in drugs and diets has been closely linked to efforts aimed at exploring the possibilities of enhancing our capabilities. The world of drugs is all about the brain, about the possible chemical transformations that will enable us to explore this organ, and therefore the way we sense the world. To compare the rise of interest in vitamins and raw food with drugs may seem nonsensical at first sight.

But the research on vitamins and oils and diets has been based in a trust that goes beyond the modern mind's need to see immediate results. Even if the effects of these ingredients are noticeable in the short term, the interest in the body reflected by all these diets is one that does not need a witness, a judge. It may take generations to absorb, to metabolize all this knowledge and affect and transform the body.

It may take hundreds of years before we can understand the evidence of particular experiments. We have vitamins, the monsters, to avoid our body from falling ill, to make us live longer, or to stretch our productive years. We have developed the science of nutrition not only to achieve a strong-machine body, but also to be able to generate a paradoxical state, one in which we are so healthy that we can work more while also having a body which makes us feel like we are living in a resort, in a state beyond labor. In my view, vitamins, like the light, represent for us the possibility of the redundancy of labor and of becoming just radiant. Becoming radiant is a way of talking about human individuals who do not structure their life around production (or consumption) but around being itself.

The monster, then, is the total externality that marks a territory for life beyond these classical ideas of the self and of labor. If drugs are all about the mind that like a skyrocket is able to take off and escape leaving behind a damaged body, the metabolic cult expressed by super food represents a body capable of making the mind last and radiate.

Oh, Well, It's Just a Story!

Oh, well, you may say, it is just a story! What does all of this has to do with art? Yes, indeed, it is merely a story, an exercise in imagining. What I am proposing to you is to look at vitamins in the same as way you look at art. Both occupy a position of total externality as regards the body, both represent a challenge to the idea of labor, and still it is difficult to think of how art is the vitamin, the monster. Historically and culturally we have been searching for constant expansion, in all sorts of fields and territories of life, and, at the same time, for balance. This involves a quite paradoxical movement, because the one drive contradicts the other. One of the hardest things to imagine for us is how to produce an image of goodness that is not static or entropic. In other words, how can we grow without advancing, conquering, destroying or taking? From Utopia to the thousands of versions of "ecological balance" movements, human beings have been trying not only to reach that new state of grace, but to find an image for it that would not be kitsch or represent bluntly this immense complexity, one for which we still do not have enough words. My idea is to propose art (the vitamin, the monster) not as an artifact, not as the object-without function, not as the site of taste, but as an organ.

Imagine art as being an organ, an organ that operates independently from us and may be part of us or relate to us, but not only that. If art is an organ, its function is exactly that: to produce an imagination of change that does not necessarily correspond with the one we inherited from Modernity. Art, being much older than our recent cultural memory, rehearses other notions of time and also synchrony, but also itself embodies the most sophisticated and challenging idea of change and transformation that we can imagine. As an organ it has been affected by an array of ideas on form, image, and culture throughout the ages, and still it managed to continue to inhabit a non-place, or a place that surpasses representation in so many ways. And an organ, like a body organ, is situated, but this being situated is something you feel, more than that you see it. And an organ, too, that has defied the great many problems Modernity posed to the human body by counterpointing it to the machine, the tool, the dream of becoming a super-body, artificial or even virtual.

Emergence Replaces Teleology

This idea of art as an organ—a third gender, if you like—addresses the need to acknowledge our ignorance about the nature of emergent processes—like art—through which consciousness, the organism, and the environment are constituted. Art as an organ is art as an emerging form of intelligence capable of transforming the way we sense (time, matter, the self, the mind, the others, the social) and of forming images and experiences of renewing our notion of life and the world.

Rather than as a discipline or a practice among other practices or a metaphysical force possessed by few, we need to conceive of art as a stomach. Art, in other words, is more like a digestive organ or a liver than an eye or an ear. An organ that posses a non-conscious form of will or intelligence, or, if conscious, a consciousness that is not identical with any known language. If we envision art as a digestive organ, just for the sake of the idea here presented, it is not difficult to see why philosophy often refers to art as being a movement. To function, art needs to produce continuous oscillations in the way matter is seen and treated, and the same happens with ideas and the chains of ideas in arguments and even in ideologies—in the clouds of belief that ideas can form to be less abstract, more of a presence to which people can relate in time and a given culture.

Consider this organ—art—as a fourth dimension. A fourth dimension that contains all possible forms, but also all possible ways of sensing the universe. In this external relation to the world—since the world as we rationally know it has three dimensions—it is not difficult to see how this organ is capable of both assuming time (through its digestive function) and embodying freedom, because it is barely conscious, barely able to know its own pre-conditions, while it is also impossible for us to limit or to enhance that monster. Yes, because this organ—which is big and small at the same time, at once alive and unconscious—is art, and art is the monster. As such this "monster" refers to a time and a space further removed from form. The beautiful name "monster" names the total impossibility of description, of applying the norm, of being subject to discussion, to labor, to a movement in history, to a gender, to a particular imagination. Monster is the name of intelligence, not seen as an agent or an active principle, but as a stomach taking its time for digesting.

Timeline of the travels and correspondence of Desiderius Erasmus and Thomas More between March 1515 and December 1516, focusing on the conception and publication of *Utopia*.

March 1515: Erasmus travels from Basel to London where he hopes to get support from his patrons. Here he may be staying in Thomas More's house, as he did in 1509. His previous stay inspired Erasmus to write *In Praise of Folly*, which he dedicated to More. 1509 was also the year in which Sebastian Brant's *Ship of Fools* was first published in English.

7 May 1515: Erasmus writes to Peter Gillis in Antwerp (Ep. 326) recommending that he welcome Thomas More during his imminent visit to Flanders. Peter Gillis is a close friend of Erasmus and acts as his secretary in Antwerp.

18 May 1515: More arrives in Bruges as an envoy of Henry VIII to meet with the ambassadors of Prince Charles and to negotiate trade agreements regarding wool.

June 1515: More and Erasmus meet in Bruges. Erasmus is returning to Basel from London and is temporarily staying in the house of John Louis de Moscheron, who is a good friend of Hieronymus van Busleyden.

July 1515: Erasmus travels to Basel, passing through Antwerp and Mechelen. This gives him the opportunity to remind his friends Gillis and Busleyden to adequately welcome More when he leaves Bruges.

21 July 1515: The trade negotiations stall and More is free to visit Erasmus's friends. The other ambassadors, Cuthbert Tunstall in particular, leave Bruges for other destinations in Flanders.

21 July – 1 October 1515: Erasmus is in Basel. Where More goes during this nine-week period is not fully documented. In his first letter upon his return to London at the end of October 1515, dated February 1516 (Ep. 396), which More sends to Erasmus, he writes that he visited both Gillis and Busleyden during his break in Flanders. He also elaborates on Busleyden's house and library in particular.*

1 October 1515: A letter is sent from More and the other ambassadors to Cardinal Wolsey, signed in Bruges. In this letter they say they are still waiting to hear from the other delegation. This suggests More had already returned to Bruges.

13 October 1515: Another letter is sent by the ambassadors to Wolsey, signed in Bruges.

21 October 1515: More writes a very long letter in reply to Martin Dorp and his attack on Erasmus. This letter is also signed in Bruges. It is considered a defence of Christian Humanism against scholasticism.

24 October 1515: More meets Wolsey's secretary on his way back to London. Wolsey's secretary confirms this.

17 February 1516: More writes to Erasmus from London (Ep. 396) updating him on their common business and giving him a short account of the people he met in Flanders. There is no mention of *Utopia* in this letter. More informs Erasmus that he has refused a pension from King Henry VIII to maintain his independence.

April 1516: Erasmus sends *The Education of a Christian Prince* to Charles V, who, following the death of King Ferdinand II of Spain, has become emperor and governs over a vast territory in Europe (Ep. 389).

June 1516: More writes to Erasmus again (Ep. 417) as he is trying to send money to him, but this is proving more difficult than was foreseen. Again there is no mention of *Utopia*, but More does refer to his poems, asking Erasmus to do with them as he pleases. These are the *Epigrammata* published with the third edition of *Utopia* in Basel in 1518.

June 1516: Busleyden writes to Erasmus referring to Erasmus's criticism of kings expressed in his last letter. Busleyden suggests Erasmus should maintain more moderate views publicly.

July–August 1516: Erasmus travels to London at the end of July and stays in More's house until 14 August. The purpose of this trip is to discuss with More and Andrea Ammonius a dispensation request to Pope Leo X. More and Erasmus probably discuss the publication of *Utopia*.

3 September 1516: More sends Erasmus his *Nusquama*, "nowhere well written," (Ep. 450) together with a prefatory letter to Peter Gillis apologising for sending it a year after their meeting in Antwerp, instead of only six weeks.

October 1516: More writes to Erasmus (Ep. 470) in early October before receiving a reply to his previous letter, recommending him to get prefatory letters for his book from scholars and men of high ranking. Here he refers to Busleyden without mentioning his name, saying that he (Busleyden) had recommended that More only publish his book after the nine years prescribed under *labor limae*. This would suggest that Busleyden was aware of its existence and had had an opportunity to read a part of it previously.

2 October 1516: Erasmus replies to More's September letter (Ep. 461) informing him that all care will be taken with publishing the book and that Gillis loves it. Erasmus had probably already read most of it during his stay in London and had informed More of his appreciation.

31 October 1516: More again writes to Erasmus (Ep. 471) and warns him of his many enemies and that he should be very careful with republishing his work. He says he is happy that Peter Gillis likes his *Nusquama* and wants to know what Tunstall and Busleyden think.

1 November 1516: A letter is sent from Gillis to Busleyden in which he refers to Busleyden's "intimate acquaintance with More" and later says "for by intimate contact you really know him for a man of superhuman and almost divine genius." In the letter, Gillis states *Utopia* "is recommended to the world by your patronage." Gillis calls Busleyden, Maecenas, indicating that Busleyden perhaps paid for the publication of *Utopia*. This letter appears at the beginning of the first edition of the book.

November 1516: A letter from Busleyden to More is sent to Erasmus on 9 November in reply to his request to send a prefatory letter for the book. According to Busleyden *Utopia* "withholds itself from the many, and only imparts itself to the few." Busleyden at the end refers to More as "glory of your Britain and this world of ours." This replicates a note that More wrote on the frontispiece of Busleyden's own collection of writings, during his stay at his home. In the note More calls Busleyden "rare glory of his native country."

12 November 1516: Gerardus Noviomagus writes to Erasmus (Ep. 477) assuring him that everything is being done to complete the publication of *Utopia* and that he is sending him an image of the island for him to correct.

16 November 1516: Erasmus writes to Gillis (Ep. 482) informing him that the book is in the press.

4 December 1516: More writes to Erasmus (Ep. 486) expressing his happiness about the comments he is receiving about *Utopia* and shares a dream, in which he is King of the Utopians.

16 December 1516: The book is printed with the prefatory letters of Peter Gillis to Busleyden, Busleyden to More, and More to Gillis, as well as some poems.

Note
* There is no way to clarify how much time More spent in Antwerp and Mechelen during this period. The editor of the Yale edition of *Utopia*, J.H. Hexter, supposes that More made two visits to Antwerp, the first at the end of July, just after leaving Bruges, and the second around 12 September. The second date he deduces from More's own words in the introduction to *Utopia* where he says he arrived in Antwerp after having already been four months away from home, and we know he left London on 12 May. There is no reason to think that More was not telling the truth in his statement. Hexter's reconstruction suggests that during the first visit More and Gillis had time to conceive *Utopia* and that during his second visit More presented Gillis with the first draft. So the possibility that More was in Mechelen writing the book in between those visits to Antwerp can be considered. Busleyden was very accustomed to hosting scholars at his home. – NS

Bibliographical references in the Fooling Utopia Library
For the epistles referred to in the timeline:
— *The Epistles of Erasmus*, Vol. 2, English translation by Francis Morgan Nichols, Longmans, 1904.

For the letters of Thomas More and Hieronymus van Busleyden:
— *The Correspondence of Sir Thomas More*, edited by Elizabeth Rogers, Princeton University Press, 1947.
— Henry de Vocht, *Jerome de Busleyden, Founder of the Louvain Collegium Trilingue, His Life and Writings edited for the first time in their entirety from the original manuscript*, The Brepols Press, 1950.

For an interesting reconstruction of More's travels in Flanders:
— Appendix II in *Yale Edition of the Complete Works of St. Thomas More*, Volume 4: *Utopia*. Edited by Edward Surtz S.J. and J. H. Hexter, Yale University Press, 1965.

FOOLING UTOPIA
Catalog of CONTOUR 7:
a Moving Image Biennale
in Mechelen

Editor: Nicola Setari
Contributors: Chus Martìnez,
W. J. T. Mitchell, Hilde Van Gelder
and Katarzyna Ruchel-Stockmans
Editorial coordination:
Hannes Dereere and
Marion Prouteau (DF)
Translations and Copy editing:
Ton Brouwers, Martine Bom,
Alison Mouthaan, Elisabeth
Cluzel and Alex Brighton
Graphic design:
Luc Derycke and Stijn Verdonck,
Studio Luc Derycke
Photos of artworks:
Kristof Vrancken, Elio Germani
(for Ana Prvački and Grazia
Toderi) and Milena Vergara
Santiago (for Angel Vergara)
Photos of venues: Stijn Swinnen,
Milena Vergara Santiago
(for Mechelen Cultural Centre)
Proofreading: Duncan Brown

Special support for the pro-
duction of the catalog: Vadim
Grigorian, Pier Luigi and Roberta
Lanza, Andrea Montanari
and Alice Setari, Bernard and
Laurence Soens, Pier Alberto and
Marina Testoni

Special thanks to the Dena
Foundation for Contemporary
Art for assisting with the editorial
coordination of this catalog.

Published by:
MER.Paper Kunsthalle
Geldmunt 36
B-9000 Gent
www.merpaperkunsthalle.org

Texts © the authors, Art
© the artists, Photography
© the photographers, © Contour
& MER. Paper Kunsthalle
for this edition

ISBN 978-94-9232-108-4
D/2015/7852/30

The curator would like to thank
Charlotte Bonduel, Marcel and
Ernesto Setari, and Tommaso and
Giuliana Setari for their ongoing
support and insights throughout
the making of the exhibition. He
also wishes to thank the supporters of the catalog, without whom
this publication would not have
been possible.

Exhibition Colophon

CONTOUR 7

A Moving Image Biennale
in Mechelen
29 August – 8 November 2015

Curator: Nicola Setari
Advisors: Chus Martìnez, W. J. T.
Mitchell, Hilde Van Gelder
Artists: AaBbPp, A Dog Republic
& RAM Radioartemobile, Sander
Breure & Witte van Hulzen,
Andrea Büttner, Jan Fabre,
Michael Fliri, Chiara Fumai,
Johan Grimonprez, Fabrice Hyber,
Rabih Mroué, Ana Prvački,
Michael Rakowitz, Gilad Ratman,
Albert Serra, Slavs and Tatars,
Nedko Solakov, Javier Téllez,
Grazia Toderi, An van. Dienderen,
Angel Vergara, Gilberto Zorio

Team

Director: Steven Op de Beeck
Production and public mediation:
Alyssa Decq
Communication and press:
Hannes Dereere
Production assistance:
Edoardo Cimadori, Lola Daels,
and Laura Tack

Special thanks to Natalie Gielen,
Lieze Eneman, Katleen Vermeulen,
Jailee Rychen, Sam De Wit, Lars
Van Vlasselaer, Quinten Verhelst,
and Jo Clarysse

Web design: Studio RGB
AV: Vidisquare and Eidotech
Installation: AORTA, Wankel
and Artouché
35mm film: Filmprojektion Mondt
Lighting: PRO FORMa
Polystyrene: Twinplast

Lenders: Braverman Gallery,
Tel Aviv
Peter Kilchmann Gallery, Zürich
Galleria Raffaella Cortese, Milan
Sfeier-Semler Gallery, Beirut
and Hamburg
Carl Michael von Hausswolff
and Leif Elggren
Mario Pieroni and Dora Stiefelmeier
(RAM Radioartemobile)
Kraupa-Tuskany Zeidler, Berlin
Nathalie Obadia, Paris
Museum Voorlinden, Wassenaar
Private collection H.G. Knokke
Private collection Brugge
Rhona Hoffman Gallery, Chicago
and Jane Lombard Gallery,
New York
Universiteitsbibliotheek Leuven
Koninklijke Bibliotheek
van België
Foundation LIMA

Full list of sponsors:
Studio Luc Derycke, Studio Rgb,
Designosource, Moonshack,
Academie Mechelen, Stedelijke
Musea Mechelen, Emmaüs
Vzw, Kazerne Dossin, Frans
Masereel Centrum, Uit in
Mechelen, Toerisme Mechelen,
Beaufort 2015, Triënnale Brugge
2015, Open Monumentendag
2015, Mmmechelen Feest Vzw,
't Atelier

CONTOUR 7 thanks its wonderful volunteers, guards and guides.

Board members of Contour:
Heidi De Nijn, Marie-Louise
Grouwet, Koen Leemans,
Bert Leysen, Stijn Maes,
Hans Martens, Luc Pelgrims,
Greet Pluymers, and Philippe
Van Meerbeeck

This publication was first
presented at the Utopia and
Europa Salon, which opened
on October 7, 2015 in Mechelen.
The salon was divided into three
public debates that took place
in the exhibition spaces of
CONTOUR 7 and was realised in
collaboration with the Directorate
General Culture and Education
of the European Commission
and the Representation of the
European Commission in Belgium.

START
CONTOUR 7
29.08–08.11.2015

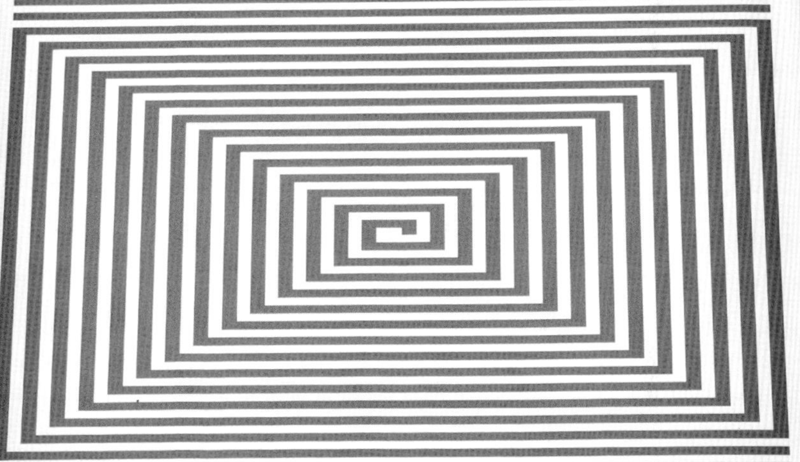

BIENNALE VOOR
BEWEGEND BEELD
A MOVING IMAGE
BIENNALE
WWW.CONTOUR7.BE   #CONTOUR7

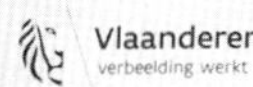
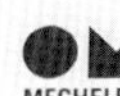
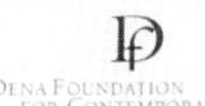
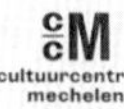
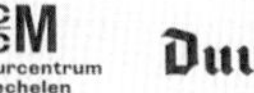
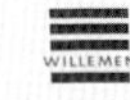
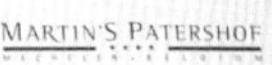
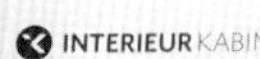
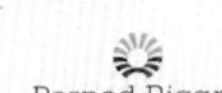
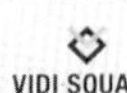

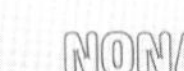
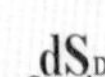

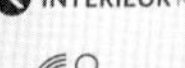
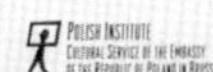
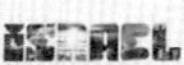

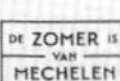
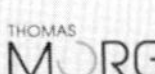
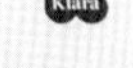
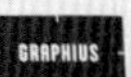

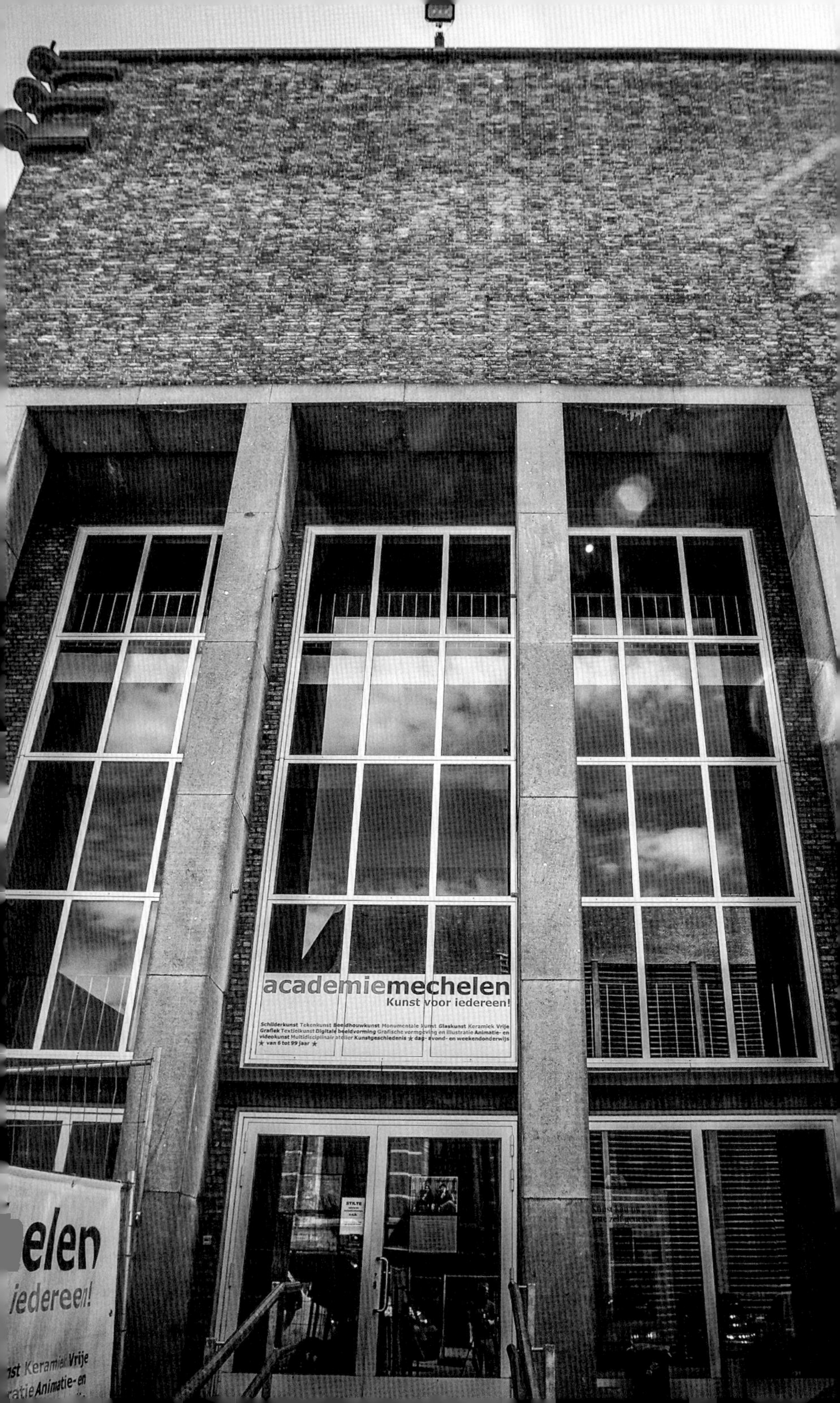

academiemechelen
Kunst voor iedereen!
Schilderkunst Tekenkunst Beeldhouwkunst Monumentale Kunst Glaskunst Keramiek Vrije Grafiek Textielkunst Digitale beeldvorming Grafische vormgeving en illustratie Animatie- en videokunst Multidisciplinair atelier Kunstgeschiedenis ★ dag- avond- en weekendonderwijs ★ van 6 tot 99 jaar ★
elen
iedereen!
st Keramiek Vrije
ratie Animatie- en

Mechelen Academy

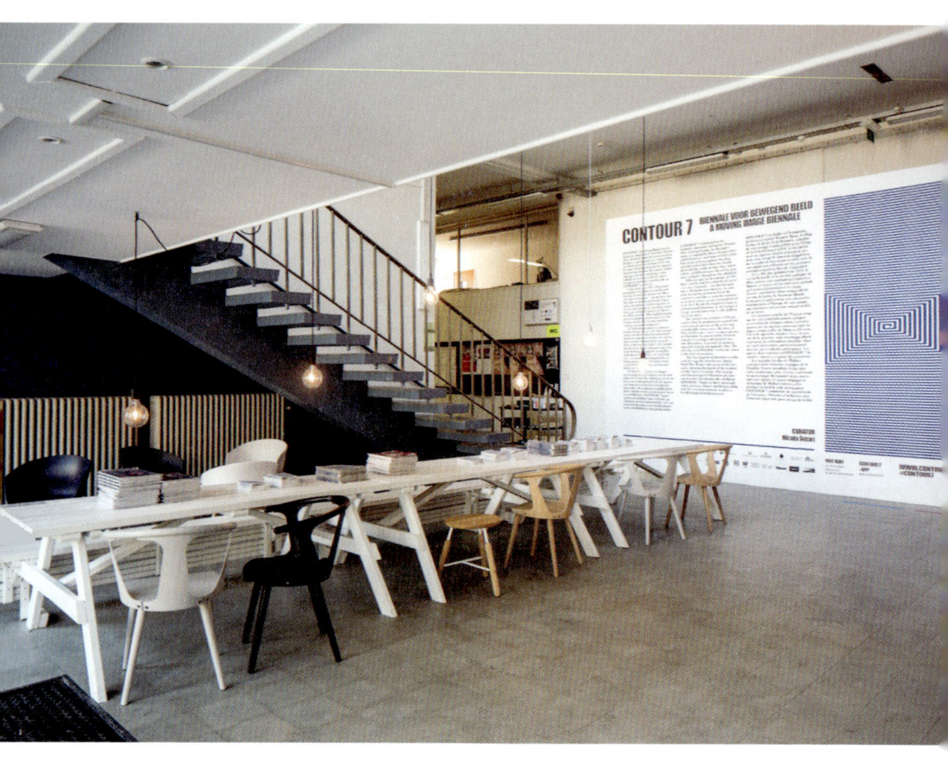

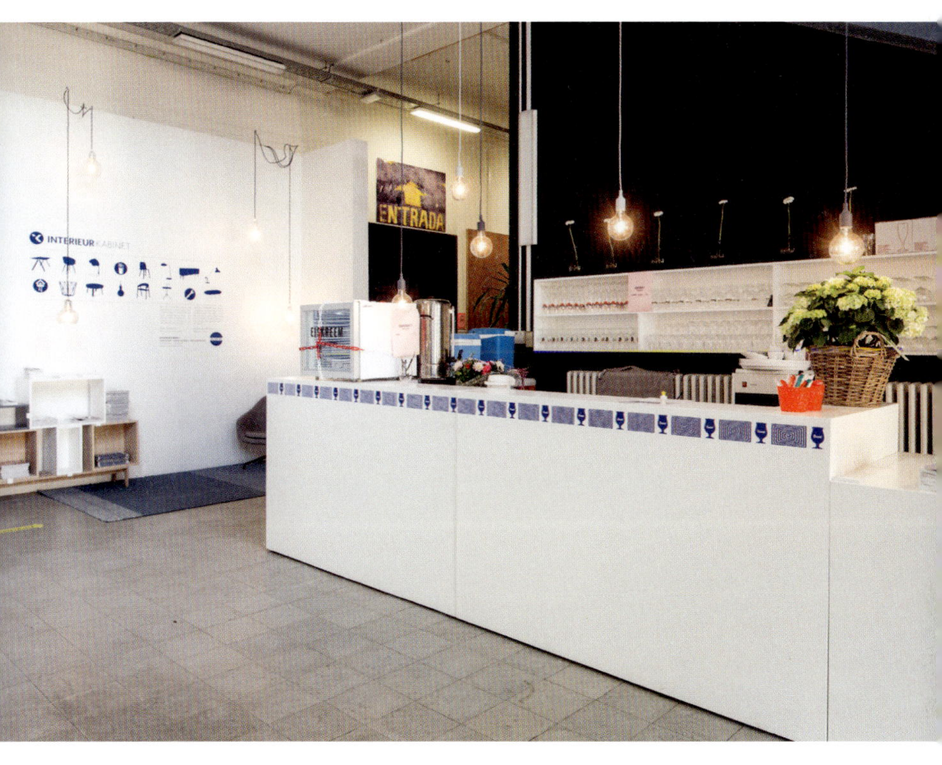

Starting Point CONTOUR 7
Mechelen Academy
Interior design by Interieurkabinet Mechelen

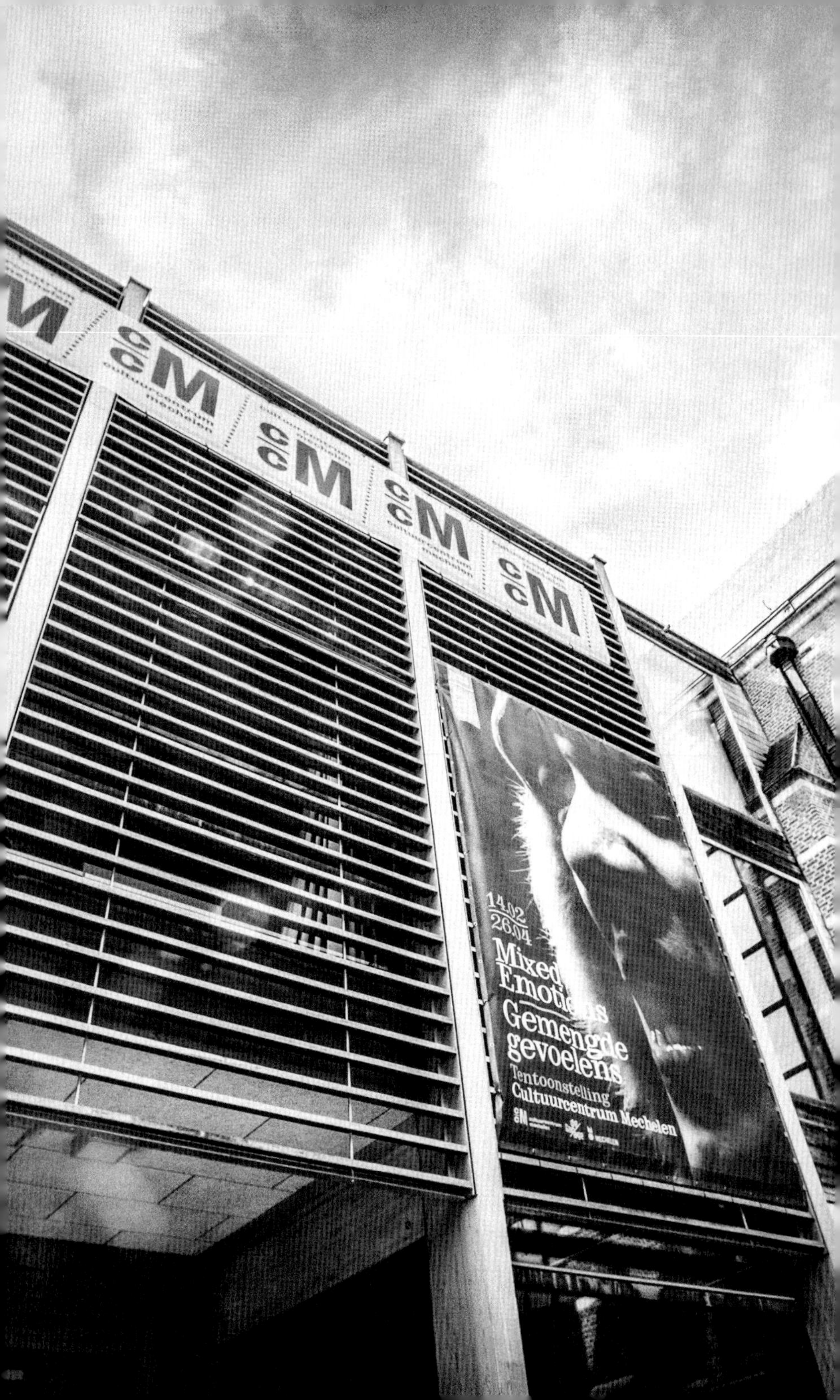
cultuurcentrum mechelen
14.02
26.04
Mixed Emotions
Gemengde gevoelens
Tentoonstelling
Cultuurcentrum Mechelen

Mechelen Cultural Centre

The site occupied today by the Mechelen Cultural Centre is steeped in history. It was once home to a large monastery complex with inner courtyard, guest rooms, and infirmary that was founded by Wouter II Berthout in 1231 and rebuilt in 1342 after a fire.

Following destruction and plundering, building work started on a new church in 1606. With the help of the city and its citizens, the church was embellished with (among other things) Margaret of York's mausoleum, sculptures by sculptor Frans Langhemans, and paintings by the Flemish baroque painter Antoon Van Dyck.

In 1796 the Order of the Friar Minors was banished and large parts of the monastery were demolished. Today the Cultural Centre houses the remains of the seventeenth-century church reminding the people of Mechelen of the Order.

Grazia Toderi

Grazia Toderi takes as her starting point the view at night from the tower of Sint-Rombout's Cathedral, which was never completed but still measures 97m in height. For her, this place is an imaginary vantage point from which Thomas More observed, studied and drew the island of Utopia. The idea came to her by comparing the first image of the island of Utopia published in the 1516 edition of the book with maps of Mechelen from the same period. She also makes reference in the title of the work to the nickname of the inhabitants of Mechelen, "Moon Extinguishers," which was given to them in the seventeenth century after a drunkard put the entire city into alarm by saying that the tower was on fire. The fire-fighting operation was stopped once everyone realized that it was the reflection of the moon on the glass of the tower producing bright lights on a misty evening, rather than an actual fire. The "foolishness" of the city's residents, far from being a negative trait, testifies to their utopian spirit.

In her video, projected onto the ceiling of the rotunda of the Cultural Centre, the contours of Mechelen blur into a suspended luminous island, a rotating horizon, which makes Belgium look like one big city. A recurring formal element in her videos, the rotation also suggests the movement of celestial spheres, transfiguring the physical lights of the city, into a spiritual and existential dimension. The horizon is in fact traversed by an axis of lights moving across a line that doesn't follow the general rotation. For the artist these rigid movements signal the arrivals and departures to and from Mechelen. Many of those departures where forced, when in the 1940s, during the Nazi occupation, the city was used as a transit zone for the deportation of Jewish and Roma people to Auschwitz. The question mark that towers and also rotates over the layers of images invites the viewer to interrogate history in its positive and negative narratives. This work was chosen to symbolically open the exhibition parcours of CONTOUR 7.

– NS

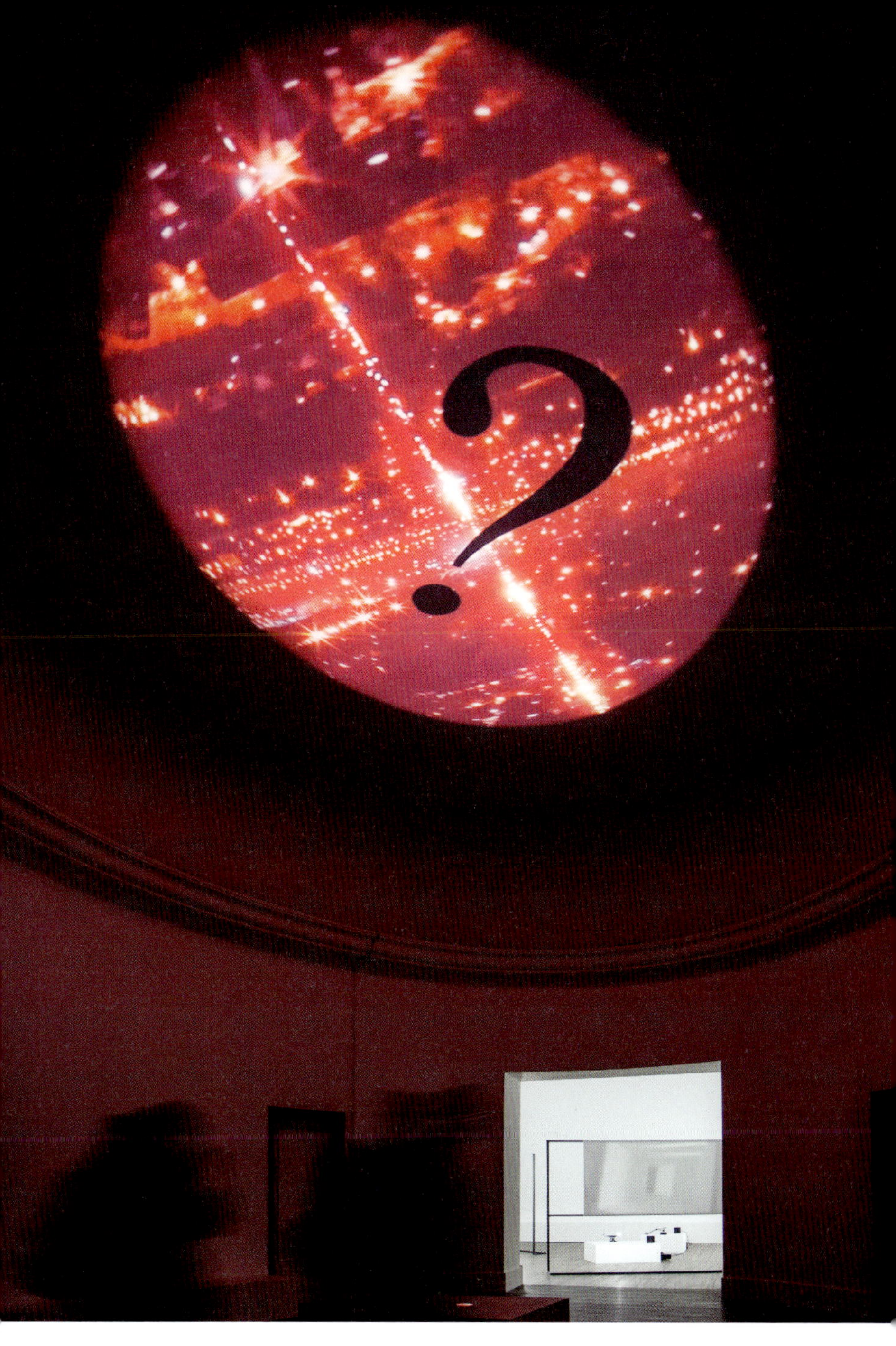

Moon Extinguishers, 2015
video installation, sound, 10′ 00″
Commissioned and co-produced by CONTOUR 7 /
Supported by Istituto Italiano di Cultura, Brussels

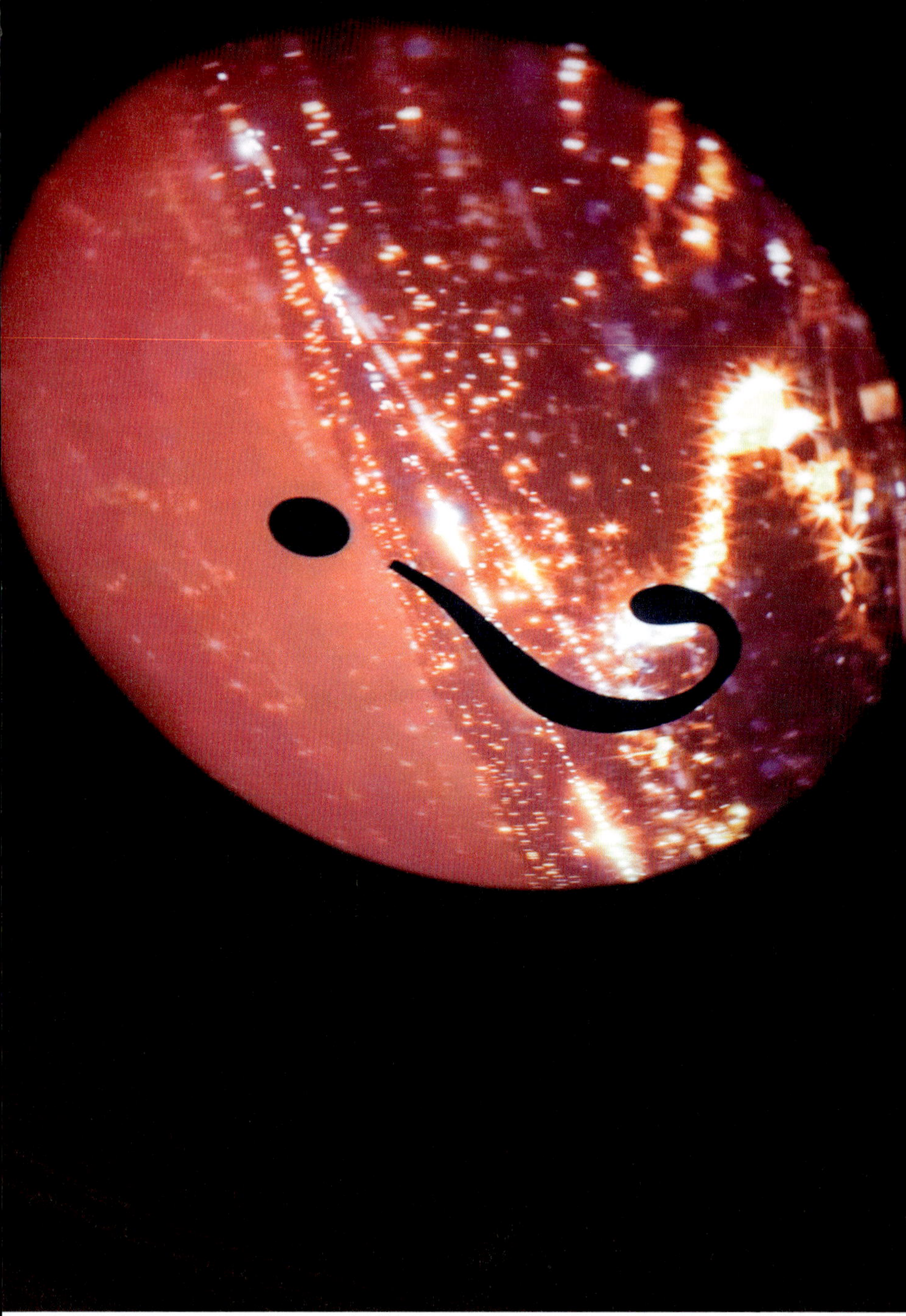

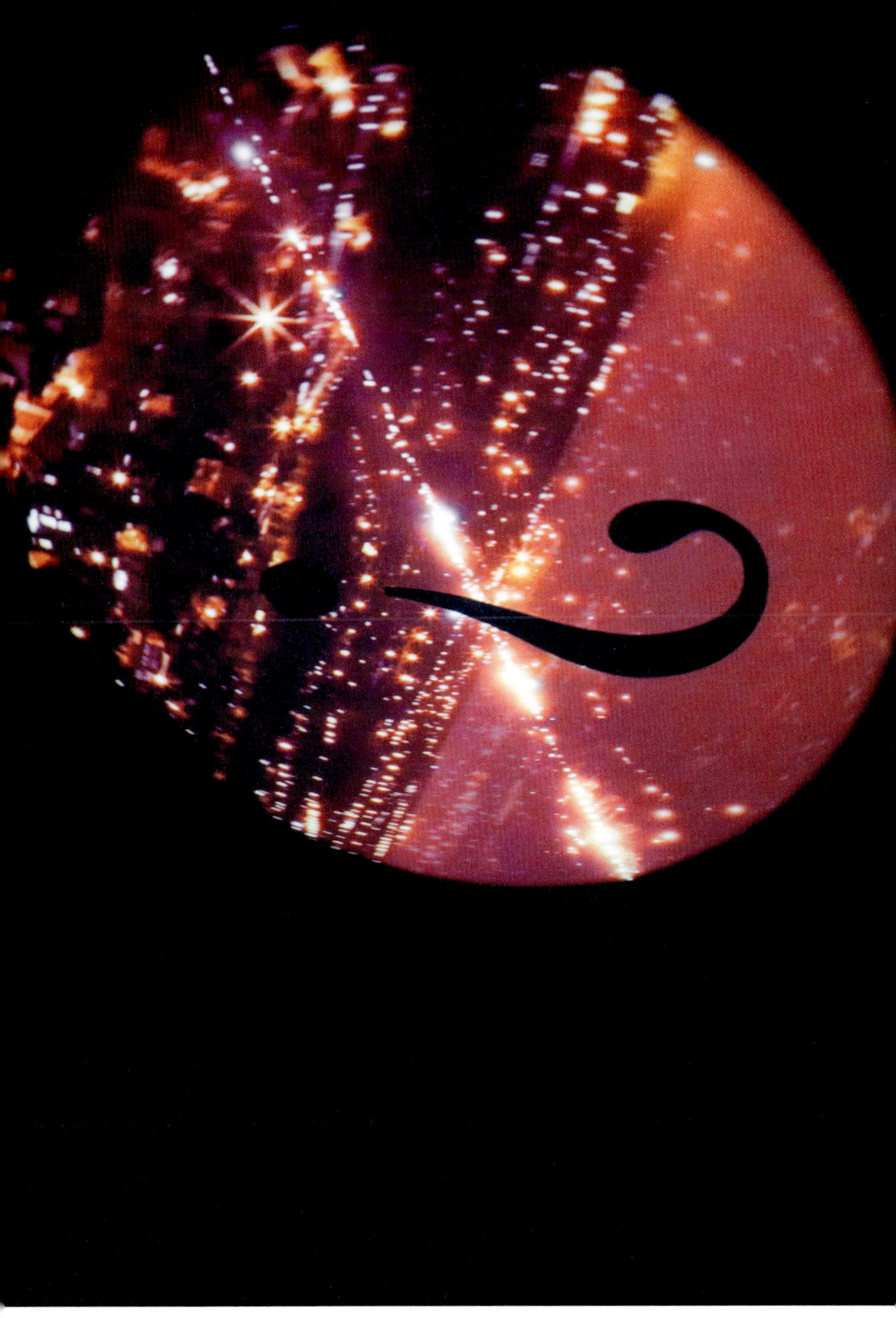

Moon Extinguishers, 2015
video installation, sound, 10′ 00″
Commissioned and co-produced by CONTOUR 7 /
Supported by Istituto Italiano di Cultura, Brussels

Andrea Büttner

The 1960s counter-culture often resorted to music as a way of expressing social contestation. Music was seen not only as an elevated and harmonious aesthetic experience, but was also used to voice anger and discontent. The quintessence of that tendency has been the destruction of the instrument on which the music is played as the last, concluding act of the piece. Surprisingly, not only guitars have fallen victim to such creative-destructive drive: beginning with Fluxus performances in the early 60s, notably by George Maciunas, there is a distinct history of artists committing piano destructions, choosing the noble and expensive instrument in order to radicalize their provocative act. Andrea Büttner invites new consideration of this tendency in her bold piece entitled, ironically, *Piano Destructions*. Shown next to historical footage of artistic performances focusing on the destruction of an instrument, nine female musicians perform in choir several piano pieces by Frédéric Chopin (1810–1849), Robert Schumann (1810–1856), and Claudio Monteverdi (1567–1643). The Romantic compositions evoke ideas of artistic genius and individuality, while the two Renaissance pieces by Monteverdi, Maciunas' favorite composer, were originally written for several voices and only later translated for piano. Here, the nine distinct instruments merge in one voice, mediating their individuality in a collective act. The pianists' gestures, smiles and gazes demonstrate a sense of community or even conspiracy. While both piano performance and piano destructions are associated with typically male activity, these female pianists are intently oblivious of that charged history. Counterbalancing the weight of that legacy, they invite us to enjoy the music in its pure beauty. As the video is shown in the context of the history of piano destructions, viewers might expect an interruption of the music ending in a destructive act. Frustrating that expectation, the piece instead offers a short respite from aggression and antagonism through an aesthetic experience which in Thomas More's utopia was considered to be the highest form of pleasure.

– KRS

BIO The work of German artist Andrea Büttner (°1972) includes woodcuttings, screen prints, reverse glass paintings, sculptures, videos and performances. She attempts to create connections between art history and social issues, with a particular interest in notions of poverty, shame, sexuality, vulnerability and dignity, and the belief systems that underpin them.

Büttner's work often references religious communities, drawing attention to the relationship between religion and art. Her previous public exhibitions have featured in the Museum for Modern Art in Frankfurt, Tate Britain in London, and Museum Ludwig in Cologne. She has participated in dOCUMENTA 13, the Sao Paulo Biennale and won the Max Mara Prize in 2010.

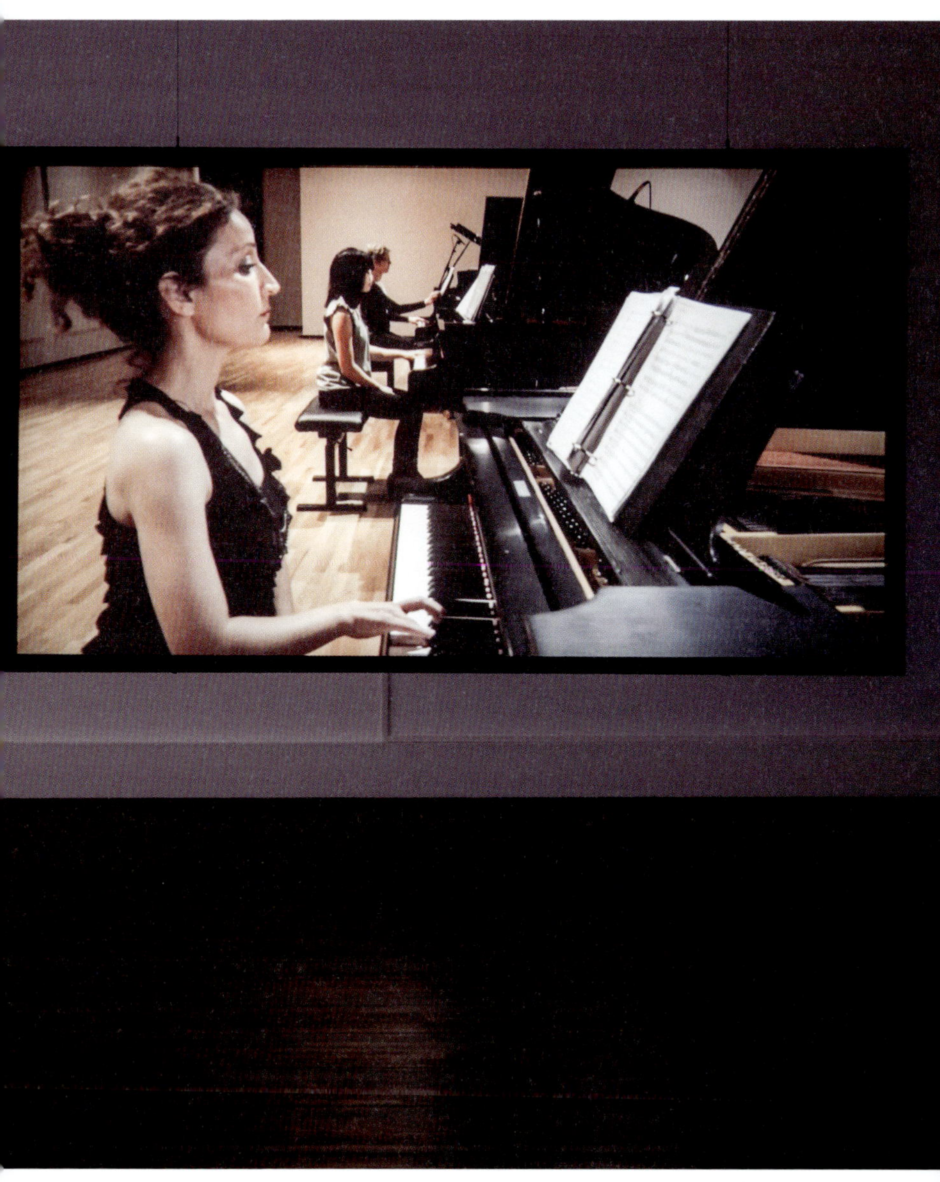

Piano Destructions, 2014
five-channel video installation, sound
Commissioned and produced by Walter Phillips Gallery and The Banff Centre,
Alberta / Supported by Goethe-Institut, Brussels

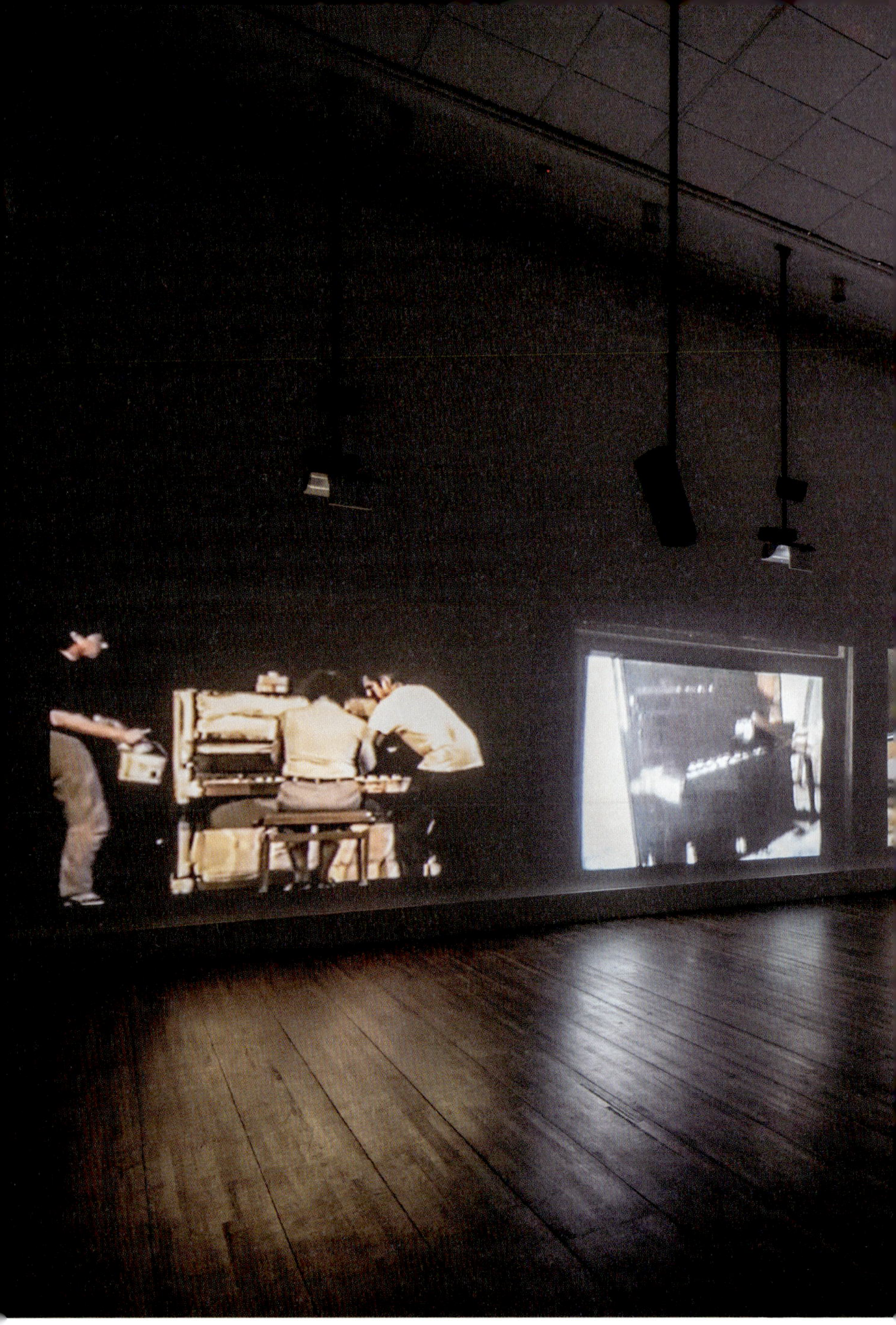

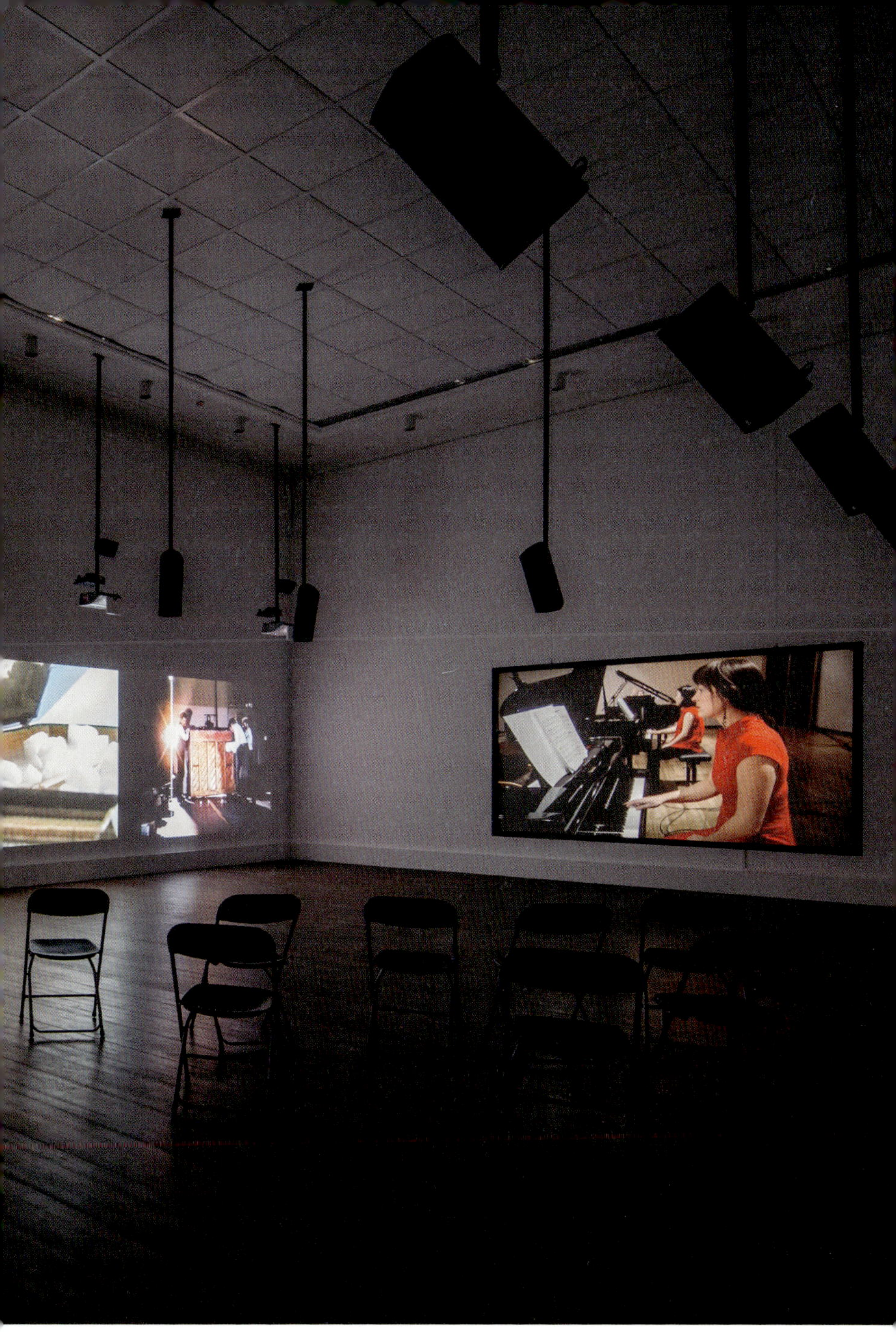

Piano Destructions, 2014
five-channel video installation, sound
Commissioned and produced by Walter Phillips Gallery and The Banff Centre,
Alberta / Supported by Goethe-Institut, Brussels

Gilberto Zorio

The Italian artist Gilberto Zorio proposes a singular perspective on the question of utopia. The installation consisting of partly fluorescent letters on a metal bar, lit by two different types of lights, transports us into the center of the visual language characteristic of Arte Povera. The minimalist arrangement of elementary forms, combined with the integrity of prime materials, is the signature style defining that now canonical current in art history. Gilberto Zorio works predominantly with such essential materials as stone, wood or metal, arranging them in basic, often symbolic shapes. The recurring motifs in his practice are a star, a javelin, and a canoe, but he also repeatedly uses language. The work *E' utopia, la realtà, è rivelazione* (1971) included here is exactly such a combination of elementary shapes and words. While the three terms: utopia, reality, and revelation are continuously lit by spot lights, the halogen lights are turned on and off at regular intervals. When they are on, they reveal the connecting words written with fluorescent letters. The full inscription thus reads: "It's utopia, reality is revelation." It is the reality, taken in its richness and simplicity, which may reveal itself as the source of epiphany. Yet Zorio adds more to that equation: this revelatory aspect of reality is in fact the utopia people search for. In Zorio's installation we find the most affirmative voice in the whole exhibition. It thus offers a counterbalance to the critical, somber, or mocking tone of the more recent art practices. It suggests that sometimes the answers should be sought in the ordinary and the mundane, because in the end it is where everything commences and terminates.

– KRS

BIO Italian artist Gilberto Zorio (°1944) is associated with the Arte Povera movement in Italy at the end of the sixties: a radical artistic stance of a group of artists towards the established values and institutions of the time, including government, industry, and popular culture.

In his work Zorio combines language and alchemy. His interest in the concept of "energy" led him to explore transformative natural phenomena, such as evaporation or oxidation. His sculptures, paintings, and performances are often regarded as metaphors for revolutionary human activity and creativity.

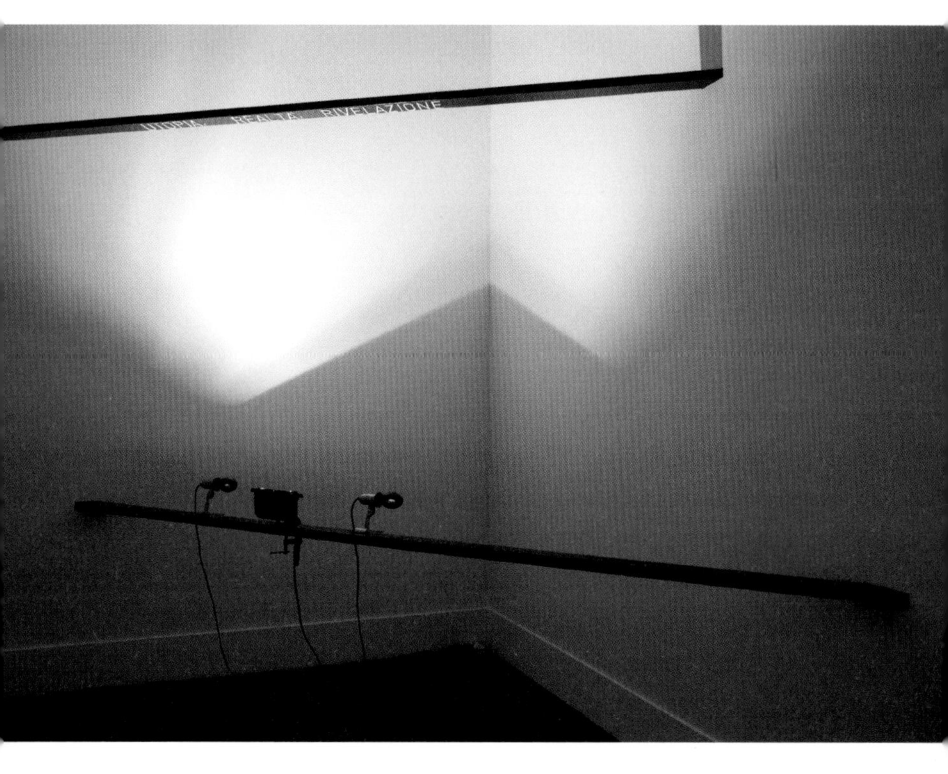

E' utopia, la realtà, è rivelazione, 1971
phosphorescent "wax" (cera), fluorescent letters, iron, timer, halogen, lamp, Wood's lamp
Courtesy the artist / Supported by Istituto Italiano di Cultura, Brussels

E UTOPIA, LA REALTÀ, E RIVELAZ

E' utopia, la realtà, è rivelazione, 1971
phosphorescent varnish, fluorescent letters, iron, timer, halogen, lamp, Wood's lamp
Courtesy the artist / Supported by Istituto Italiano di Cultura, Brussels

An van. Dienderen

The filmmaker An van. Dienderen works at the intersection between documentary, anthropology, and visual arts. While exploring various documentary strategies, she also investigates the medium of film in a self-reflective way. Her new work *Lili* not only tells a story, but also offers us a unique access into a rather overlooked aspect of the filmmaking process. What we see might seem like a quite uneventful moment in the creation of cinematic—real or fictional—worlds. Or is it? The girl named Lili, who rests somewhat cluelessly on a high chair in a film studio, appears to be increasingly bored. She is a China girl. She poses in front of a camera, motionlessly and with her eyes wide open. She has no dialogues to memorize or a character to impersonate. All she is required to have for the role is an impeccably white complexion. Of course, it is always better if she is pretty. Although her images will not be seen by a large public, the camera operators and technicians, who are usually male, prefer to look at pretty girls. China girls serve as models in a technical exercise preceding the actual filming, namely the calibrating of the colors of the camera and printing process. Nobody knows for sure why they are called China girls, as they are never actually Chinese. Perhaps because sometimes, when a live model was lacking, porcelain dolls were used for the task. Or perhaps it is because their skin is supposed to be as white as porcelain. With the film *Lili*, An van. Dienderen questions the supposedly neutral character of this highly problematic and ideologically charged practice. If the film tonality is adjusted to the white complexion, other skin colors look unnaturally dark. Black actors appearing next to white actors need to wear insanely thick layers of make-up, otherwise they will appear pitch black with only white patches of teeth and eyeballs. For this very reason, Jean-Luc Godard famously refused to use Kodak film stock when working in Mozambique. Can technology itself be racist? An van. Dienderen contends that the medium itself should be examined from its technical aspect, because it matters what we consider a norm, be it in the skin color, the gender relations involved in the film process, or an average beauty standard.

– KRS

BIO Belgian filmmaker An van. Dienderen (°1971) has made several internationally acclaimed documentaries, and writes on visual anthropology, cultural diversity, and urbanisation. Her work focuses on the relationship between artistic processes and society.

She investigates the opposition of fact and fiction, imagination and observation, and representation and experience, using the importance of the image in our multicultural society as the point of departure. The work of An van. Dienderen shows the absurd, poetic, and often touching stories that these oppositions can hold in everyday life.

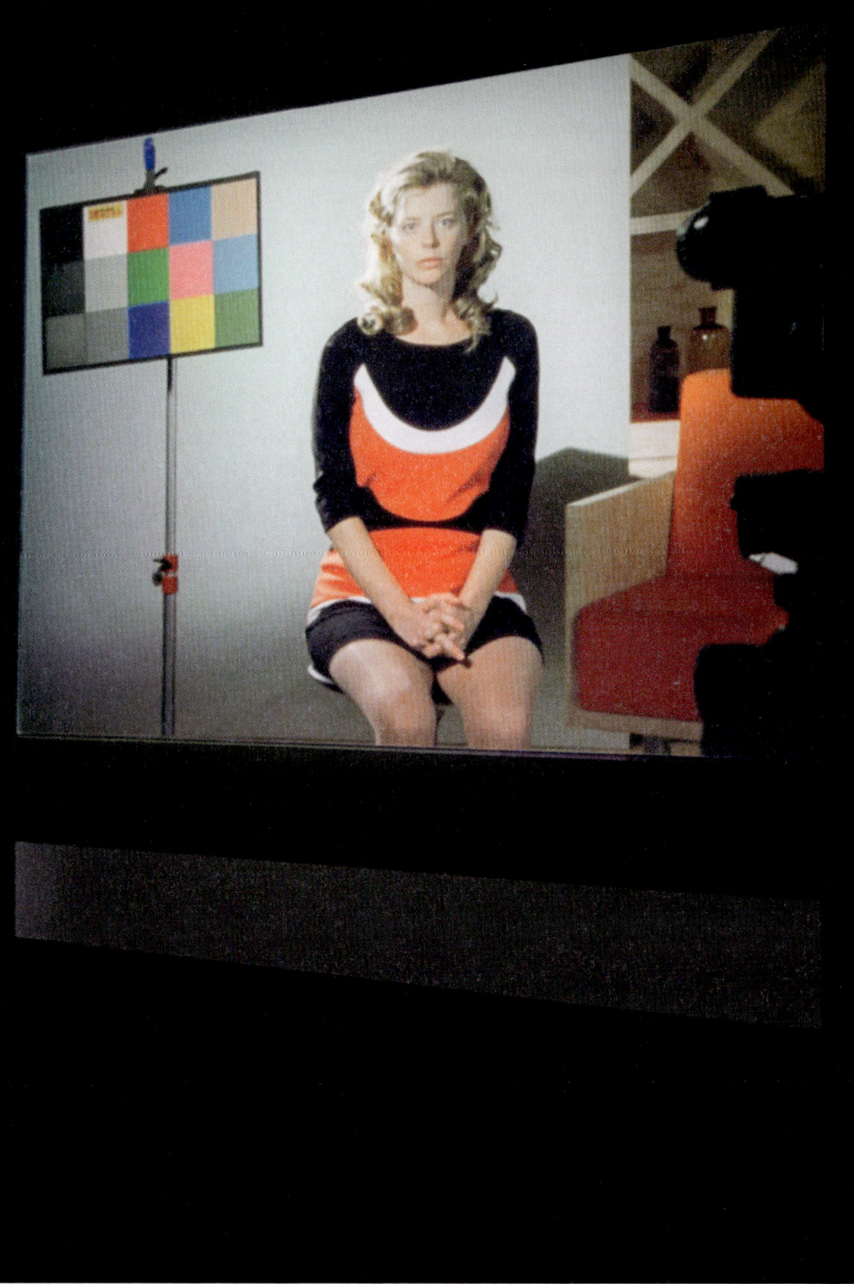

Lili, 2015
film, sound, 11′ 15″
Commissioned and co-produced by CONTOUR 7 /
Produced by Elektrischer Schnellseher / Supported by VAF, VRT, Argos,
On & For Production, Bella Belli and School of Arts (Ghent)

Gilad Ratman

The multiscreen installation by Gilad Ratman transports us into a strangely unreal world populated by small drones, flying haphazardly within an indoor space made entirely from styrofoam. These architectural structures are being cut and sliced by means of a hot wire, which makes the scene even more enigmatic. Drones are remotely operated electronic devices, which today may first call to mind sophisticated military and surveillance operations. But drones are also strongly tied to the natural world. They not only resemble insects but are modelled on their mechanics and behavior. Even the characteristic buzzing sound is similar to that of a bee drone, which, by the way, also gave it its name. Operated by a group of people isolated behind windows, with only their headless torso in view, holding remote-controls in their hands—the drones sometimes seem to be competing or fighting against each other. At other times, their flight patterns appear to be independent from each other or even random. Yet most surprisingly of all, they sometimes also seem to behave like a swarm. Without any central decision making, members of a swarm act in a similar way, thus creating a self-organizing system. Even when there is no visible hierarchy, they communicate and connect, which allows them to act together. In biology this fascinating and pervasive phenomenon has been described as emergence. The activities of drones, in themselves designed to imitate nature, can in return be suggestive of human behavior. The installation evokes an ambiguous human world, where cooperation, competition, decision-making, and control are transforming into each other, and becoming hard to trace and distinguish. The cutting of architectural structures, on the other hand, contrasts with the fluid and organic transformations of the drone structures. Ratman has a continuous interest in examining the fine line dividing the world of animals and that of humans. In *Swarm*, he investigates the possible connecting points between humans and technology. Ultimately, observing drones and their ability to act as an algorithm-guided super organism, becomes an exercise in better understanding the potential of social relations to transform into swarm-like structures. The menacing and uncanny effect such comparisons between drones and people might produce is a way of opening up a space in which we can inquire into social relations and interactions as they form spontaneously, in a bottom-up movement. At the same time, it is impossible to forget the drones' ubiquitous presence in contemporary surveillance, war, and destruction, which brings the installation closer to the theme of the monstrous.

– KRS

BIO   Israeli artist Gilad Ratman (°1975) lives and works in New York and Tel Aviv. His videos and installations search for ways to deal with untenable aspects of human behaviour by exploring the appearance of "pain," "struggle," and "the wild" within the friction of the real and the imaginary. Pushing narrative to its borders and allowing for a fractured chain of events to take place, Ratman investigates the possibilities of the cinematic apparatus. Cause and effect are abandoned in favor of a non-narrative space where the poetic and the pathetic can coexist.

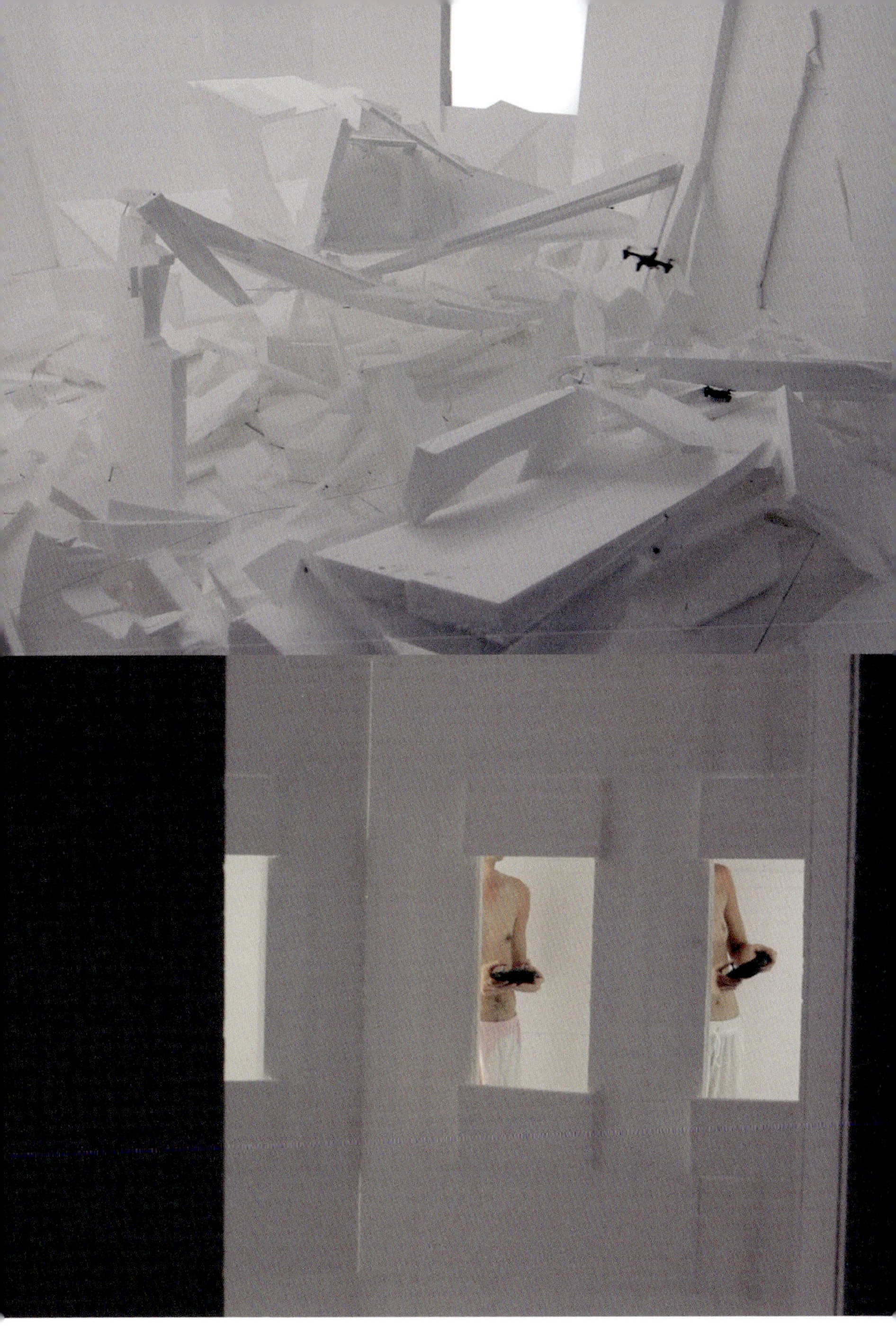

Swarm, 2015
multi-channel video installation, sound, 4′ 00″
Courtesy Braverman Gallery, Tel Aviv and the artist /
Co-produced by CONTOUR 7 / Supported by Israeli Embassy, Brussels /
Polystyrene thanks to Twinplast

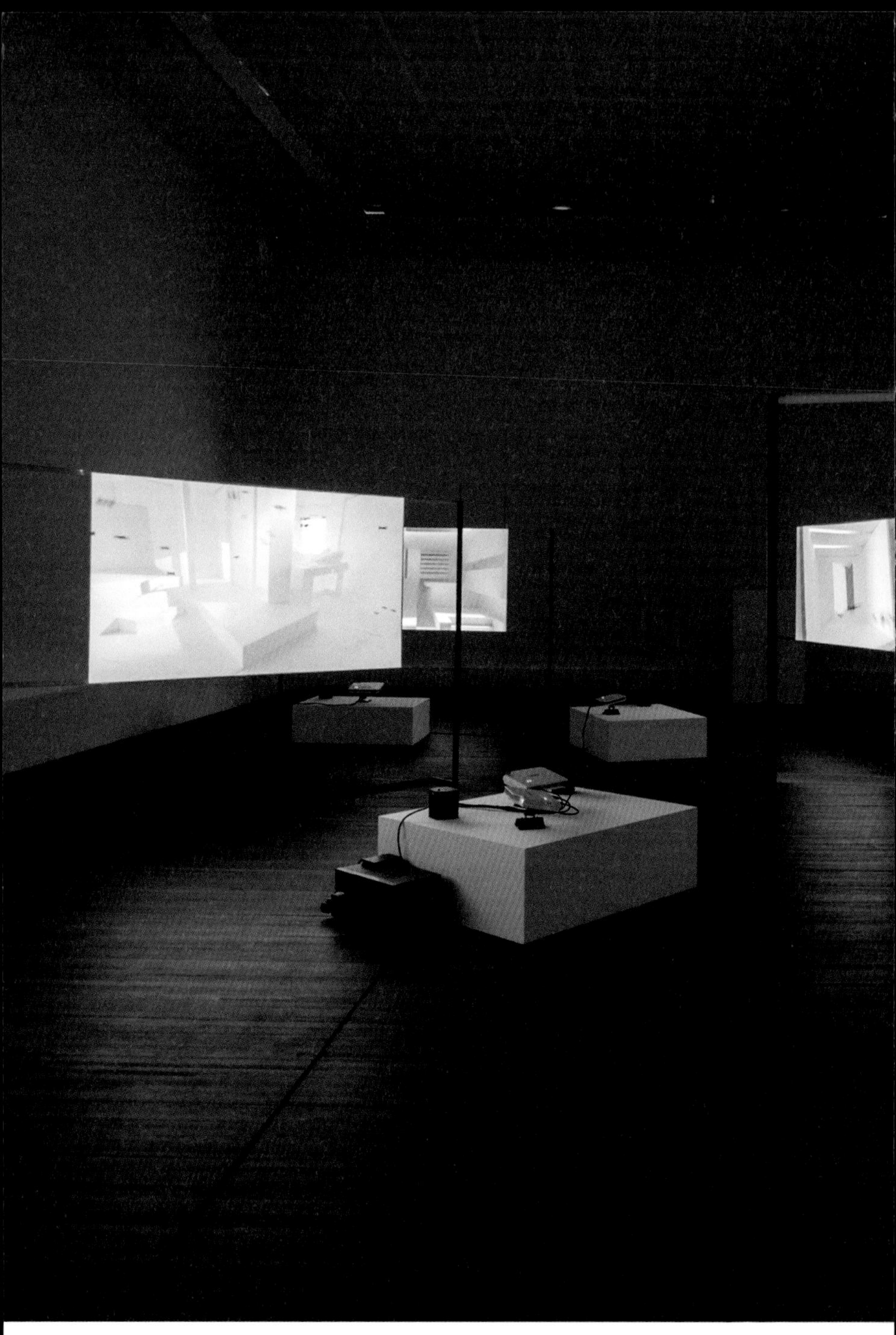

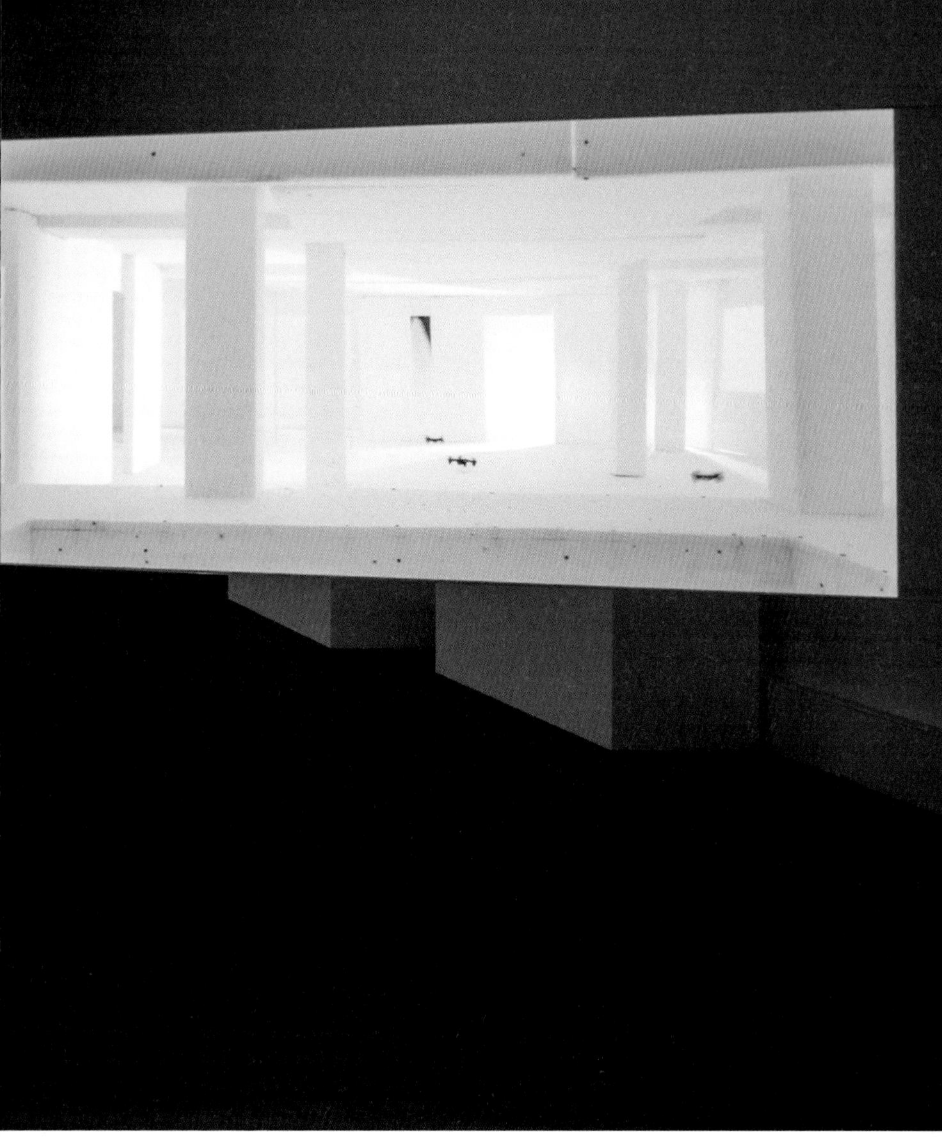

Swarm, 2015
multi-channel video installation, sound, 4′ 00″
Courtesy Braverman Gallery, Tel Aviv and the artist /
Co-produced by CONTOUR 7 / Supported by Israeli Embassy, Brussels /
Polystyrene thanks to Twinplast

Javier Téllez

Various utopias invented in European literature have always proposed visions of an improved world, similar to ours, only more accomplished. Every new artistic medium, on the other hand, has had as its ultimate goal to seamlessly render reality. When photography and film were invented, they were embraced as the new media promising an immediate access to the real world. They were praised because they successfully superseded older media. Javier Téllez revisits such an older, nineteenth-century medium called panorama in order to address the very topical political issue of today, namely migration. The question of how to organize a harmonious society without excluding some of its members is thus confronted with a reflection on the artistic medium. The panorama is a monumental, circular painting which once also held the promise of transporting the spectator into the middle of historically or geographically distant events. The Bourbaki Panorama in Luzern, where the film was made, shows the episode from the end of the Franco-Prussian war of 1871 in which the defeated army of general Bourbaki surrendered in the neighboring Switzerland. The highly realistic painting, enhanced by three-dimensional figures and props, shows a wintery landscape in which distressed and wounded soldiers receive help from the local population. The panorama thus portrays the central aspect of the Swiss national identity, which is the idea of the humanitarian aid. In Téllez' 35 mm film, the painting comes even closer to reality by an addition of actors impersonating some of its scenes. In front of the painting moves a procession of anonymous characters in contemporary clothes. People of different skin color and origin, both men and women, walk in the counter-clockwise direction. Leading that unusual convoy is the small sculpture by Alberto Giacometti *La Main* (1947). This bronze rendition of an emaciated hand, the poignant symbol of the destructiveness of war, reconnects different moments in European history with the present-day situation of refugees. All participants in the seemingly aimless wandering are refugees currently living in Switzerland. Instead of telling their particular stories, the film invites us to revisit the principles of humanitarianism. At the same time, it recuperates the idea of realism by featuring real people in need of help.

– KRS

BIO **Growing up as the son of psychiatrists, Venezuelan artist Javier Téllez (°1969) developed a close affinity with patients who suffer from mental illnesses. We can see this continuously reflected in his art. Through installation, film, and video, he addresses the general understanding and perceptions of such marginalised populations.**

Téllez investigates how and where we draw the often rigid line between normal and abnormal, healthy and sick. His work combines pathology with art, and in doing so diffuses the often rigid difference between creativity and anomaly.

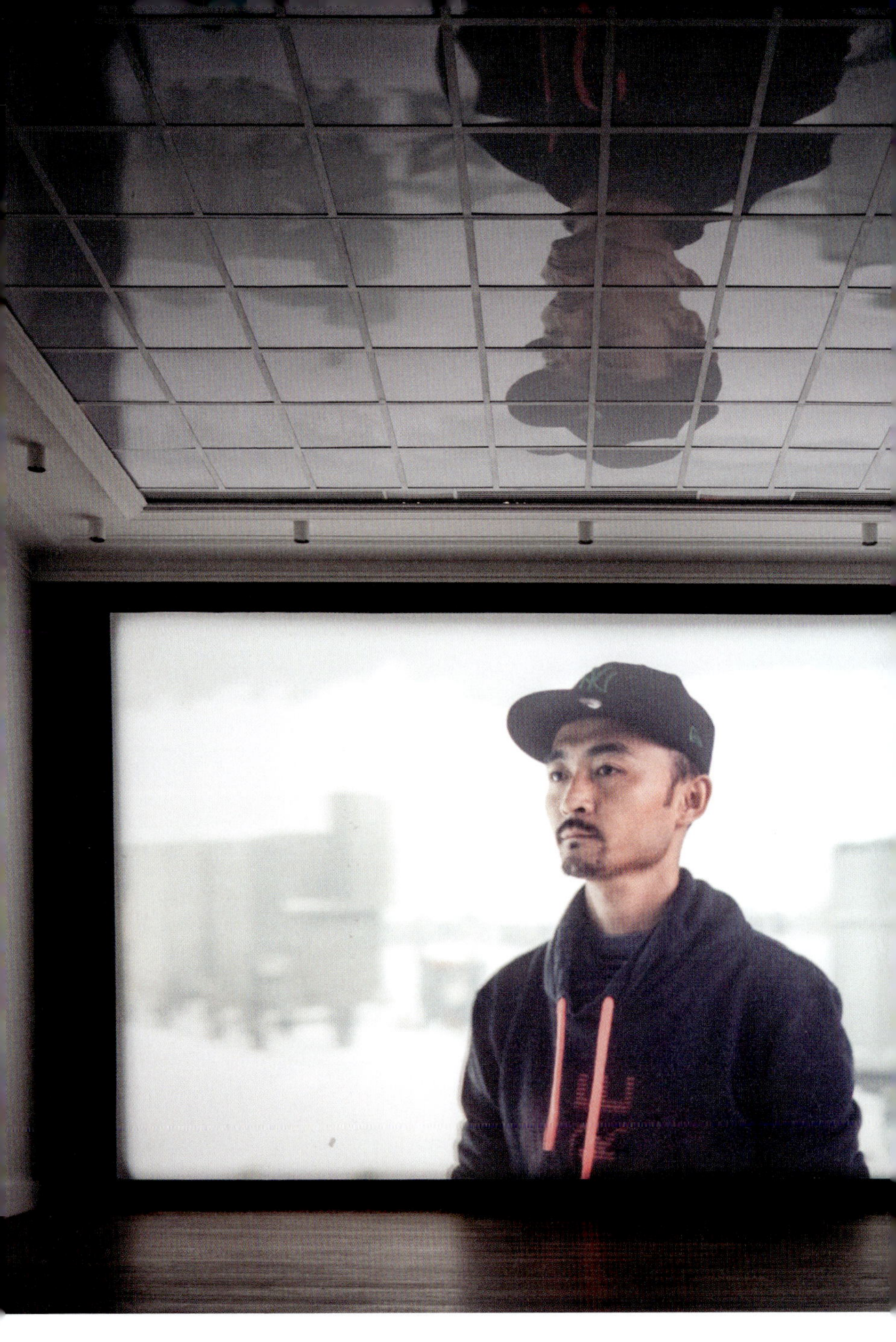

Bourbaki Panorama, 2014
35mm film projection, mute, 13′ 47″
Courtesy the artist and Peter Kilchmann Gallery, Zürich

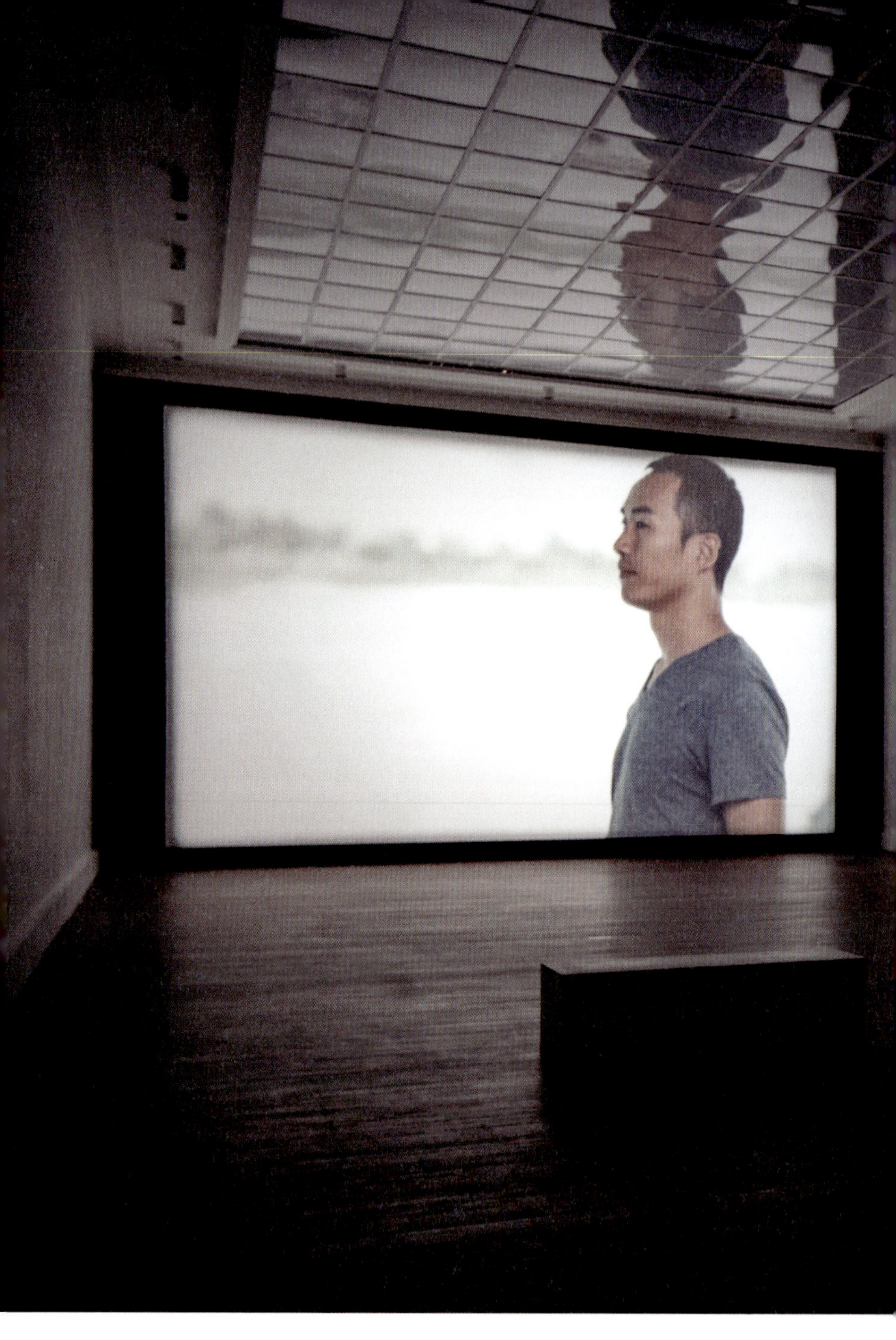

Bourbaki Panorama, 2014
35mm film projection, mute, 13′ 47″
Courtesy the artist and Peter Kilchmann Gallery, Zürich

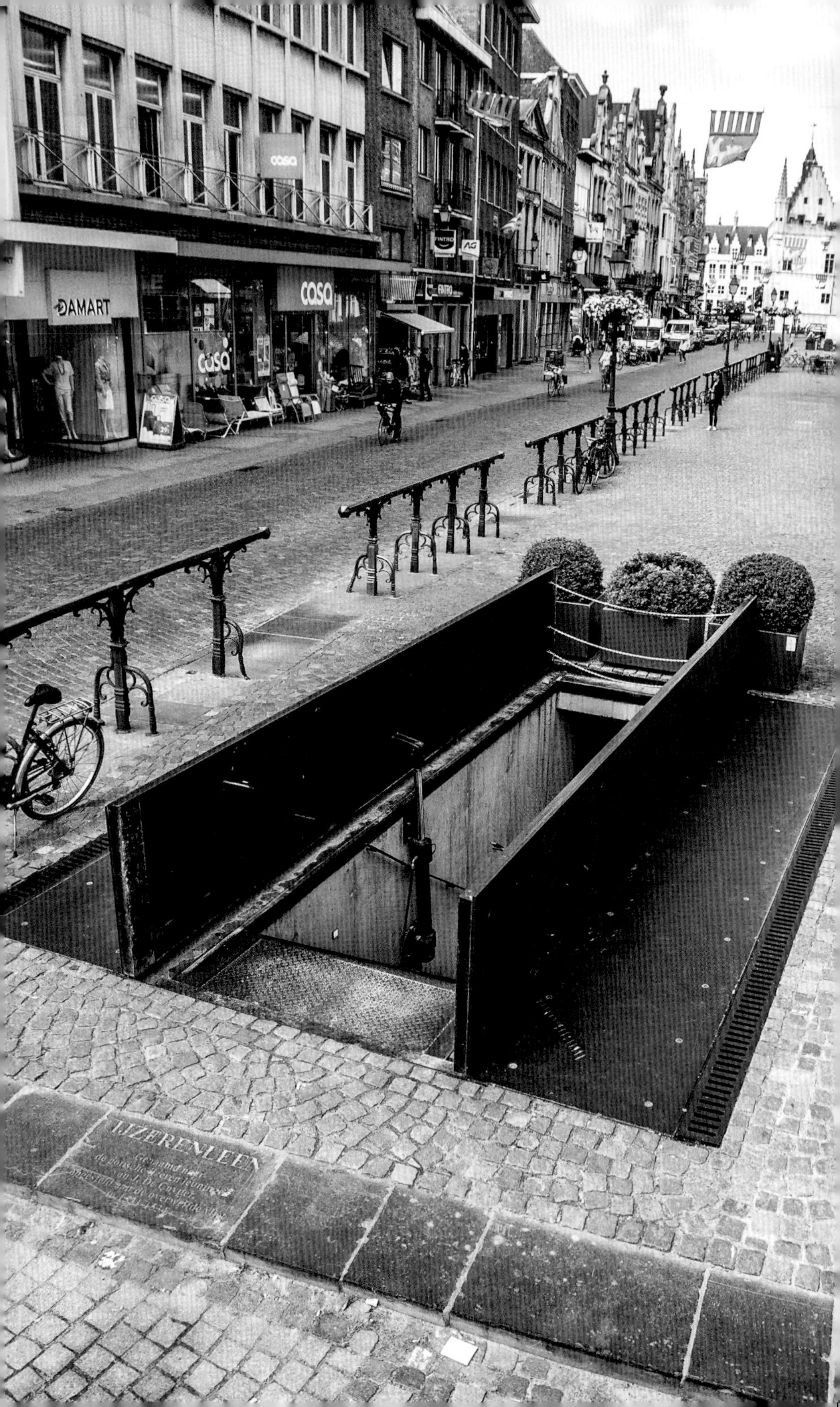

DAMART
casa
CASA
FINTRO
AG
IJZERENLEEN

De Vlietenkelder

Walking along the IJzerenleen it is easy to forget that one of the most impressive relics of Mechelen's history lies concealed beneath the paving stones. Only the decorative elements hint at the underground corridor complex. On descending the steps from the busy shopping street, one is struck by the peace and serenity of the place.

The existence of the former city canal or inlet (*vliet*) reminds us that Mechelen originated partly because of its favorable location at the confluence of several waterways. The city canal on the IJzerenleen was filled in and vaulted over in the sixteenth century. It was restored during the summer of 2012. Mechelen has had a turbulent history and the Vlietenkelder has played a crucial role in difficult times. During the Second World War, for instance, it served as an air-raid shelter protecting its citizens against attacks from above.

Michael Fliri

Fliri is a performing-video artist who brings us into the realm of surreal situations by staging acts in his videos that border on the absurd, while appearing as visual transfigurations of yet-to-be-pronounced parables. For CONTOUR 7, he pushes the envelope of such experimentation by combining his fascination for masks, the physical void they embody, and their cultural or fictional history with a paradoxical quote by Thomas More: "I Pray to God I'm a False Prophet." This introduces into his work an unstable referentiality to a historical figure, who as we know at the end of his life was martyred. When, after being tortured, More was forced to pronounce on political matters of the time, he responded with silence and was subsequently beheaded. In his video, Fliri appears to stage a contemporary form of martyrdom, where the beheading is replaced by the seemingly forced impression of his face, never visible in the video, into a composite soft material, producing an effigy reminiscent of the kind that would be used to memorialize the face of saints and kings. The effigy is then molded into a wooden mask portraying a disproportionate and slightly monstrous figure.

What is emblematic of Fliri's practice is that it remains suspended in a space that allows us to draw links to contemporary realities, such as the beheadings carried out by ISIS members, to the futuristic environments imagined by science fiction, where the question of identity theft and preservation seem always to be in play, as well as to mythological narratives and pre-modern rituals. His work, in other words, has an extra-temporal character.

In Fliri's micro-narrative for *I Pray I'm a False Prophet*, victim and perpetrator seem to find a common space in between the effigy of one and the mask of the other. The color and material signifiers and codes are inverted: dark black and a soft composite for his effigy and light cream and heavy wood for his obverse. Today's martyr was yesterday's monster as they rest together in a special case that is a central element with which the video opens and closes.

– KRS

BIO   Italian artist Michael Fliri (°1978) was born in the German-speaking region of the Italian alps, in South Tyrol. Travelling up and down the mountains, but also travelling North and South to study abroad in Germany and Norway, have influenced his artistic practice. His work is often in between two poles, two ideas.

Fliri uses different media, such as performance, video, photography, and sculpture. He researches the notions of metamorphosis and masquerade: the protagonists in his work—often Fliri himself—undergo a certain change or transformation. This transition can be seen as an encounter of two opposite worlds.

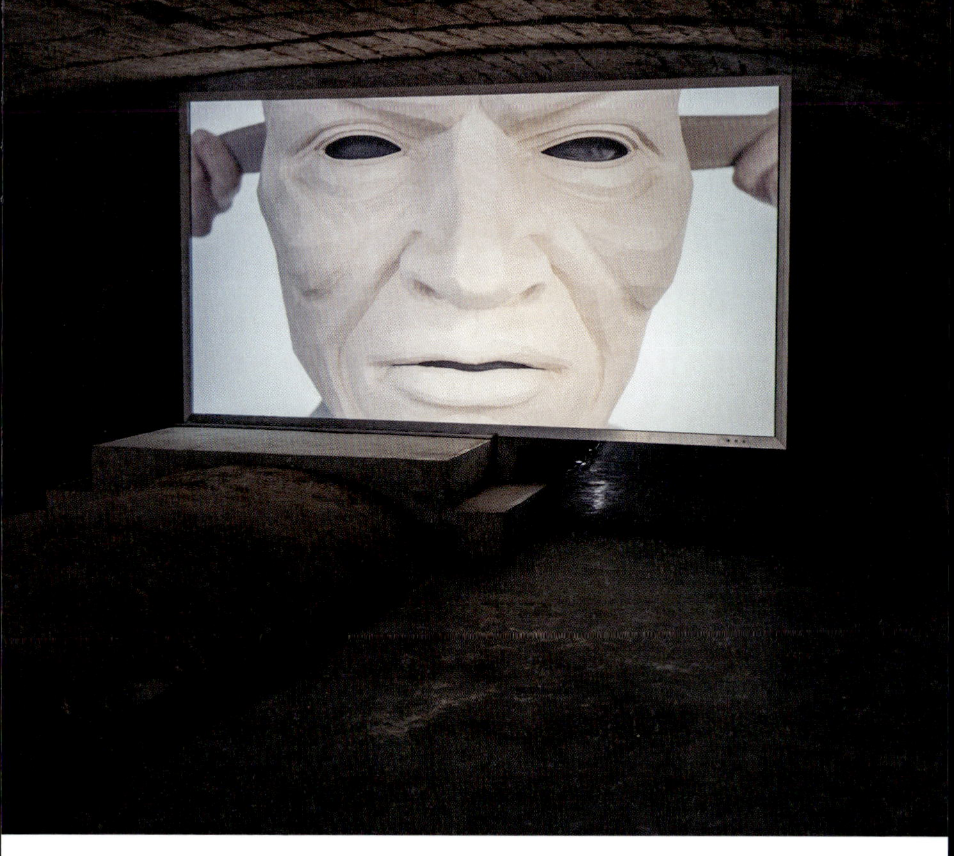

I Pray I'm A False Prophet, 2015
video, sound, 2′ 00″
Courtesy the artist and Galleria Raffaella Cortese, Milan / Commissioned and
co-produced by CONTOUR 7 / Supported by Dena Foundation for Contemporary Art
and Cultural Department of the Autonomous Province of Bolzano South Tyrol

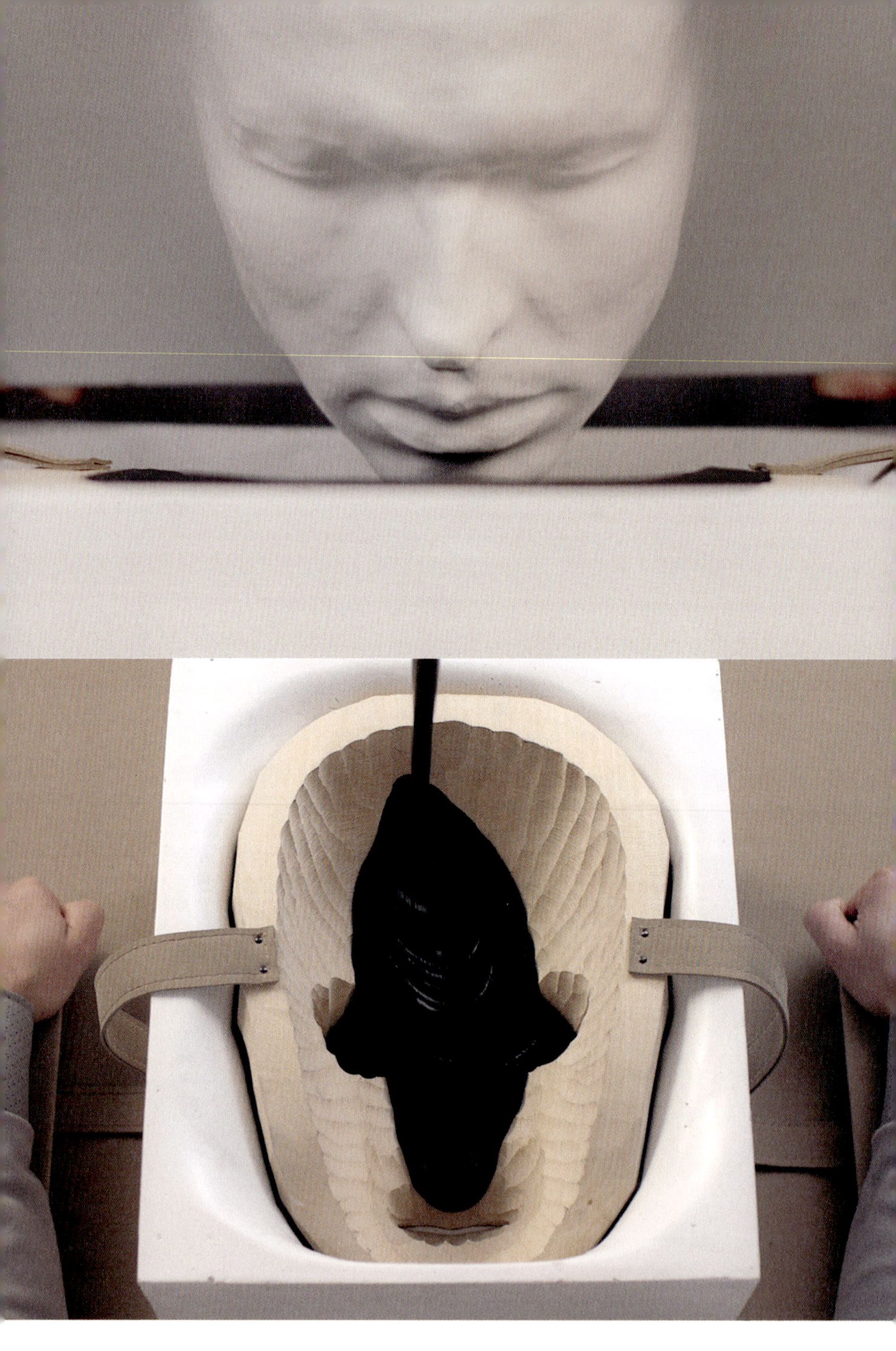

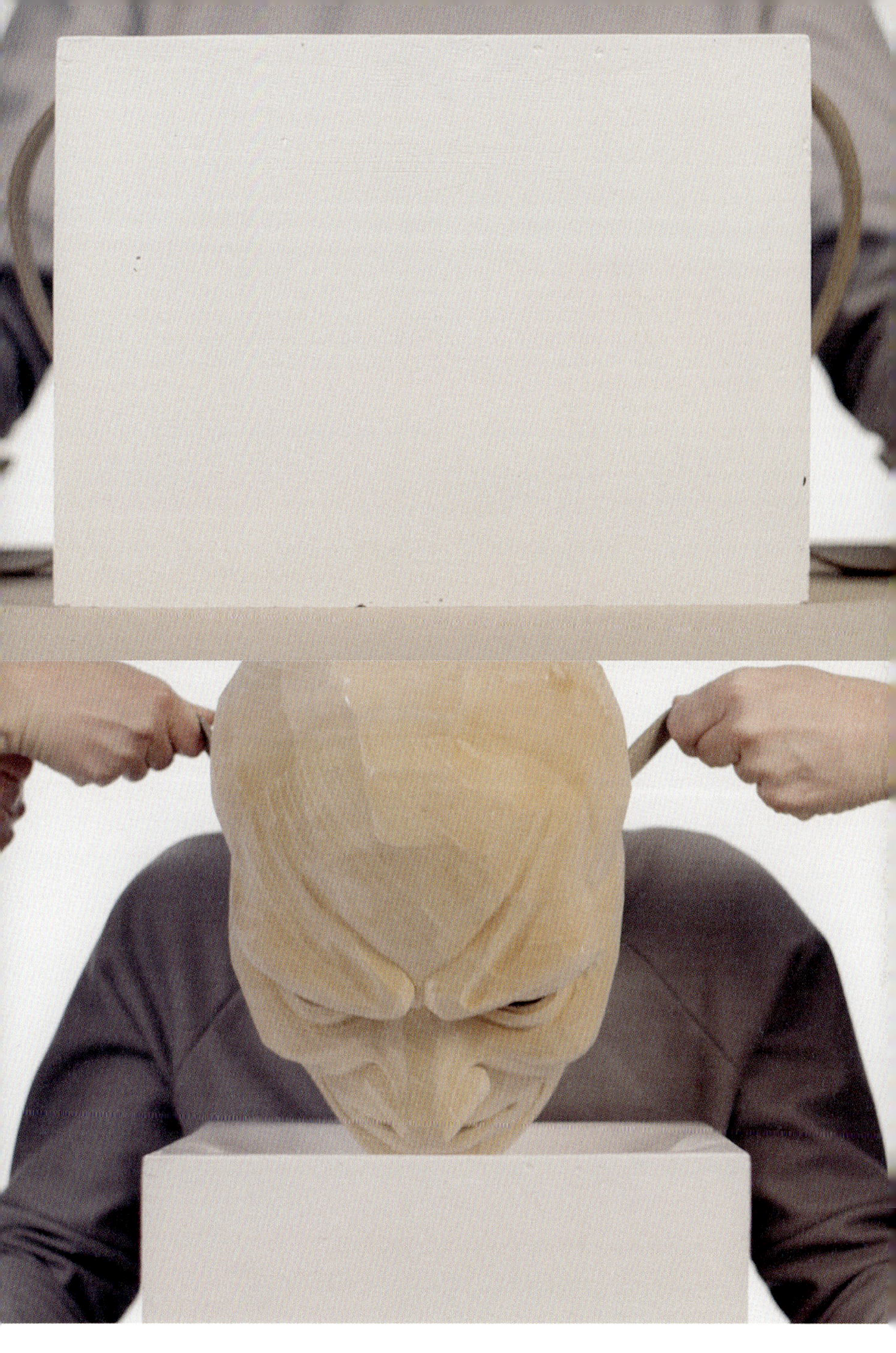

I Pray I'm A False Prophet, 2015
video, sound, 2′ 00″
Courtesy the artist and Galleria Raffaella Cortese, Milan / Commissioned and
co-produced by CONTOUR 7 / Supported by Dena Foundation for Contemporary Art
and Cultural Department of the Autonomous Province of Bolzano South Tyrol

Rabih Mroué

On first sight, the issues that animate Rabih Mroué's work have little in common with the forward-looking character of utopian thinking. Driven by the imperative to confront his country's tragic history, he often unavoidably exposes the monstrosity of human actions. Having a background in theater and performance, Mroué actively combines fact and fiction in his practice. The space where his works are presented is significant for its links to the more somber chapters of the local Belgian history. The Vlietenkelder was used as a bomb shelter during the Second World War, when Mechelen underwent heavy bombardments. Equally, the memory of the city's transit and concentration camp, from which Jews were sent to Auschwitz, resonates throughout the bleak histories told by the Lebanese artist. The four works exhibited here deal, each in different ways, with daunting and often traumatizing memories from Lebanon's past through storytelling and role play. The most recent piece, *Crocodile who Ate the Sun* (2015) consists of a series of photographs and a written commentary. In 1982 the Israeli army dropped leaflets on Beirut prior to their planned bombardments, urging the civilians to flee the city. The artist returns to that episode after many years, but he is unable to find the original leaflets. Instead, he makes replicas and invites friends to tell their stories from that very day. The partly torn, folded, scribble-covered leaflets stand for the various memories of the Israeli attack on Beirut. Mroué's need to record these micro histories is triggered not so much by a nostalgic desire to reconstitute the past. Rather, it is prompted by a much graver loss. As he searched for that memorable leaflet, he learned that a good friend of his had gone missing. When one is faced with such an adversity, the recollection of the episode with the leaflets functions as a substitute that helps to forget the more dramatic part of that history. In the video entitled *Old House*, showing a demolition of a building in Beirut, this is exactly the reason Mroué gives for recollecting the past. His goal is not to remember, but to make sure he forgets. The day-to-day catastrophe of people

who disappeared or went missing is the subject of another work entitled *Noiseless*. Here, the artist inserts his photograph in the numerous newspaper announcements on missing persons. The original photographs merge with the artist's face to become an unrecognizable blurry shape. In this performative gesture, Mroué transposes the act of playing a role of somebody else onto the visual language of photography and video. As in several of his earlier performances, he reflects on the limits of an individual identity and on the border between the individual and the collective. While all of these recollections and musings remain bleak and unpromising, the effort of the artist is directed at rescuing the small moments of respite or happiness. The video *Two Hours without Wars* is homage to a short ceasefire during the Israeli war on Lebanon, precisely for the duration of the final football match of the World Cup. If a durable change is unthinkable, small episodes of bliss seem to be the last resort and a source of hope.

– KRS

BIO   **Lebanese artist Rabih Mroué (°1967) is a theater director, visual artist, and playwright. Mroué played an important avant-garde role in Lebanese theatre, which he took to new and unknown territories, away from the conventional institutions and European influences.**

His visual art sprouted from his theatre practice, which often contains video and installation art. In the videos of Mroué, time and montage play a crucial role. Using text and photography are characteristic of his installations.

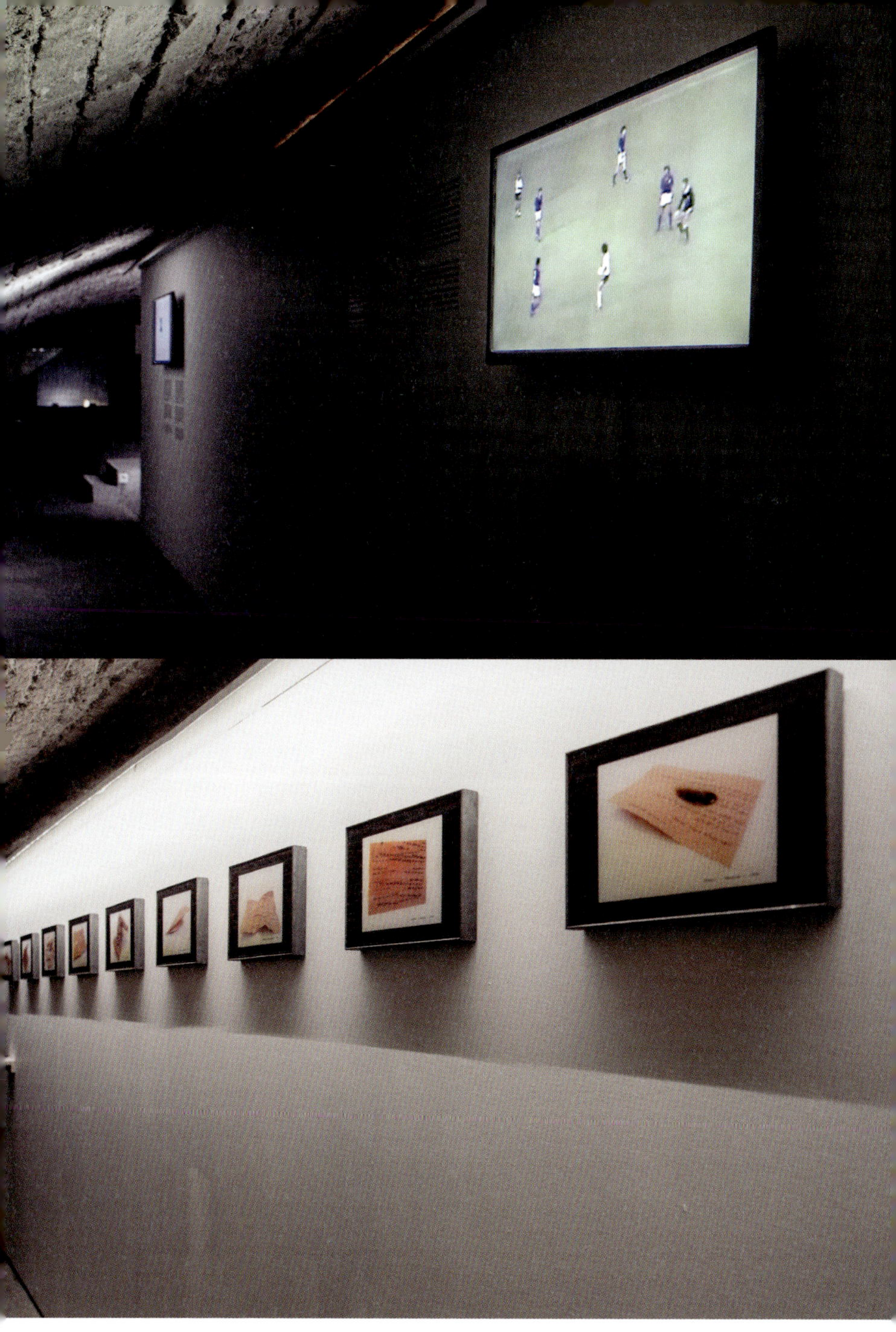

Two Hours Without War, 2014
video, sound, text, 2′ 12″
In cooperation with Arts Centre NONA

The Crocodile Who Ate The Sun, 2015
12 × diasec photos in frame, text, pamphlet
Courtesy the artist and Sfeier-Semler Gallery, Beirut and Hamburg /
In cooperation with Arts Centre NONA

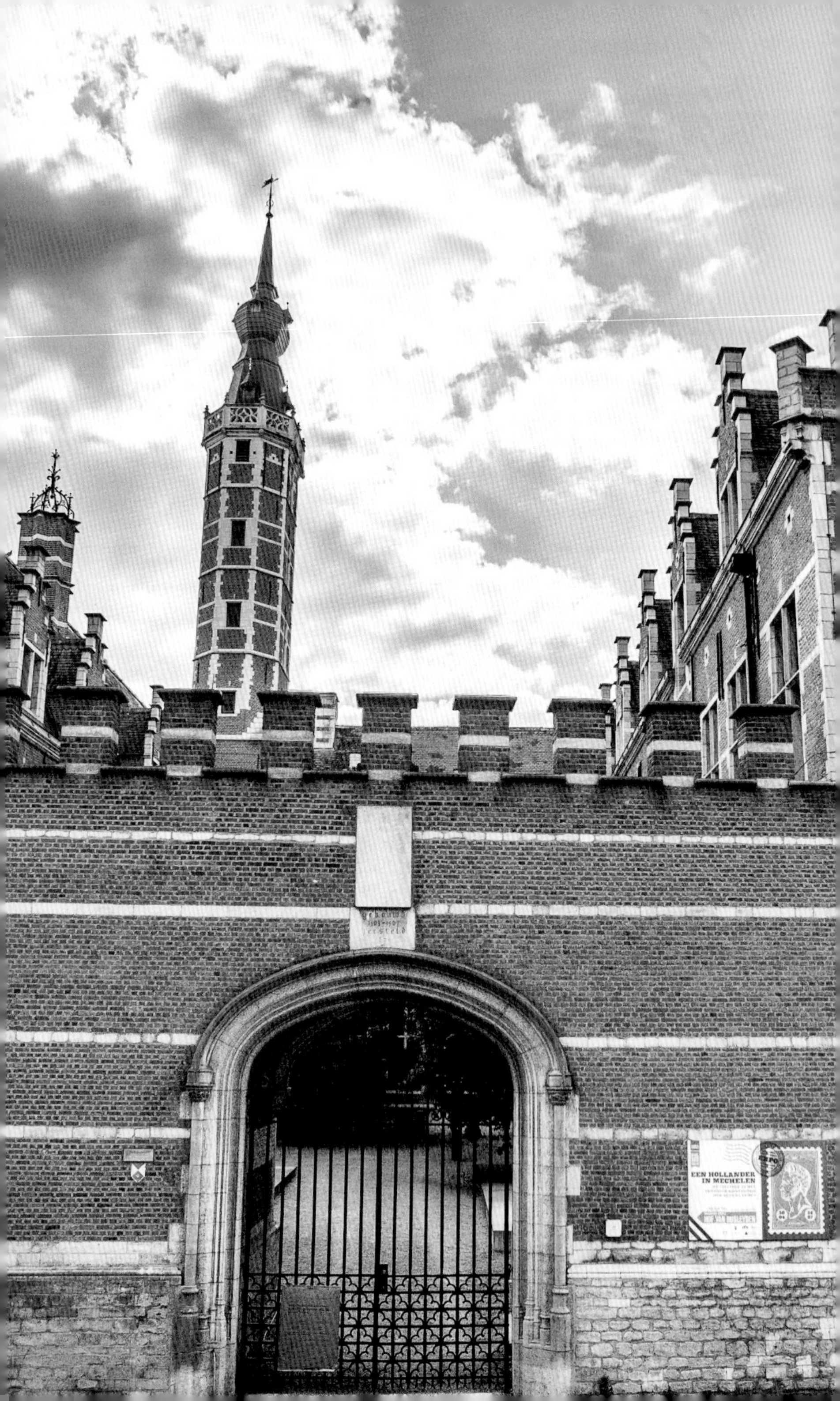

The Hof van Busleyden

The Hof van Busleyden was built at the beginning of the sixteenth century for Hieronymus van Busleyden, ecclesiastical jurist, and member of the Great Council, the supreme court of the Low Countries. A Maecenas and humanist, he was also a good friend of Desiderius Erasmus and Thomas More.

Between 1619 and the First World War the building housed an organization known as the Berg van Barmhartigheid—or Mountain of Charity—which loaned money to the poor on an interest-free basis. All but the walls of the building were destroyed during the First World War. Later on it was rebuilt and became the city museum.

It is possible that Thomas More strolled in the garden in 1515 contemplating his book *Utopia*. He even wrote a poem about the beauty of the Hof van Busleyden. So it is no coincidence that exactly five hundred years later it was chosen as one of the locations to host the Biennale dedicated to More.

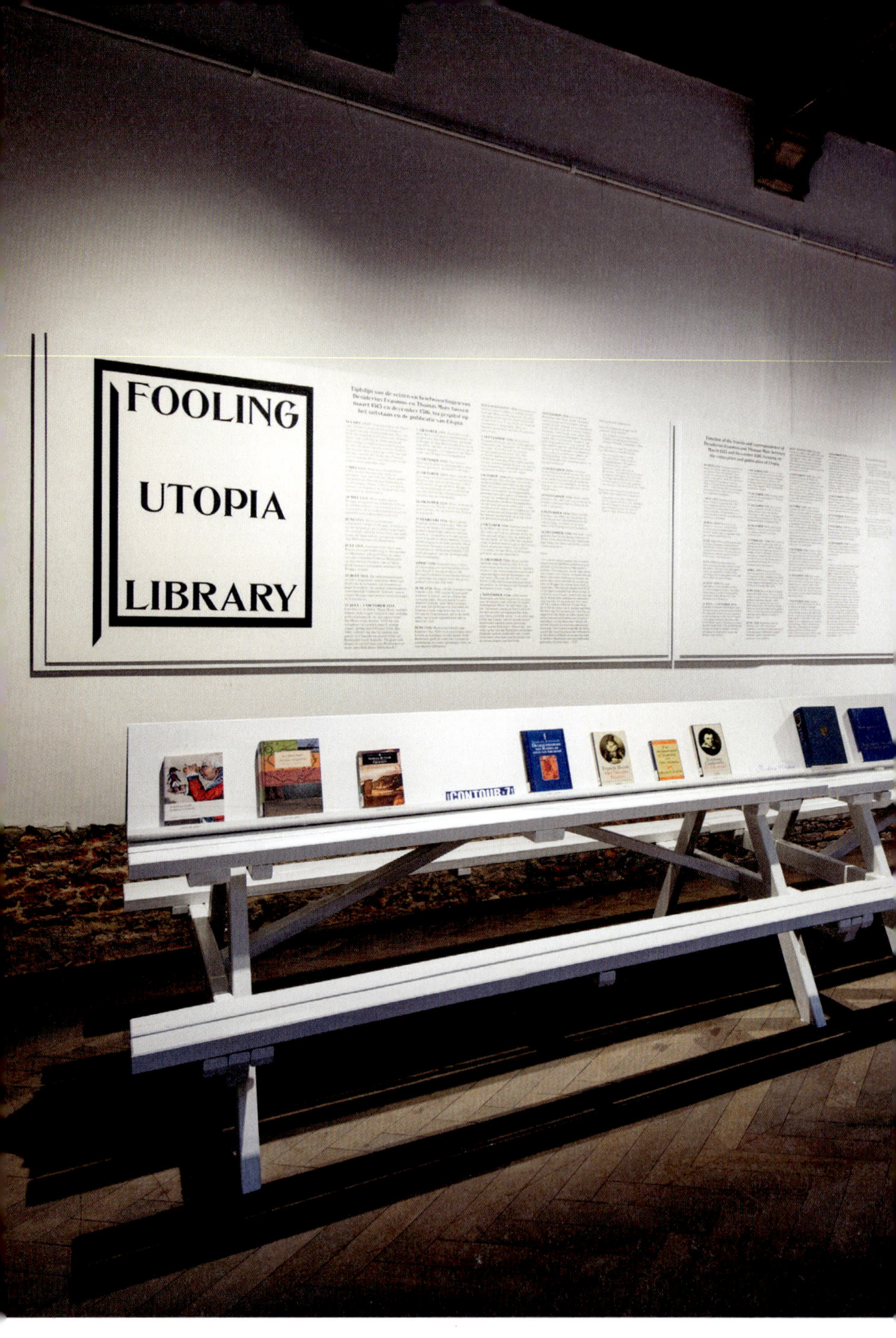

FOOLING
UTOPIA
LIBRARY

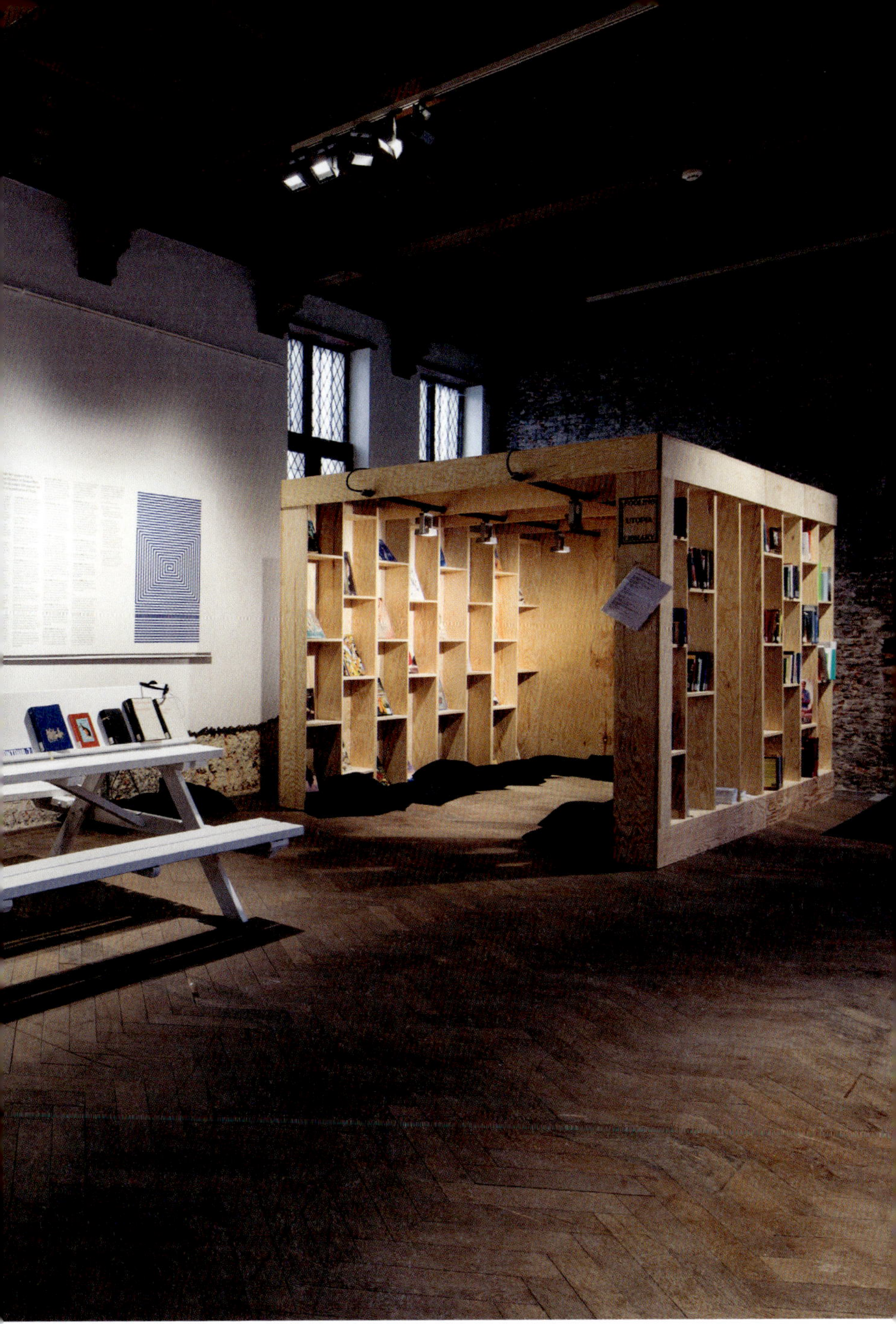

Fooling Utopia Library
Made possible with the kind support of KBR Royal Library of Belgium,
University Library of KU Leuven, Library Mechelen, Youth Section
Library Mechelen and many others.

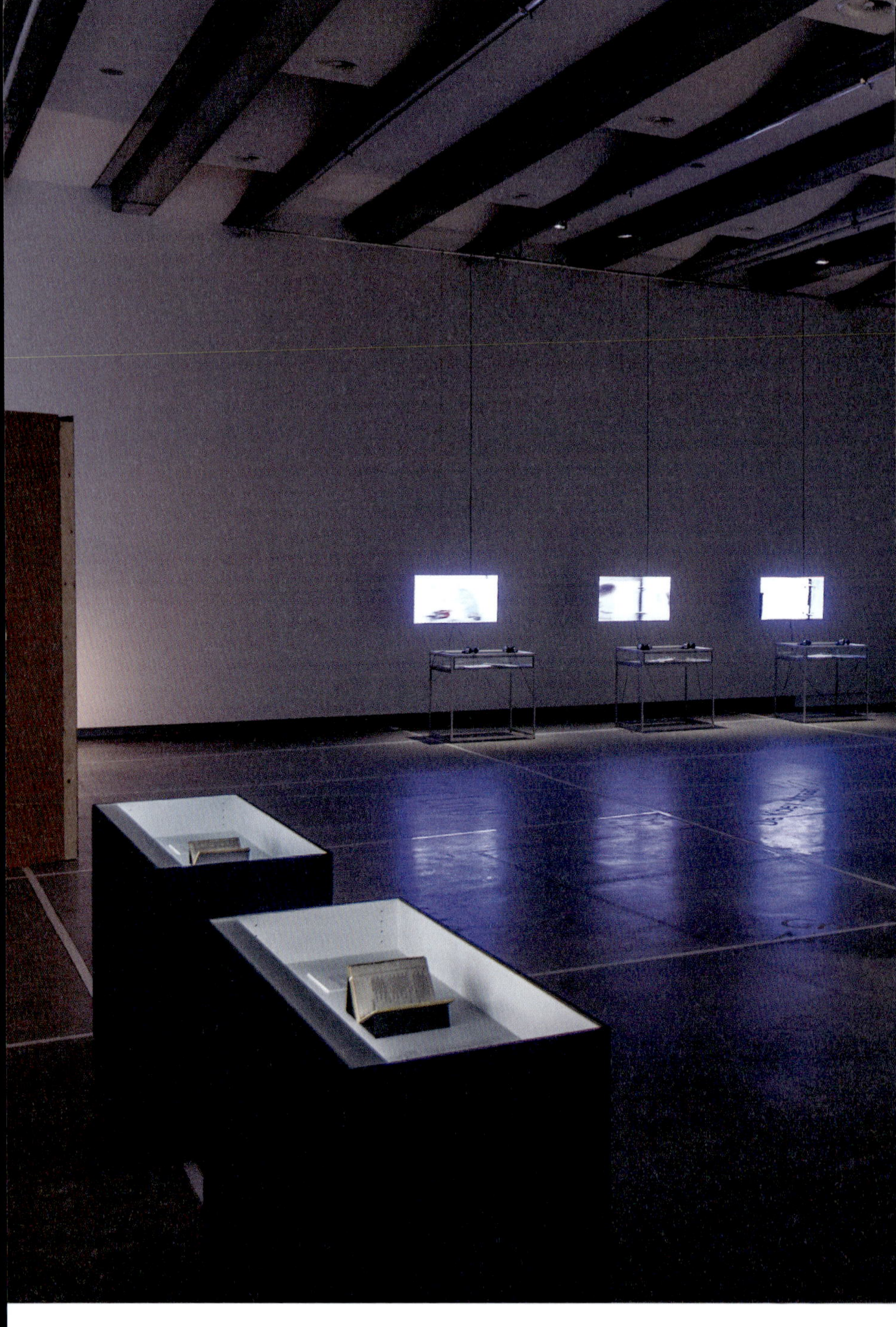

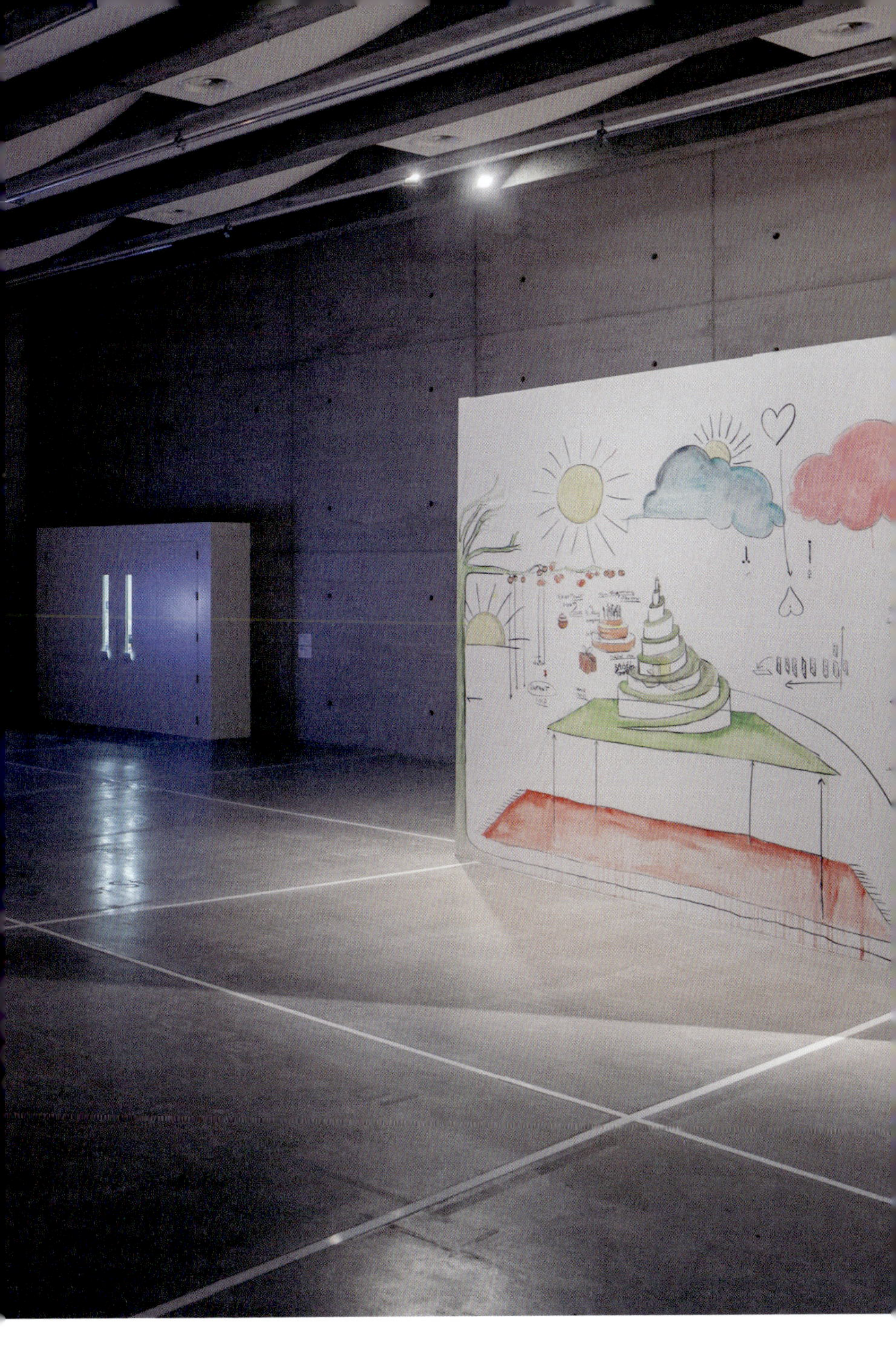

Downstairs exhibition room at Hof van Busleyden

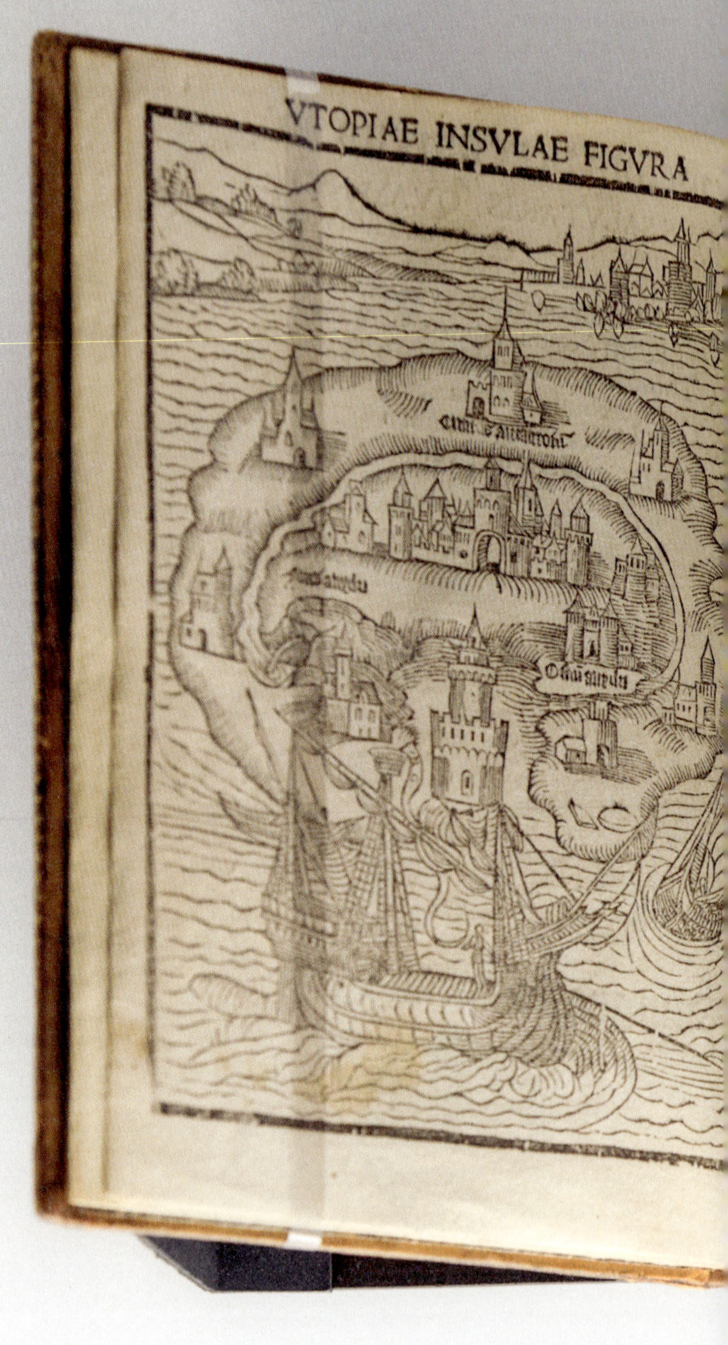

VTOPIAE INSVLAE FIGVRA

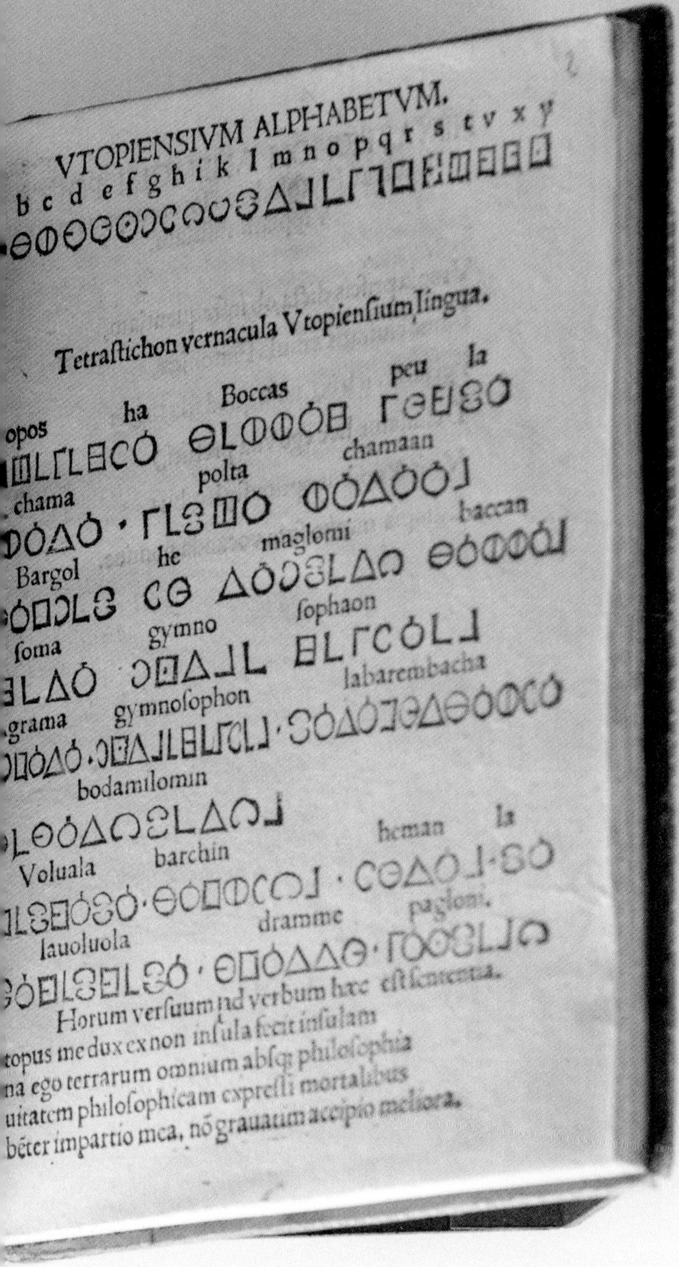

VTOPIENSIVM ALPHABETVM.

a b c d e f g h i k l m n o p q r s t v x y

Tetrastichon vernacula Vtopiensium lingua.

Vtopos   ha   Boccas   peu   la

chama   polta   chamaan

Bargol   he   maglomi   baccan

soma   gymno   sophaon

grama   gymnosophon   labarembacha

bodamilomin

Voluala   barchin   heman   la

lauoluola   dramme   pagloni.

Horum versuum ad verbum hæc est sententia.

Vtopus me dux ex non insula fecit insulam.

Vna ego terrarum omnium absq; philosophia

Ciuitatem philosophicam expressi mortalibus

Libenter impartio mea, non grauatim accipio meliora.

A Dog Republic and RAM Radioartemobile

A Dog Republic was founded in 2011 by artists Jean-Baptiste Decavèle, Nico Dockx, Helena Sidiropoulos, architect Yona Friedman, and musician Krist Torfs. In 2012 a first manifest was discussed amongst them and Yona Friedman's invisible dog Kopec—led to the constitution of their republic. Since then, they have organized various demonstrations in New York, Middelburg, Antwerpen, Oostende, Munich, Paris, and Marseille, where they have written and published some revolutionary papers in collaboration with designer Thomas Mayfried. What binds all of these demonstrations and their related documents is the act of establishing other modalities of thinking and working, thereby questioning our existing structures and the values of art, economy, politics and social relations.

For CONTOUR 7 they invite you to participate in a barking conversation that will be recorded during improvised live encounters during the opening weekend, as well as through an online application that can be visited at any time at the website of the biennale. All collected barking sounds and speeches will be distributed in one of the (exhibition) rooms in Hof van Busleyden and later published as a limited vinyl edition. This call to overcome the gap between humans and animals, although clearly playful and provocative, can nevertheless be seen as a critical gesture towards today's social, economic and political conditions which are developed by neoliberalist programs and ideas. They situate these barking conversations as a complementary and critical tool for imagining radically new and very different political, philosophical and artistic discourses.

Il Monumento al Borghese Corragioso (1971) by Jannis Kounellis and *UTOPIA/ The Kingdoms of Elgaland-Vargaland* (2003) by Carl Michael von Hausswolff and Leif Elggren ironically reflect on the possibility of social change. Kounellis created a monument to the courageous citizen, a glass jar containing arsenic in a cloth bag, as a curious homage to social subversion. Elggren and von Hausswolff founded their fictitious Kingdoms of Elgaland-Vargaland as a form of critique towards their home country. Seeing the existence of the king and queen of Sweden as rather silly, they established an entirely new state in order to become its kings. Their parody of a kingdom thus exists through an elaborate set of rules on nationalism, citizenship, and political power. It also boasts an impressive list of citizens—those who would gladly exchange their real identity cards for an entry into that imagined country. RAM Radioartemobile, an art space in Rome and Internet radio created by Dora Stiefelmeir and Mario Pieroni, presents a RAM Radioartemobile's sonic archive that stands for multifarious projects and events and is featured through a playlist on Utopia and Europe.

– KRS

BIO   **A Dog Republic was initiated by artists Jean-Baptiste Decavèle (°1961), Nico Dockx (°1974), Helena Sidiropoulos (°1979), architect Yona Friedman (°1923), and musician Krist Torfs (°1980), in 2011. After many conversations in Paris and Antwerp on the subject of constituting their very own republic, they teamed up with some other dogs for a series of "demonstrations" at a.o. Ludlow38 in New York, Esther Donatz Gallery in Munich, and the 55th Venice Biennale. Together with graphic designer Thomas Mayfried, they are working on a series of artist books.**

Founded by Mario Pieroni and Dora Stiefelmeier in 2003, RAM Radioartemobile is a platform for contemporary art in Rome and is dedicated to sound research and exhibitive activity aimed at the creation of an international network. RAM sets up exhibitions and projects in collaboration with both public and private spaces all over the world, juxtaposing visual and sound art.

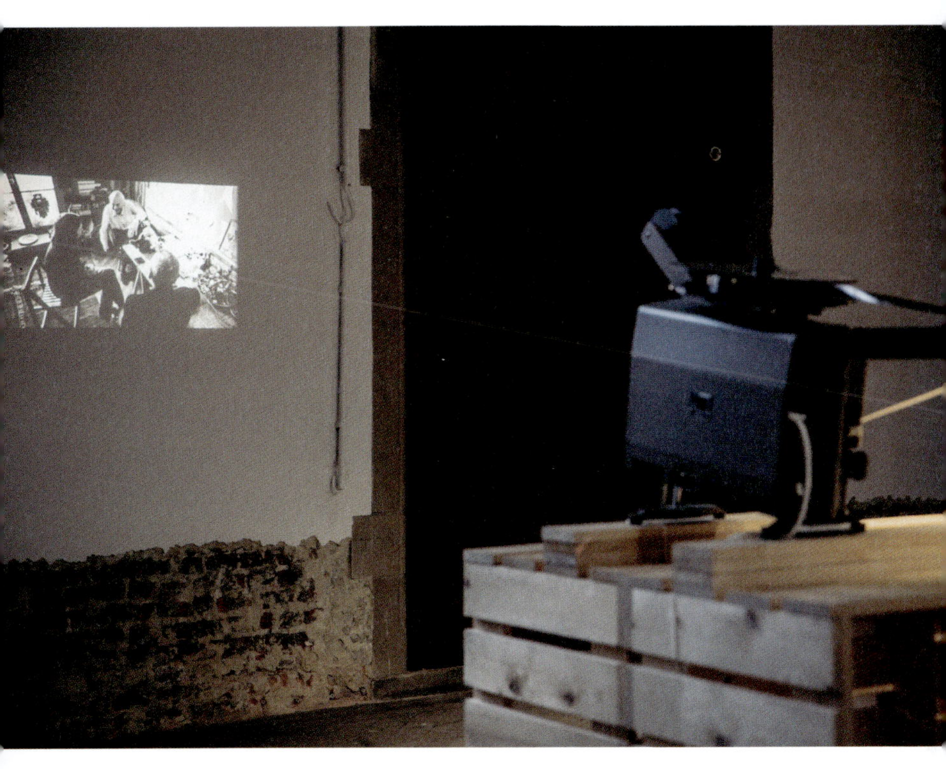

A Dog Republic
Let's Talk Peace!, 2015
16mm film, multi-channel sound installation
Commissioned and produced by CONTOUR 7

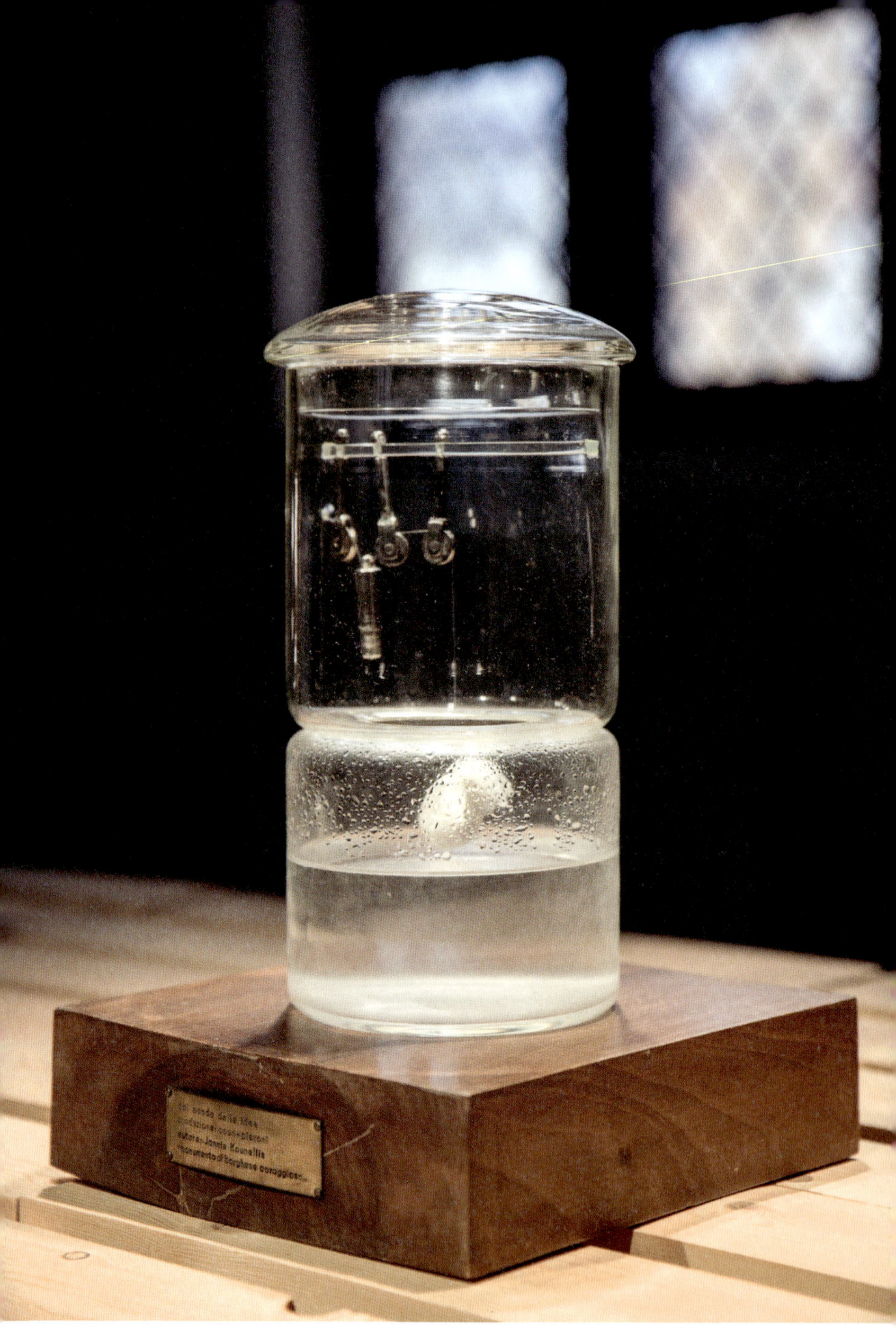

RAM Radioartemobile
Jannis Kounellis
Il Monumento al Borghese Coraggioso, 1971
glass, metal, fabric, wood base
Courtesy Mario Pieroni and Dora Stiefelmeier

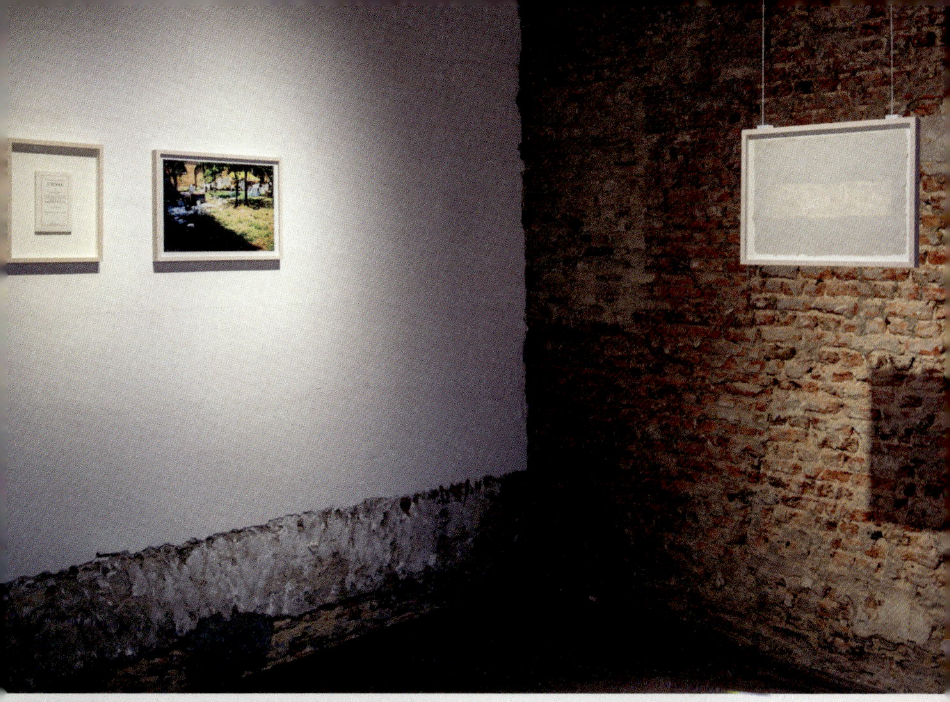

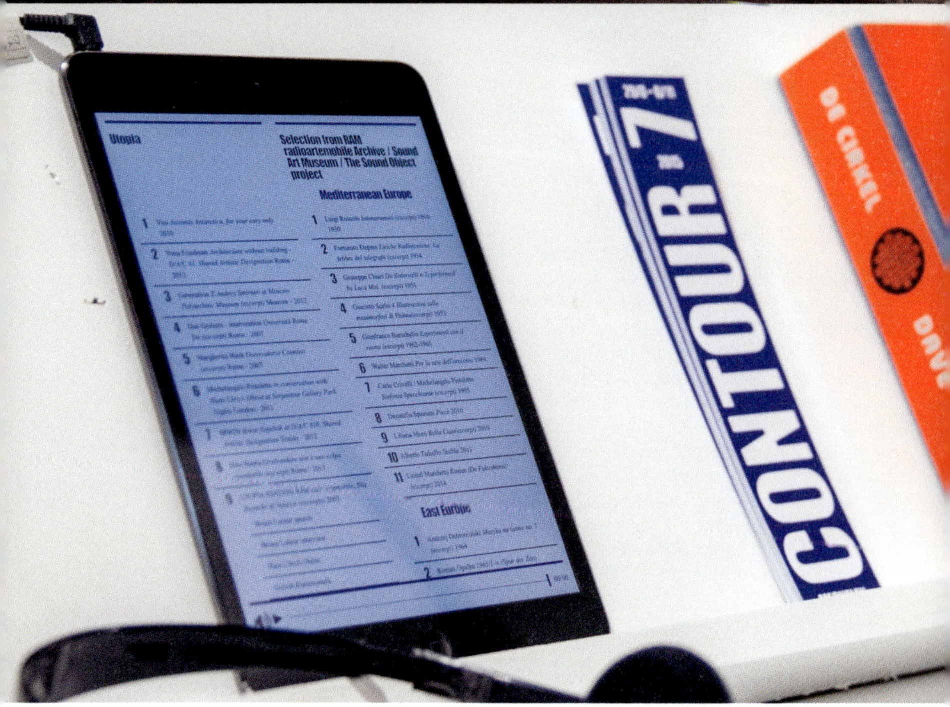

Carl Michael von Hausswolff & Leif Elggren
Utopia / The Kingdoms of Elgaland-Vargaland, 2003
handmade paper, photo, book
Courtesy the artists

RAM Radioartemobile, Special Utopia
and Europa playlist for CONTOUR 7
Also available at http://contour7.radioartemobile.it

AaBbPp

The artist collective AaBbPp pursues a collaborative approach to art-making through a variety of projects and initiatives. The video made by Tomas Pozemis is based on the stop-motion show for children entitled *Magic Roundabout*. After the originally French series had been translated into English in the late 1960s, it quickly acquired the status of a cult classic due to its multilayered narration. Read by one voice only, the dialogues often contained gags and snippets of bitter commentary on the economic situation and various political issues in Great Britain. Different characters in the series met in a colorful park remarkable for its fairground carrousel called the magic roundabout. It is this rotating movement of the roundabout which must have attracted Pozemis to re-appropriate the footage from the popular children's picture. In his remix, the figures and scenes are still visible, but the original voice-over has been replaced by DJ Kelli Hand's early House and Techno music from Detroit. Devoid of the narrative content and reworked through color mixing, the footage acquires a dreamy, hallucinatory quality. In his practice as a DJ, Tomas Pozemis is interested in reinvigorating vinyl culture, in which the rotating movement of the plate remains an essential ingredient of music. The children's roundabout thus becomes a metaphor for music as such, while its repetitive, circular movement combined with bright red, green, and blue colors, creates a hypnotic effect. Next to the video, the AaBbPp collective presents a series of hats which is part of an ongoing project inspired by historical headwear from different parts of the world. The form of the three hats presented here is derived from an old Chinese headpiece, which is transformed into a new model. The fabric, pattern, and accessories give each item a unique character. The project has an online platform, which subversively appropriates the conventions of a web shop. Through it, the AaBbPp collective investigates new possibilities for collaboration and artistic research.

– KRS

BIO   AaBbPp is the Vilnius-based collective founded by Lithuanian artists Gintaras Didžiapetris (°1985) and Elena Narbutaitė (°1984) in 2015. AaBbPp pursues a collaborative approach to art-making, an alternative to the current neoliberal economic structures.

The collective spans a wide range of media, such as video, print, photography, and sculpture. They investigate questions of art and perception, history and the accessibility of the past, and the relationship between fact and fiction.

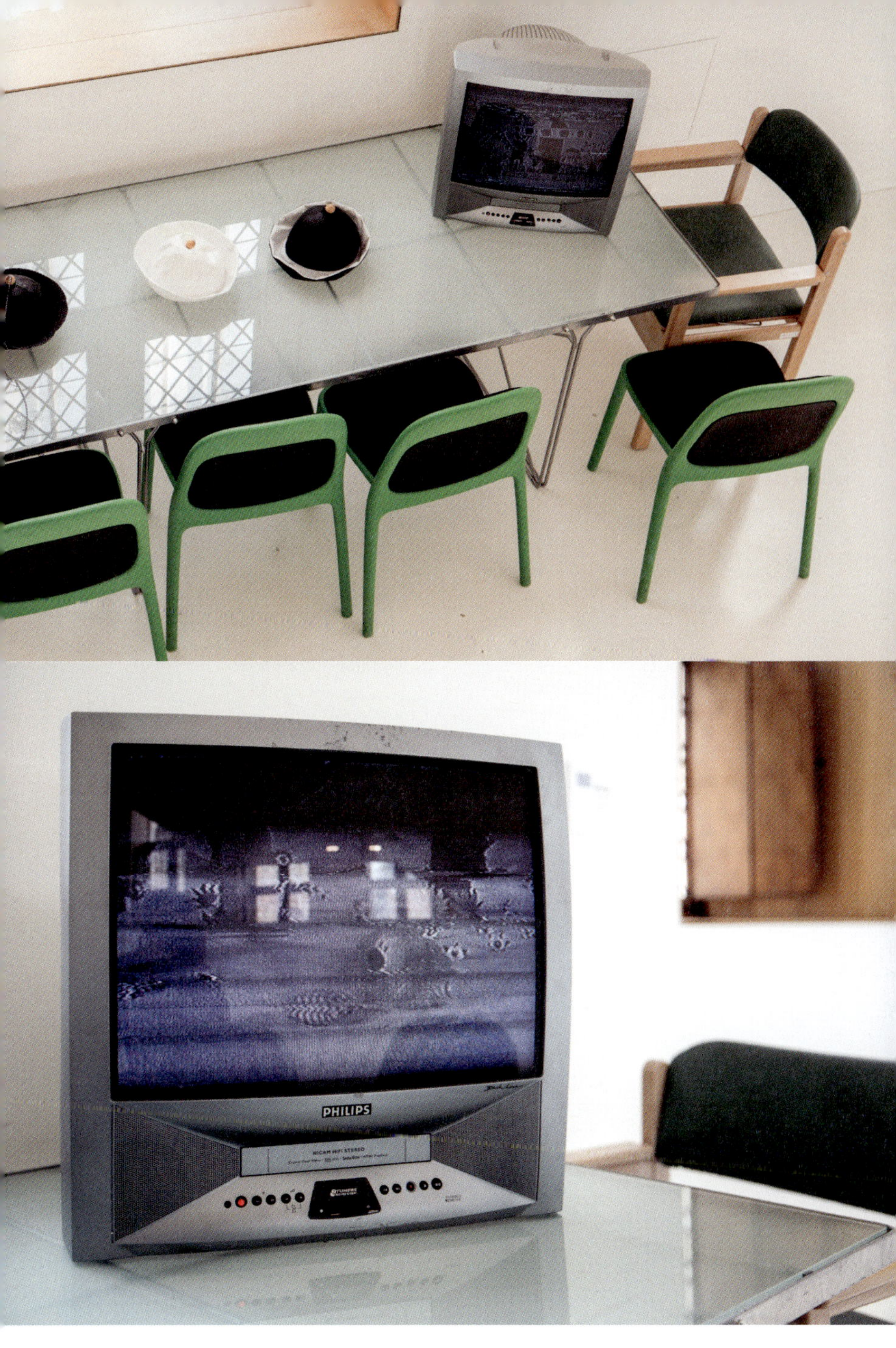

Three Official Hats, 2015
monk hood, leaf hood, ripped hood
Commissioned and produced by CONTOUR 7

Thomas Pozemis, Acid Round About, 2015
vhs, tv screen, sound, 98′ 32″
Commissioned and produced by CONTOUR 7

Slavs and Tatars

In their knowledgeable appropriation of different cultural traditions from the broadly understood area of Eurasia, Slavs and Tatars excavate lesser known ideas for a better common life. Linguistic idiosyncrasies and peculiar affinities between distant traditions are the core of their practice, resulting in singular installations and objects. *Hung and Tart*, a lavishly executed glass model of a tongue, is an example of their multifaceted and often humorous practice. Together with the installation *Lektor*, this work is part of a larger project *Mirrors for Princes* dealing with medieval guidebooks for rulers. The aphoristic prescriptions, heard in different languages, on how to use one's tongue with moderation are meant as guidance towards happiness and fulfillment. Such instructions for rulers on etiquette and self-control existed both in the Muslim and the Christian world. Suffice it to mention Machiavelli's *Prince*, which is perhaps the best-known Western example of that tradition. The text fragments used here are taken from the eleventh-century monument of Turkic literature entitled *Kutadgu Bilig* (Wisdom of Royal Glory). The original Uighur language of the text is layered with several voice-overs, creating a multilingual cacophony. The title *Lektor* refers to a wide-spread method of voiceover for foreign films used in Poland and other Eastern European countries. Instead of dubbing or subtitling, a single monotonous voice-over would be audible simultaneously with the original version, creating a space of rupture between host and home language. It creates a playful and irreverent mixture where translation offers hospitality. The approach of Slavs and Tatars towards their historical material has little in common with respectful preservation, but should rather be seen as a forcible resuscitation of the past. The diverse cultural traditions, both ancient and very recent, are confronted with each other in the search for new models of reading, seeing, and thus being, together, within the contemporary context.

– KRS

BIO   Slavs and Tatars is an art collective devoted to an area beginning East of the former Berlin Wall and ending West of the Great Wall of China. The combination of European, Slavic, and Asian identities is a main focus in their work, in which they consistently explore different media and neglect fixed disciplines and style conventions.

Originally organised as a reading group in 2006, the collective lives and travels in a region that has been realigning itself since the collapse of Soviet Communism and which experiences escalating tensions between Eastern and Western identities. Populations, allegiances, and languages are all in transition. In exploring the area's expansive historical narratives and transnational relationships, Slavs and Tatars create something associative, intimate, and playful.

Qum Rabat, 2015
video, loop, 22″
Courtesy the artists and Kraupa-Tuskany Zeidler, Berlin / Supported by Polish Institute, Brussels

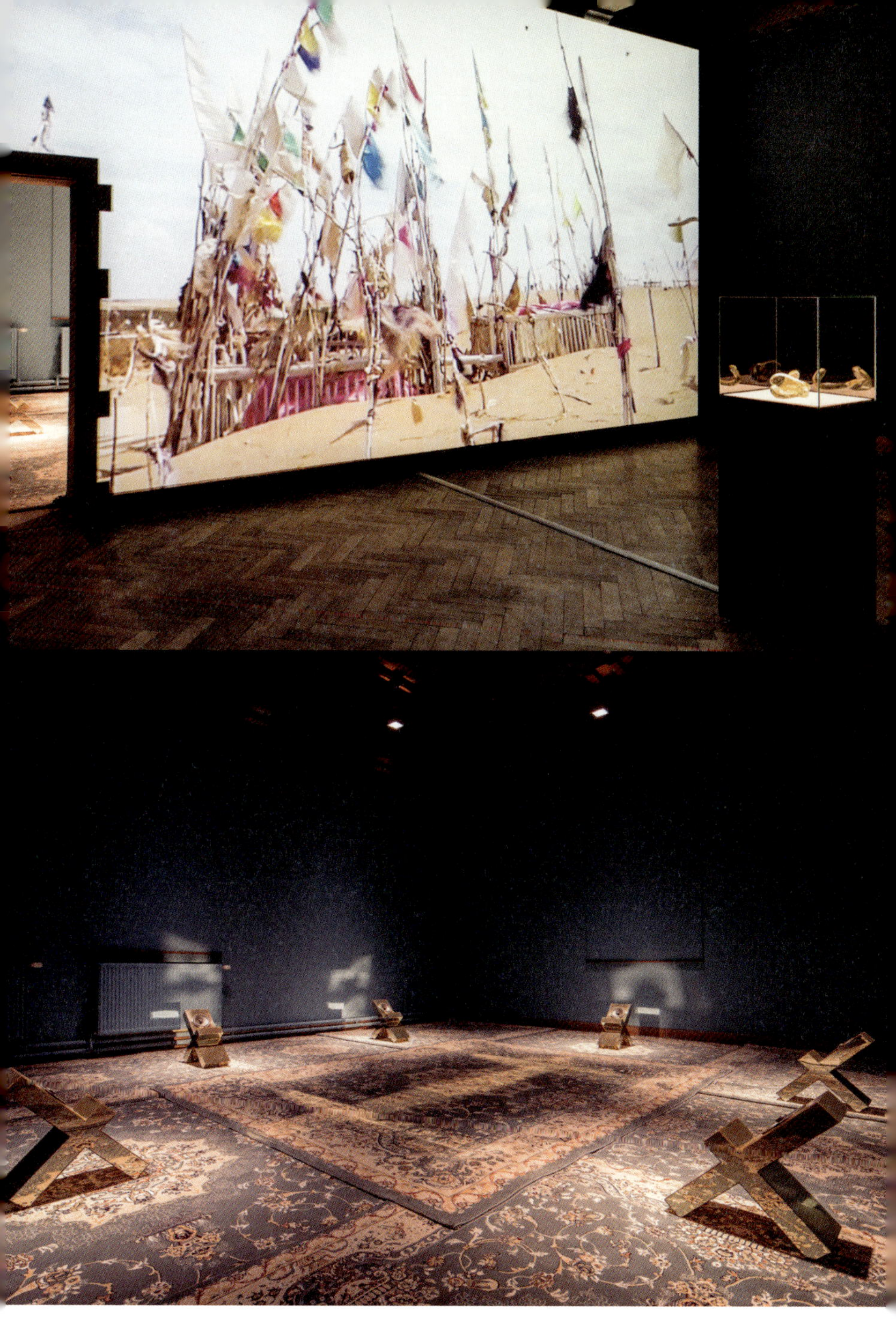

Hung and Tart (Full Acacia), 2014
handblown glass
Courtesy the artists and Kraupa-Tuskany Zeidler,
Berlin / Supported by Polish Institute, Brussels

Lektor (Speculum Linguarum), 2014–Today
six-channel sound-installation, plexiglass, speakers, 36′ 29″
Courtesy the artists and Kraupa-Tuskany Zeidler, Berlin /
Supported by Polish Institute, Brussels

Albert Serra

In CONTOUR 7 Albert Serra presents a new
two-channel installation based on *The Lord
Worked Wonders in Me* (El Senyor ha fet
en mi meravelles, 2011), a slow-paced film
based on conversations and encounters. It
features the crew of his earlier film on Don
Quixote entitled *Honor of Knights* (Honor
del Cavalleria, 2006) as they travel through
La Mancha in central Spain. The amateur
actors are shown eating and talking together,
or simply killing time while waiting for the
beginning of a new film production. In his
characteristic style, Serra allows for the film
narration to be stretched in long duration
scenes. Lingering on the landscapes or
interiors where a conversation faded, the
filmmaker visibly delights in long takes. The
actors talk about politics, drugs, and love,
but they also engage with the story of Don
Quixote and Sancho Panza. Their real-life
problems, fragmented recollections, and
simple gestures of sociability become inter-
mingled with the fictional story of Cervantes.
In his earlier film on Don Quixote Serra
refrained from retelling the whole complex
narrative from the seventeenth-century literature. Instead, he focused on the relationship
between the knight-errant and his squire.
Even the love story and the figure of Dulcinea
was omitted. For Serra, the narrative serves
as a point of departure for the creation of a
unique picture. In it, he combines a particular
sensitivity for arresting, carefully framed
images with a subtle reflection on the delu-
sional idealism of Don Quixote. The viewer
is drawn into the world of the ordinary and
unpretentious lives of the film's real/fictional
character. In *The Lord Worked Wonders in
Me* it does not even matter that the new film
which the crew is supposedly preparing will
never actually be realized (unless it's maybe
the film you are watching?). The really significant events happen in the unimportant, dull
intervals and seemingly lost moments of waiting of a crew pretending to live the collective
utopia of Art, that is, to live inside a film.

– KRS

BIO   Albert Serra (°1975) is a Spanish
film director and producer. His work
has emerged as a highly original voice
in contemporary cinema. Similar to
several unconventional filmmakers
before him, he also engages in projects
for contemporary art venues. He
was selected to be the icon of new
avant-garde cinema at the Cannes Film
Festival in 2009 and was awarded a
Golden Leopard for best film at the
Locarno Film Festival last year.

With a radical yet wonderfully
accessible form of pure cinema, Serra's
films rediscover the space and time of
motion pictures, marvellously reani-
mating mythical heroes with the clumsy
weight of existence and transforming
landscapes into meditative dramas of
light and shadow.

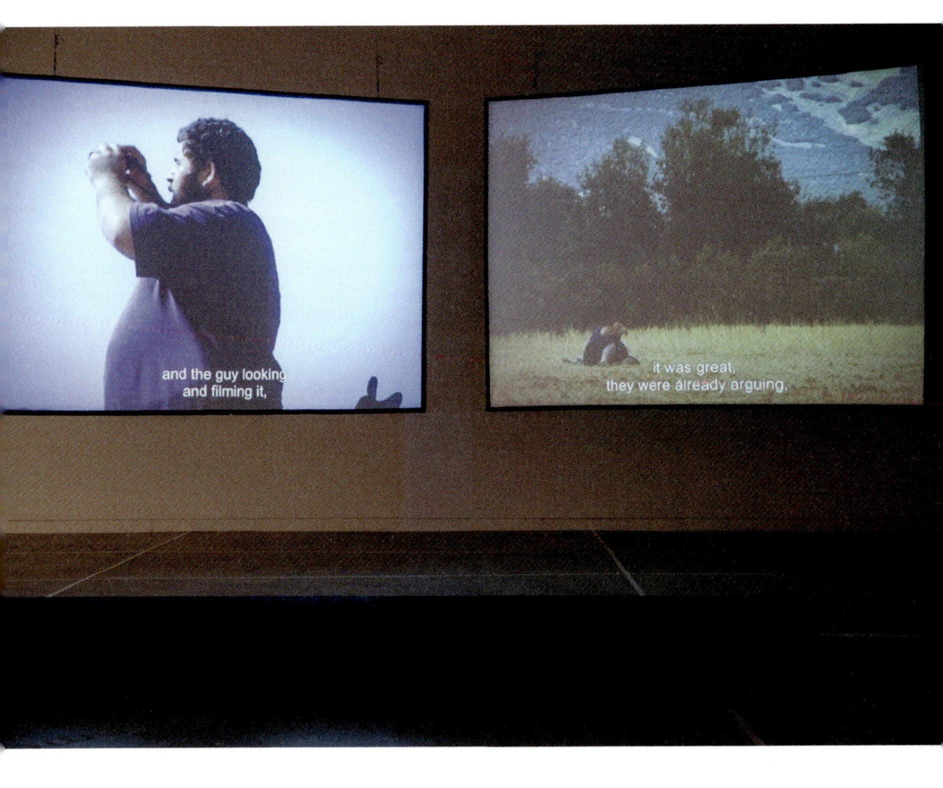

The Lord Worked Wonders in Me, 2015
two-channel video installation, sound, 69′ 00″
Commissioned and produced by CONTOUR 7

Fabrice Hyber

TV More is a multi-layered installation by Fabrice Hyber in the form of a room presented in the underground area of Hof Van Busleyden. The volume of the structure reproduces accurately on a scale of 1:1 the Hypocaustum, a dining room with frescoes in Hof van Busleyden, where More and other guests of Busleyden would share their Utopias. The outside walls are covered with painted figures and forms from Hyber's imaginary. The underlying idea is that they are contemporary versions of the themes of the frescoes in the hypocaustum. Inside the room is divided in two parts by a wall, which features a mirror glass and a door to move in between the two spaces. Visitors are invited to participate in telepathic sessions. The two spaces have a special seating structure composed of multiple monitors on which visitors can actually sit. Each one presents a short animation or video inspired by the personal Utopias that the artist asked residents of Mechelen and Brussels to share with him. The walls are also covered with drawings and notes. Hyber's idea is to imagine a space that is particularly conducive to telepathy and Utopia being nowhere is the ideal zone where minds can meet. The room also bears a resemblance to a TV studio, playing on the idea of human mediums broadcasting thoughts and sharing emotions on the channel CONTOUR 7 has chosen to be tuned into.

– NS

BIO **French artist Fabrice Hyber (°1961) is an artistic jack-of-all-trades who likes to look at his own oeuvre as a gigantic rhizomatic structure that continuously moves forward, bouncing on its own echoes and drawing from the "giant reservoir of the possible."**

Hyber, who once set up a real television station in the French Pavilion at the Venice Biennale, creates POFs (Prototypes d'Objects en Fonctionnement—Prototypes of Functioning Objects) and continuously attempts to rethink the world through a stream of images and words. Central to his work, in which he tries to catch thoughts as they are born, is the struction and reconstruction of language and communication.

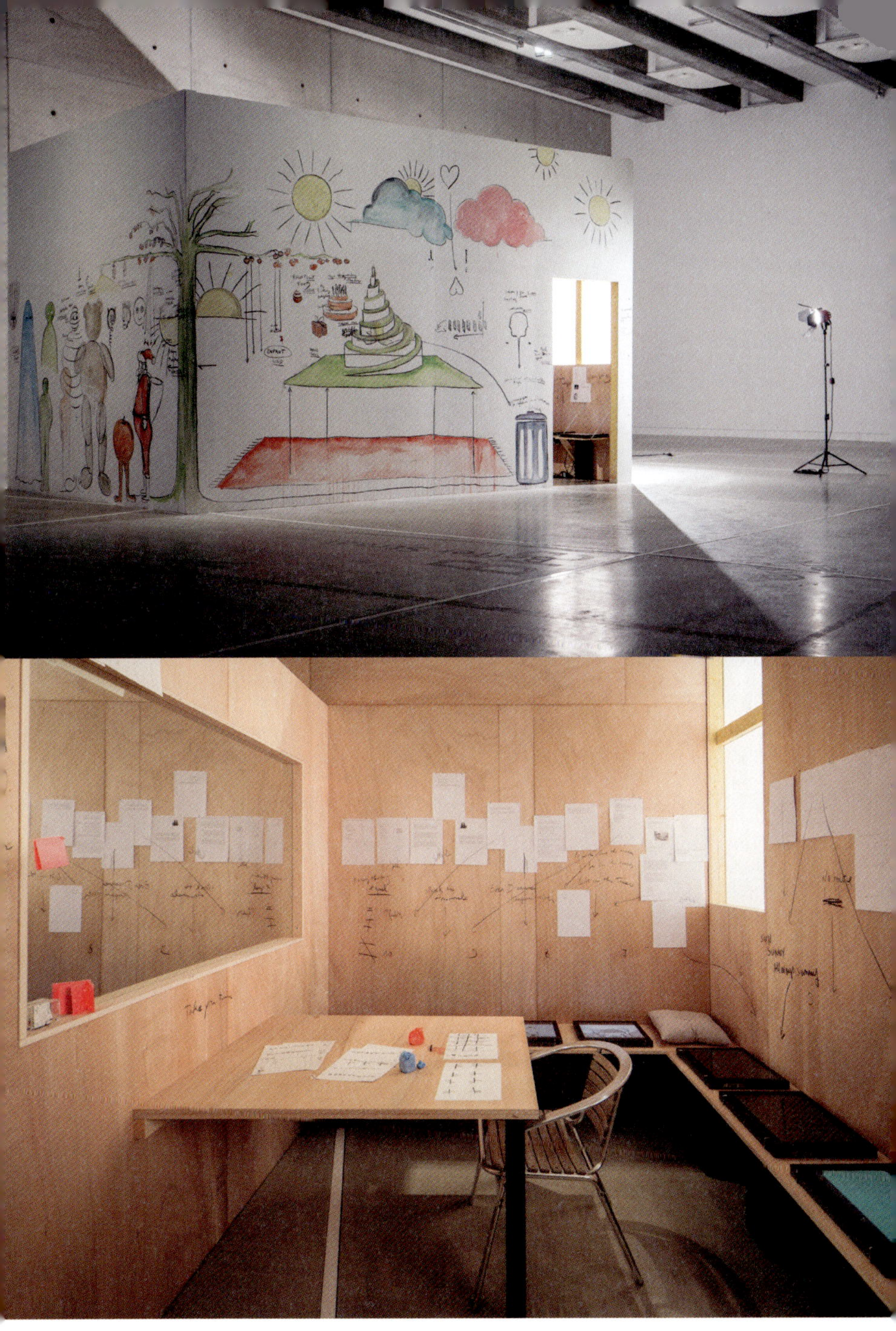

TV More, 2015
multi-channel video installation, drawings
Videos by Samon Takahashi / Courtesy Nathalie Obadia, Paris /
Commissioned and co-produced by CONTOUR 7

Nedko Solakov

In this new video installation commissioned by CONTOUR, Nedko Solakov reads from his own 1990 book *Encyclopaedia Utopia*, made shortly after the fall of the communist regimes in Eastern Europe. Twenty-five years later, the artist examines selected entries, providing commentary on his own work and on the ideas that animated him. The video has three parts corresponding to three volumes of the encyclopaedia, which are also included in the installation. In the book, encompassing variously sized drawings, text, photographs, and private documents, Thomas More's ideal island merges with the equally utopian experiment of communism in Bulgaria. Oscillating between bitter ironic, funny, vulgar, or naively pedagogical tone, the encyclopaedia becomes an occasion to irreverently mock both the literary and the actual version of the consummate society. Between numerous drawings of imaginary creatures and eerie monsters, Solakov included rules and guidelines for a happy and harmonious collective life. Some of the alphabetically ordered entries illustrate ideas proposed by More. For example, lavishly decorated clothes for slaves are juxtaposed with plain and dull garments for ordinary citizens. More designed a society in which owing or wearing golden chains and jewels is despicable because it is associated with slavery. This idea resonates in the communist ideology of abolishing private property and imposing rigorous rules of equality. Solakov muses on another such reversal of established values, namely freedom. In the tone mockingly imitating communist-style demagogy, he argues that being a slave is actually better than being a free citizen. The latter continuously fears losing his or her freedom and is thus less happy than a slave. As the artist notes in his spoken commentary, the most salient characteristic of the encyclopaedia is its ubiquitous sexual undertone. A monument is juxtaposed with an erect penis, while communist propaganda photos are interpreted in explicitly sexual terms. All of these burlesque remarks and illustrations point towards the deep disappointment with the experiment called real socialism. However,

Solakov's mockery at false puritanism and the suppressing of desires is just one aspect of the fundamental critique towards the utopian ideal. The order governing life in utopia is conditioned on the presupposition of the rational nature of human beings. Emotion, passion, and irrational drives have to be kept at bay. Frustrated allusions to the limitations of individual freedoms convey the sense of the unreality and naivety of that overly optimistic utopian vision.

– KRS

BIO Bulgarian artist Nedko Solakov (°1957) is one of the main protagonists of contemporary European art. His work combines a "classical" artistic education with conceptual elements and a strong sense for the absurd.

His funny and often touching visual art is the result of great fantasy and humor, which has kept him safe from the communist regime in his country of origin. Solakov's work includes paintings, drawings, installations, videos, texts, and performances, in which he likes to play with diverse references to the history of art.

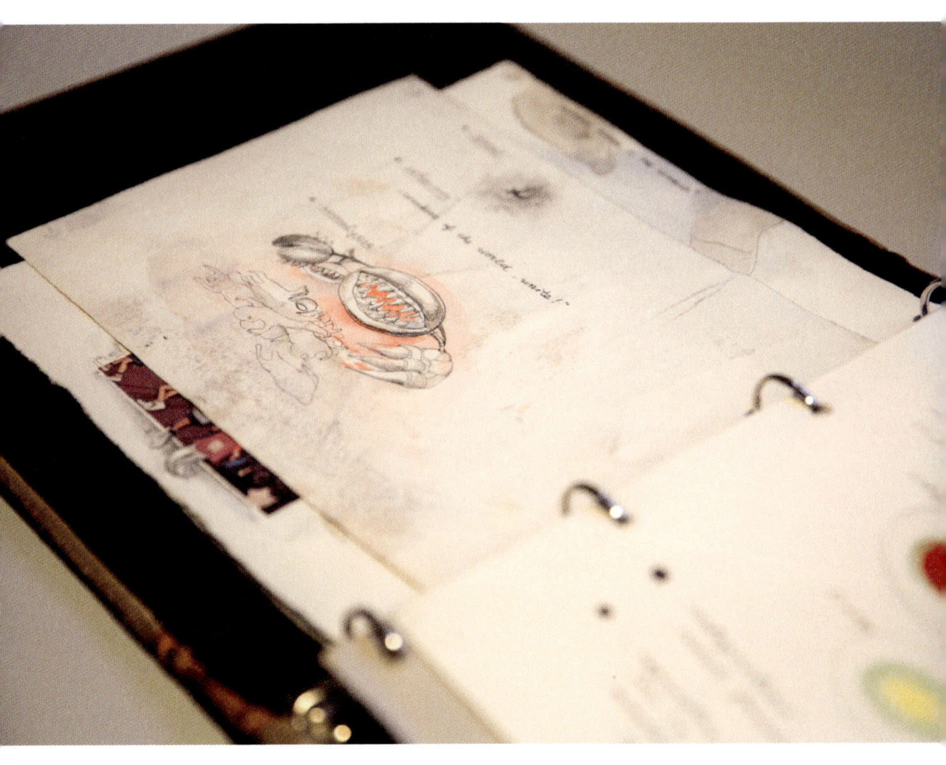

Encyclopedia Utopia, 1990
mixed media on paper and various supports;
224 pages in three volumes, handbound in leather
Courtesy Museum Voorlinden, Wassenaar

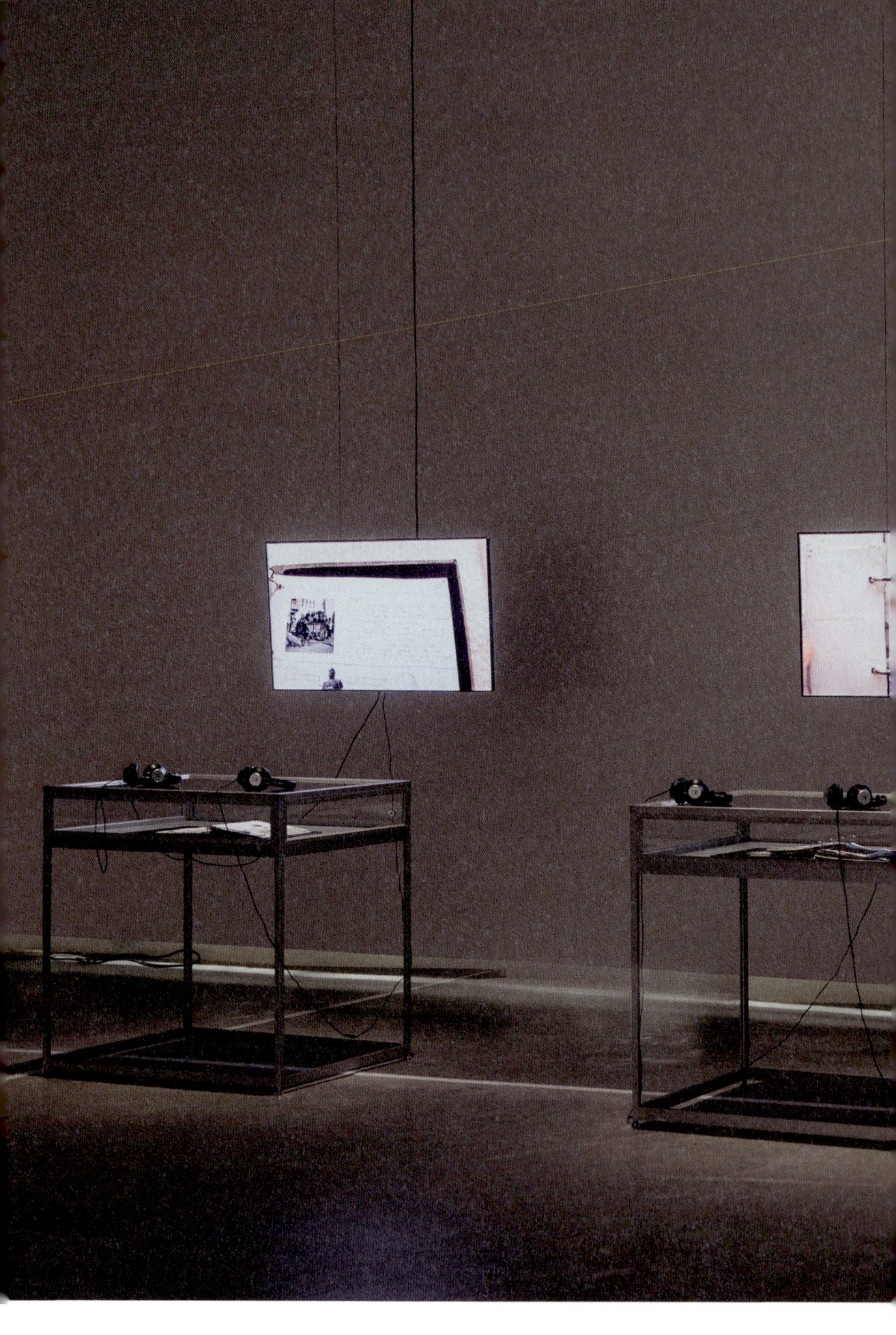

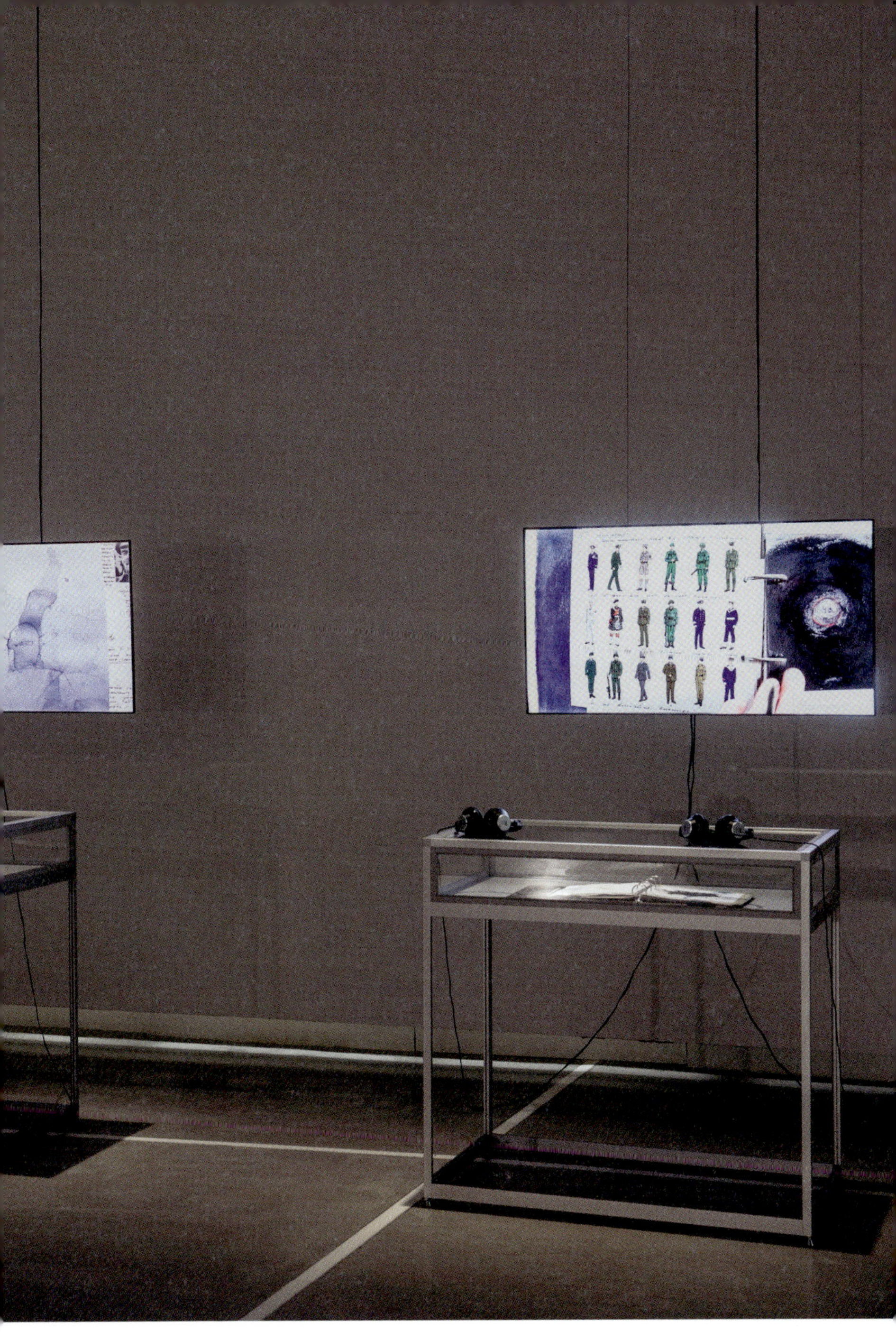

Rereading Encyclopaedia Utopia, 2015
three-channel HD video installation (31′ 40″, 26′ 46″, 25′ 56″), headphones,
three glass cases with the original books, dimensions variable.
Courtesy the artist and Museum Voorlinden, Wassenaar
Commissioned and produced by CONTOUR 7

Johan Grimonprez

In his new installation, Johan Grimonprez enters into dialogue with thinkers and scientists in the search for new ideas of the common. The questions asked in the conversations and, as always in the work of this artist, in a montage of images, pertain to the dominant role of negative factors in social organization such as fear, competition and self-interest. One of Grimonprez' interlocutors is the political philosopher Michael Hardt, who calls for the imagining of a new political organization based on the concept of love. The conversation is interspersed with footage from *Alphaville*, the dystopian film by Jean-Luc Godard, made in 1965, which offers a pertinent contrast to Hardt's theory. In Alphaville, a distant planet ruled by a powerful and tyrannical computer, love and affection are banned from social life. While Godard's film is a somber and undesirable vision of the future, Hardt seems to suggest that essentially, this is already our reality. The all-present fear makes us accept the limitations imposed on our privacy in surveillance. We also consent all too easily to the precarity of work and to the actual labor apartheid that exists for a large part of society. The philosopher suggests we should rather dare to believe that our being together can be governed by our natural sense of fairness, empathy, and collaboration. At the same time, the task of both the thinker and the artist is to remain sceptical. As the concepts of love, cooperation or democracy are also susceptible to erosion, they need to be continuously reinvented. The second project presented by Grimonprez, entitled *On Radical Ecology and Tender Gardening*, is a vlog or video blog. In it, the artist collects clips recycled from the internet and various archives on a range of issues in ecology and sustainability. The videos vary from short documentaries to news bites and commentaries. They include, for example, a story on an innovative irrigation system in a desert or a mock television news, actually broadcast by the BBC, featuring the Yes Men pretending they represent the DOW Chemical Corporation. What unites these multifarious fragments is the idea of radical ecology as a

reflection on new and responsible ways of leading our common life. The idea of tender gardening draws from Voltaire's famous advice given at the end of *Candide:* "il faut cultiver notre jardin." Putting the focus on "our" garden, Grimonprez thus unites the idea of love and tenderness, proposed by Hardt, with the pressing issues of environment and sustainability.

– KRS

BIO **The work of Belgian artist Johan Grimonprez (°1962) dances on the borders of art and cinema, documentary and fiction, and practice and theory, causing the viewer to double-take. Informed by an archaeology of present-day media, his work seeks out the tension between the intimate and the bigger picture of globalization. It questions our contemporary sublimation, one framed by a fear industry that has infected political and social dialogue.**

By suggesting new narratives through which to tell a story, his work emphasizes a multiplicity of histories and realities.

The films of Grimonprez search for those moments where representation and reality seem to coexist. They "speak to the need to see history at a distance, but at the same time to speak from inside of it." He gained international acclaim in the visual arts, and has collected numerous prizes and selections, including at the Berlinale and the Sundance Film Festival.

WeTube-O-Theque, 2015
video-library, various lengths
Commissioned by Team Vlaams Bouwmeester /
Produced by ZAP-O-MATIK

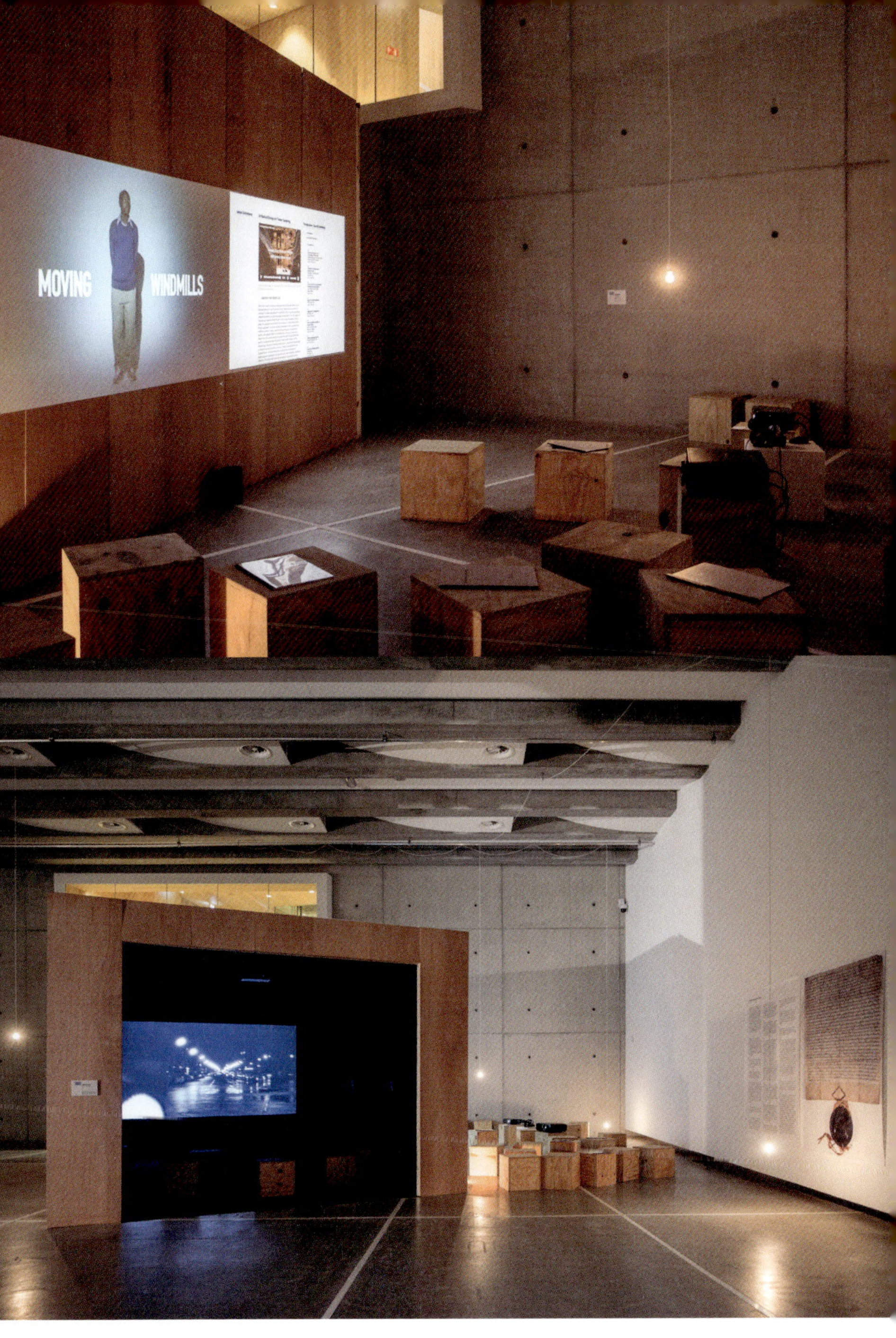

Every day words disappear, 2015
video, 15′ 11″
Edited and produced by Sabine Groenewegen
for ZAP-O-MATIK / Co-commissioned and
co-produced by CONTOUR 7 and Museumcultuur
Strombeek/Gent / Supported by Vlaamse Gemeenschap
and Vlaamse Gemeenschapscommissie

Jan Fabre

Antwerp, 10 July 1977

It is a beautiful, clear night.
The sun's day has passed
and for the past two hours the moon's day has been shining.
Today, the botanical garden in Leopoldstraat was my utopian island.
My father, Edmond Fabre, somehow convinced his workmates, the city's quick-witted
gardeners, to let me play with exotic plants and flowers all day, in preparation for a project I'll
carry out next week.
Now, 462 years later, I will go to the door of the house where Thomas More stayed in 1515 to
pay tribute to his ideal society in the Land of Nowhere.
IT WILL BE A SPECIMEN OF UTOPIAN POETRY
(IN ACTION).

Antwerp, 18 July 1977

Today, the moon's day.
Performed a simple and poetic act.
AN HOMAGE TO THOMAS MORE.
Opposite the entrance to the botanical garden, by the house in Leopoldstraat where the
English humanist discovered his Nowhereland.
(Maybe this act was an exercise in returning memory to art?)
Carl—with the red nose—Porinski filmed me with a Super 8 camera belonging to my parents.
3 reels, 3 minutes each.
I am intensely curious to see the results
and mount the magic of chemistry.
It is now 4 a.m.
AND I AM OVEREXCITED.
I hope the dictatorship of the rising sun
will burn me to sleep?

– Jan Fabre

BIO   For over 35 years, Belgian artist Jan Fabre (°1958) has held a crucial spot as an innovative visual artist, theater-maker and author. All of Fabre's works represent a strong belief in the vulnerable human body, the defence of that body and wondering how the human being will survive in the future.

Metamorphosis is a key concept in Fabre's artistic oeuvre, in which animal and human existence continuously interact. His artistry is a poetic resistance dedicated to beauty, an exercise in ways of disappearing. Throughout the years, he has created his own universe that abides by its own rules and laws, and contains its own characters, symbols, and motives.

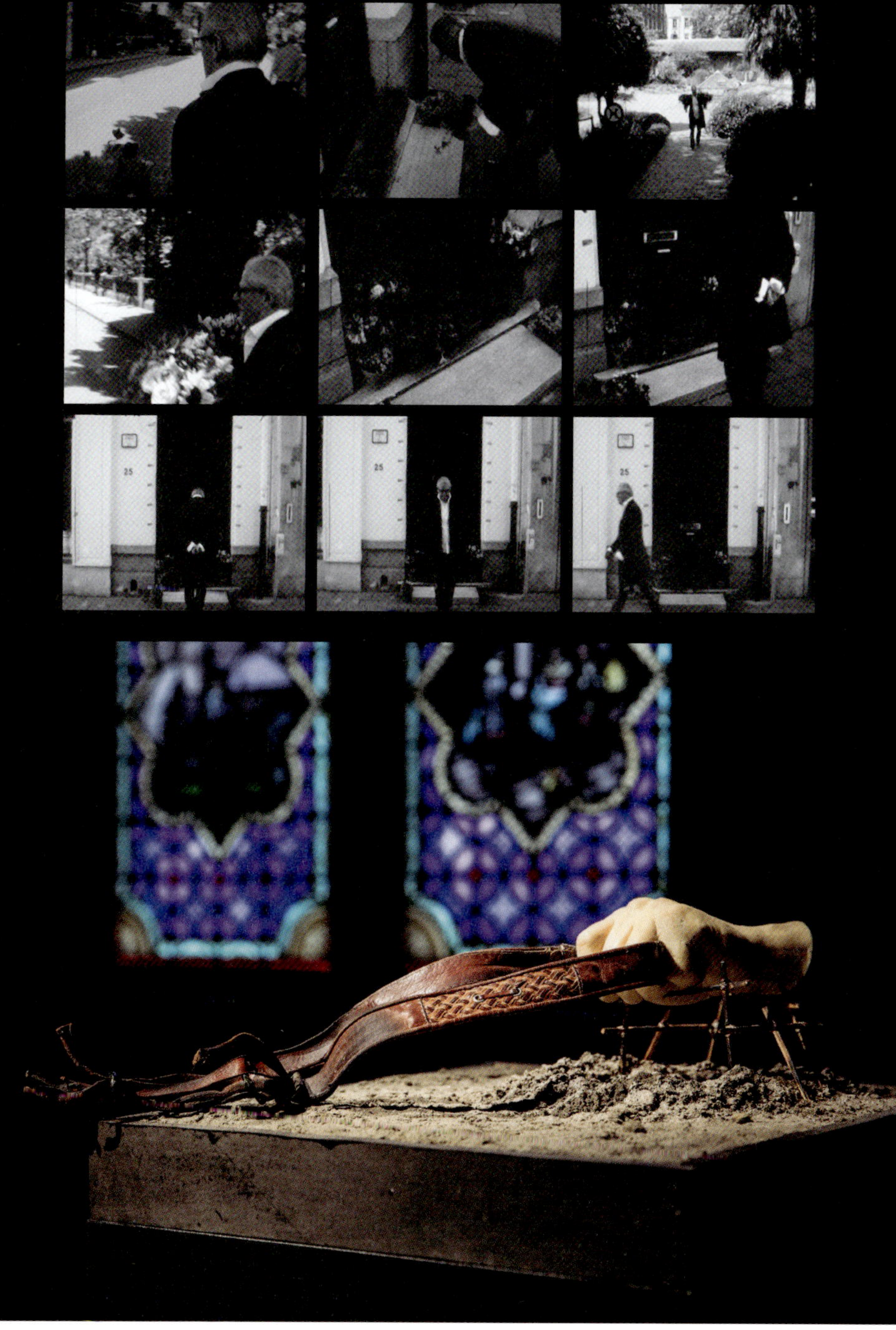

Homage to Thomas More, 1977
video, 8mm-film

Searching for Utopia II (op hol geslagen), 2005
polyester, leather belt, wood, soil
Private collection

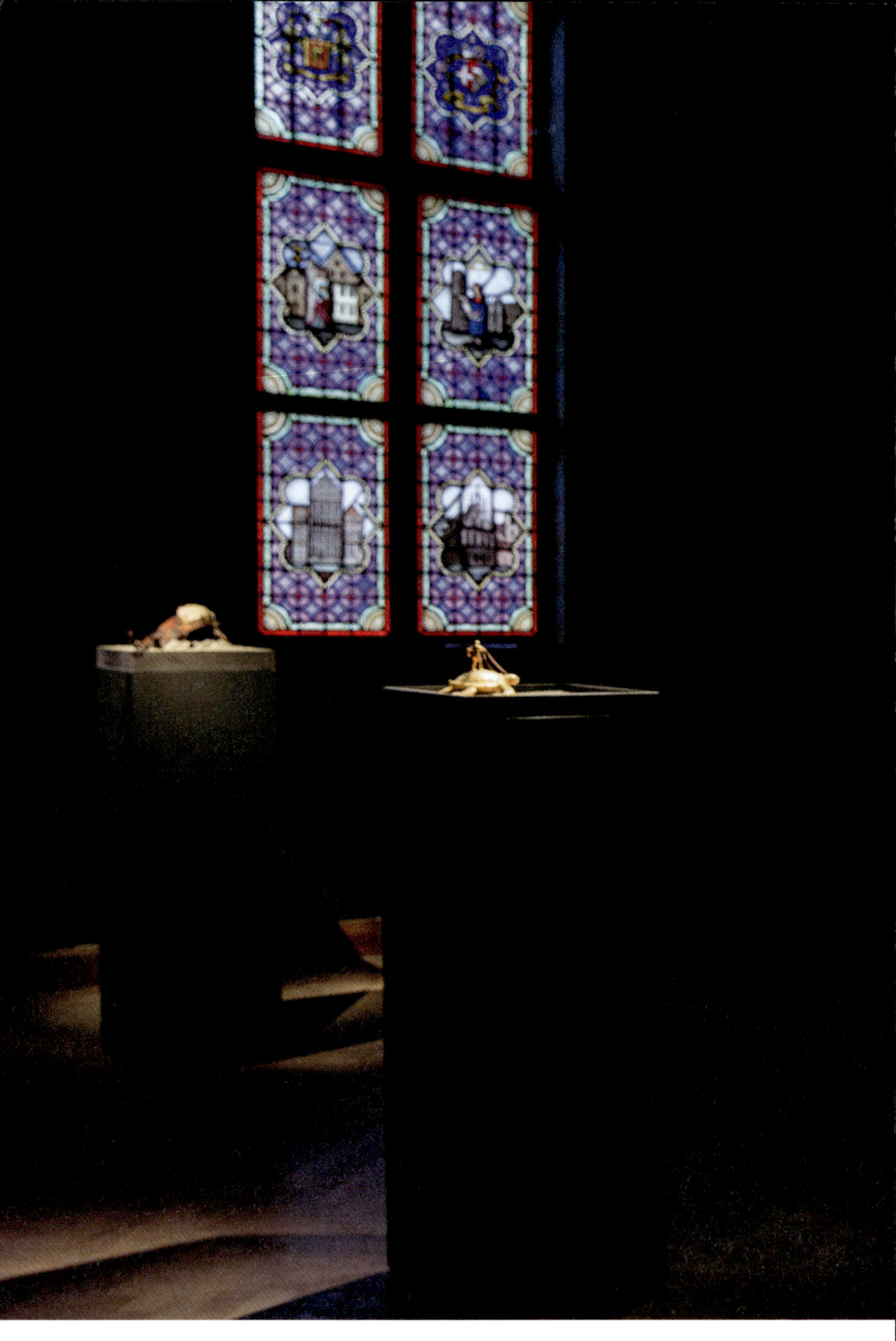

Searching for Utopia II (op hol geslagen), 2005
polyester, leather belt, wood, soil
Private collection

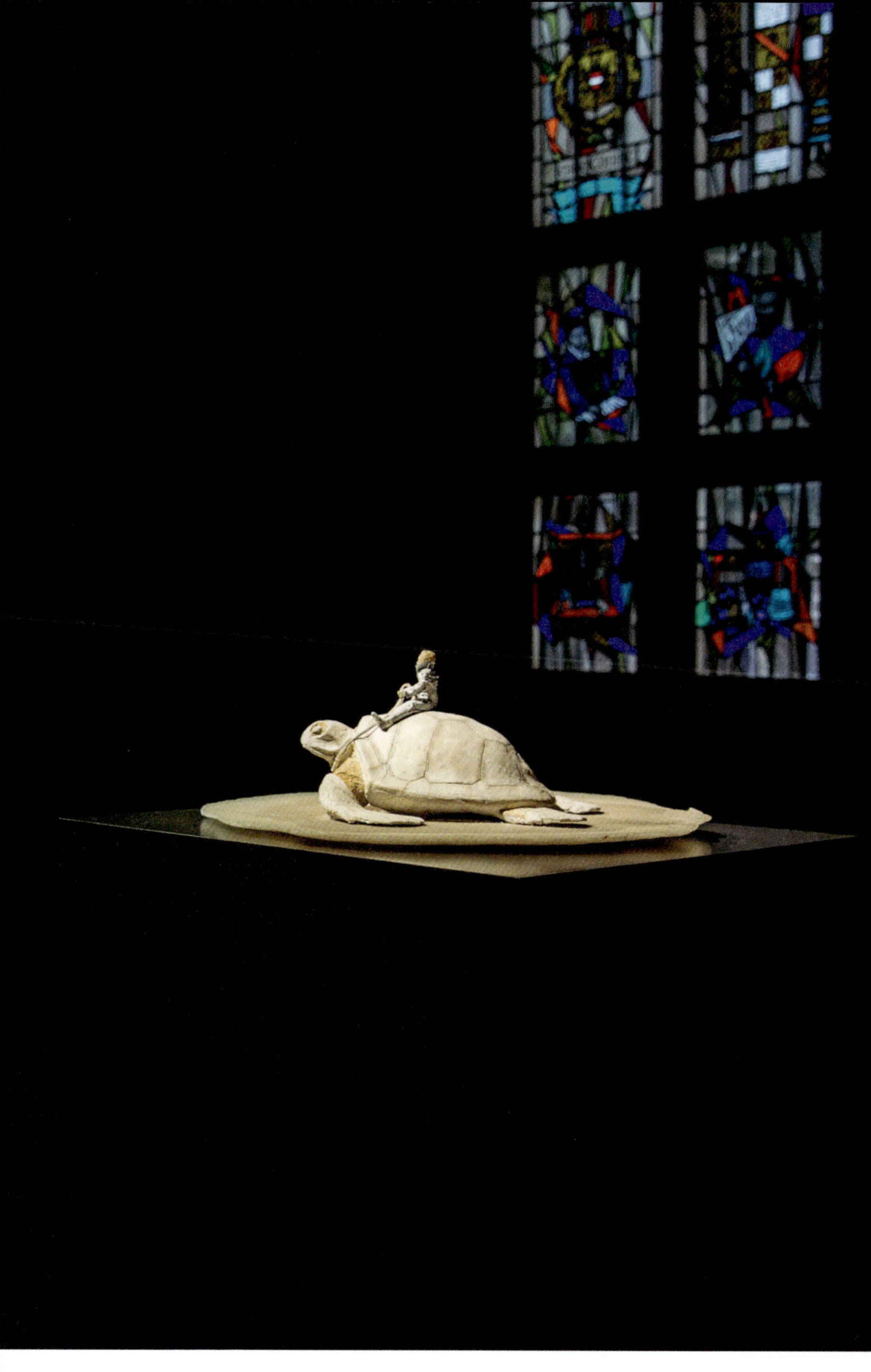

Searching for Utopia
(met kunstenaar-ruiter rechtop staand), 2002
polyester, plaster, sand, resin, gold foil, textile, wood
Private collection

Searching for Utopia
(Jantje op zoek naar Utopia of een orakelsteen), 2002
polyester, papier-mâché
Courtesy H.G. Knokke

Ana Prvački

Fig leaves have played a significant role in the history of art, covering male and female sexual organs to neutralize the erotic charge of images. Prvački's art explores ways of recharging the erotic dimension in art, while addressing forms of social intercourse and protocol. In her piece for CONTOUR 7 she presents a video with a scene from a por-nographic film shot in the 1920s, and in front of the screen she places a fig tree plant, subtly covering parts of the video, depending on the angle of the viewer. The image functions as a transgression of the social rule of the Utopians described in the title of the work, while at the same time paying homage to the convention of covering nudity in art history. As such the work offers a subtle commentary on the relationship between art, Utopia, and reality, as they all interfere with each other without allowing for a point of resolution to be possible. The work finds its point of synthesis in its audio component, however, which invites the listener into a subliminal journey back in time, covering one generation after the other of a family tree and perhaps inviting us to contemplate a primordial scene in the garden of Eden. Apparently if you repeat "grand," the word being pronounced by a basso-profondo in the video, over 70,000 times you reach the first generation of human beings on earth. Prvački's video also seems to play with the Biennale's monsters and martyrs theme as the two figures engaged in sexual intercourse in the video appear as headless, because of the frame of the film, and the repetitive movements of their bodies simultaneously evoke pleasure and pain.

– NS

BIO   Serbian artist Ana Prvački (°1976) lives and works in Los Angeles. In her work, which includes visual art and performances, she uses a gently pedagogical and comedic approach in an attempt to reconcile "etiquette" and "erotics".

Her interventions are meant to transform the viewer's perception and experience of daily life and routine, providing solutions to our everyday problems, worries, and fears. Her work explores the social anxiety and comedic potential of the so-called faux pas: the breaking of social rules and etiquette, often by an outsider. In doing so, Prvački investigates the socio-political significance of welcoming the "other."

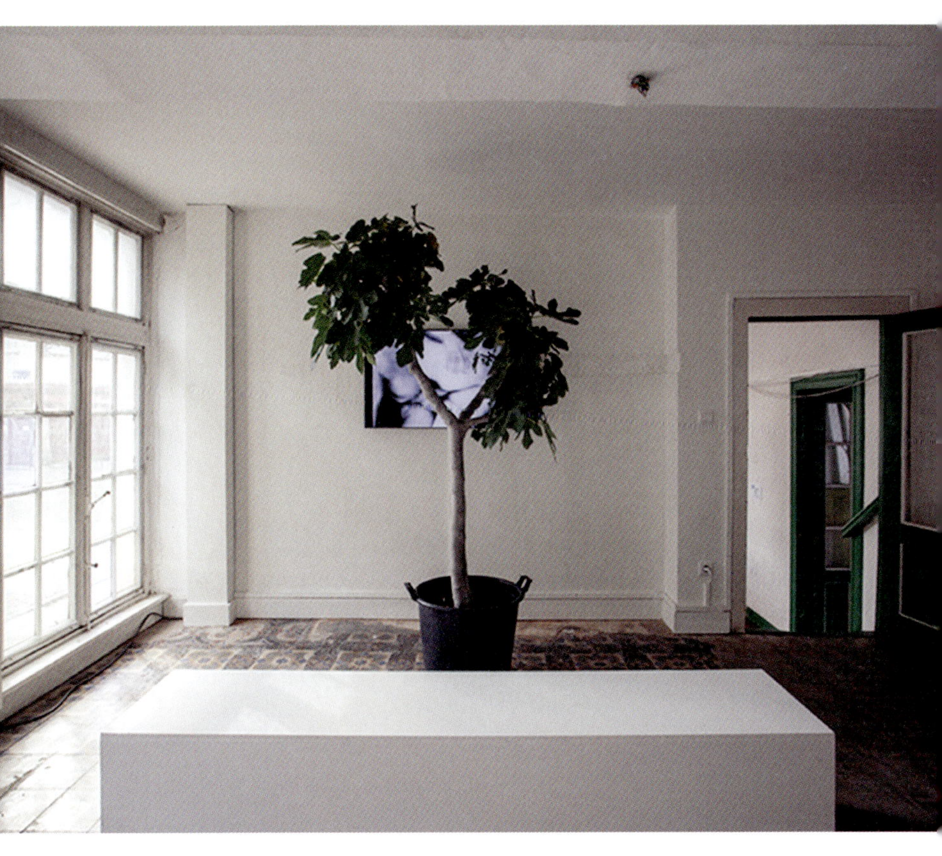

**The Family Fig Tree (for the Utopians it's important
to see their future spouse naked before marrying them)**, 2015
video, sound, fig tree, 2′ 34″
Commissioned and produced by CONTOUR 7 /
Supported by Dena Foundation for Contemporary Art

Michael Rakowitz

For CONTOUR 7 Rakowitz presents an art project-in-progress that centers on the author and singer Leonard Cohen and the ethical dilemmas of the post-Holocaust Jew in relation to Israel and Palestine. The final work will be multimedia and will include a film shot at the Chelsea Hotel, where Cohen was staying in a period during which he also traveled to Egypt and Israel to perform for the Israeli troops fighting the Yom Kippur War. In Mechelen, Rakowitz presents props for the film, fragments of a preliminary screenplay and script, derived from many of Cohen's poems and diaries. All of these materials have been realized in a strictly analog mode, using the exact same olive green Olivetti Lettera 22 typewriter that Leonard Cohen used during this time period. As often occurs in Rakowitz's practice, objects of material culture that he searches for and buys on eBay, such as photographs of Cohen playing for the Israeli army and his original typewriter, find a new mode of existence in the artist's poetic and surgical interventions in the traumas and wounds of history. Music has been a focal point of his work, often using it as an instrument for forms of collective catharsis, while giving it a twist that does not allow for the process to become unreflective.

I'm good at love, I'm good at hate, it's in between I freeze, which is a quotation from Cohen's poem *Recitation*, will culminate in a concert performed by Rakowitz with local musicians at the Ramallah Cultural Palace in Palestine. In this venue Cohen was scheduled to perform in September 2009, just days after a performance in Tel Aviv. The Ramallah date was planned to defuse the call by human rights activists for Cohen to refuse to play in Israel and was quickly canceled by the hosting Palestinian Prisoners Club as a result of the Cultural Boycott of Israel.

Rakowitz remains a fan and follower of Cohen to this day.

– NS

BIO   **Michael Rakowitz's (°1973) multidisciplinary practice engages the senses as a means of sparking discourse around pressing political, social, and historical issues. His conceptual art is deeply political and often focuses on the Middle East, the region from where his family fled.**

An American artist of Iraqi-Jewish origin, Rakowitz is known for establishing unexpected connections between Iraqi history and Western culture. In doing so, he creates entirely new and composite narratives that involve the audience in a vibrant revival of the past.

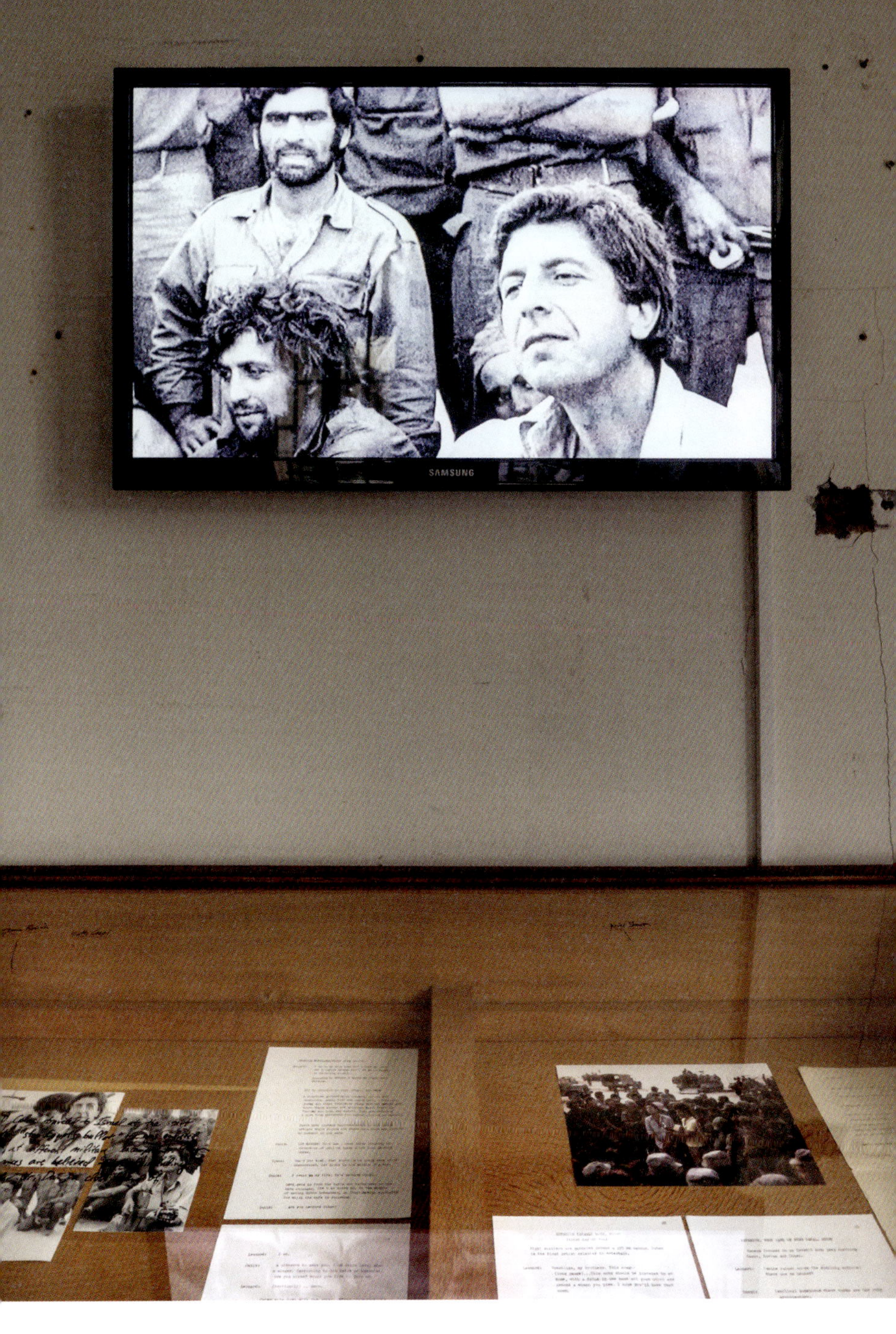

I'm Good At Love, I'm Good At Hate, It's In Between I Freeze, 2015
mixed media, script-fragments, olive green Olivetti Lettera, 22 typewriter
Courtesy the artist, Rhona Hoffman Gallery, Chicago and Jane Lombard Gallery,
New York / Supported by Dena Foundation for Contemporary Art

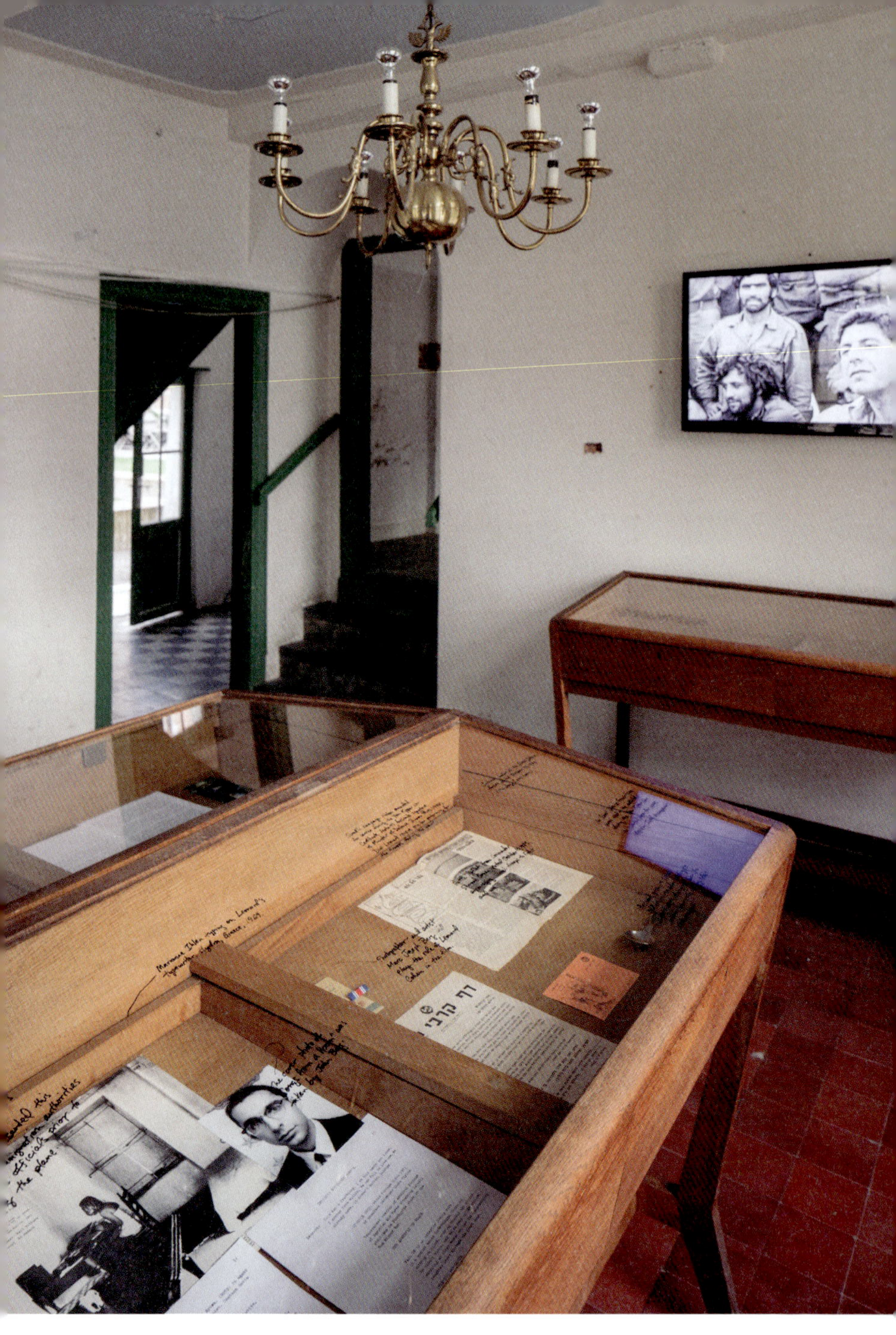

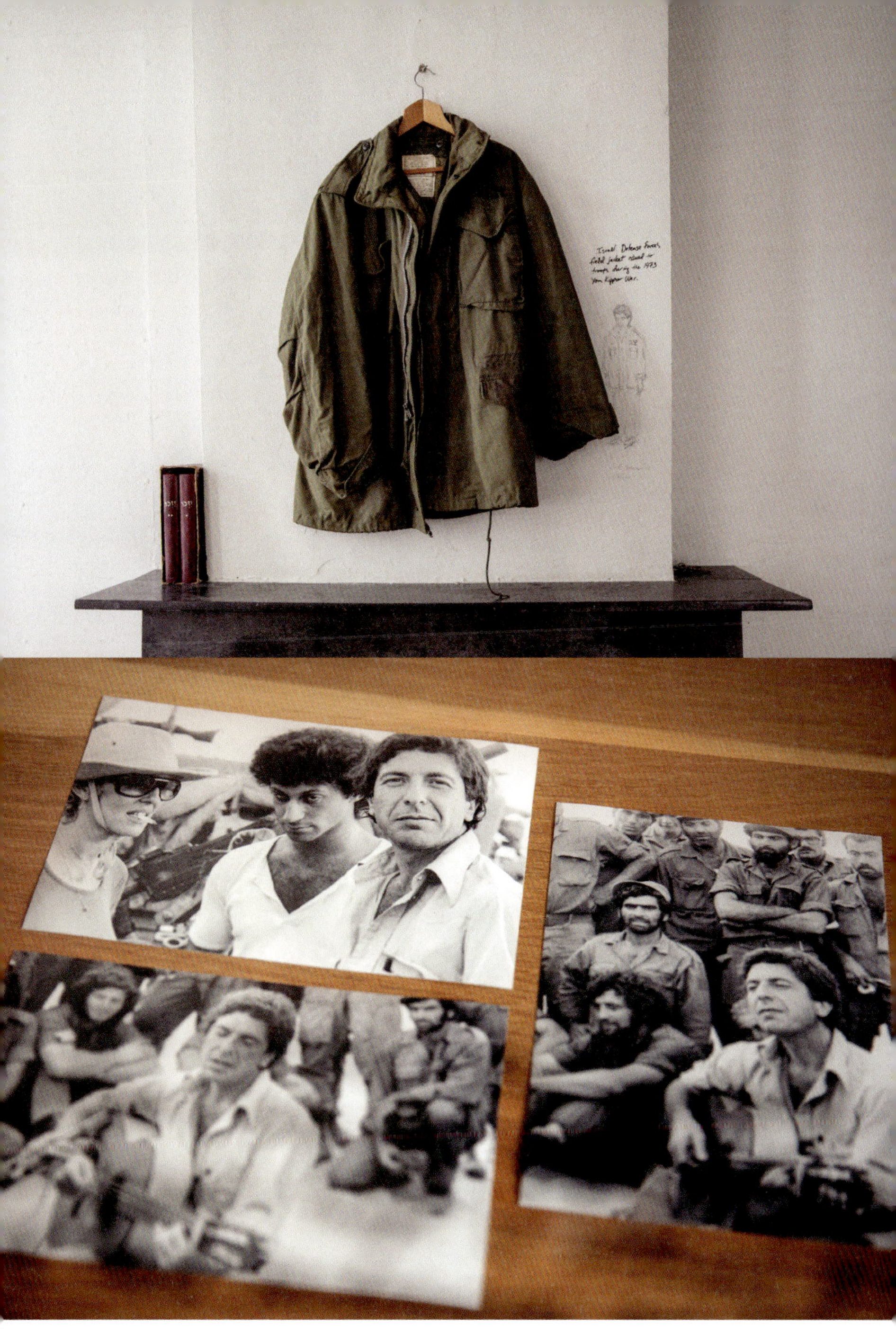

I'm Good At Love, I'm Good At Hate, It's In Between I Freeze, 2015
mixed media, script-fragments, olive green Olivetti Lettera, 22 typewriter
Courtesy the artist, Rhona Hoffman Gallery, Chicago and Jane Lombard Gallery,
New York / Supported by Dena Foundation for Contemporary Art

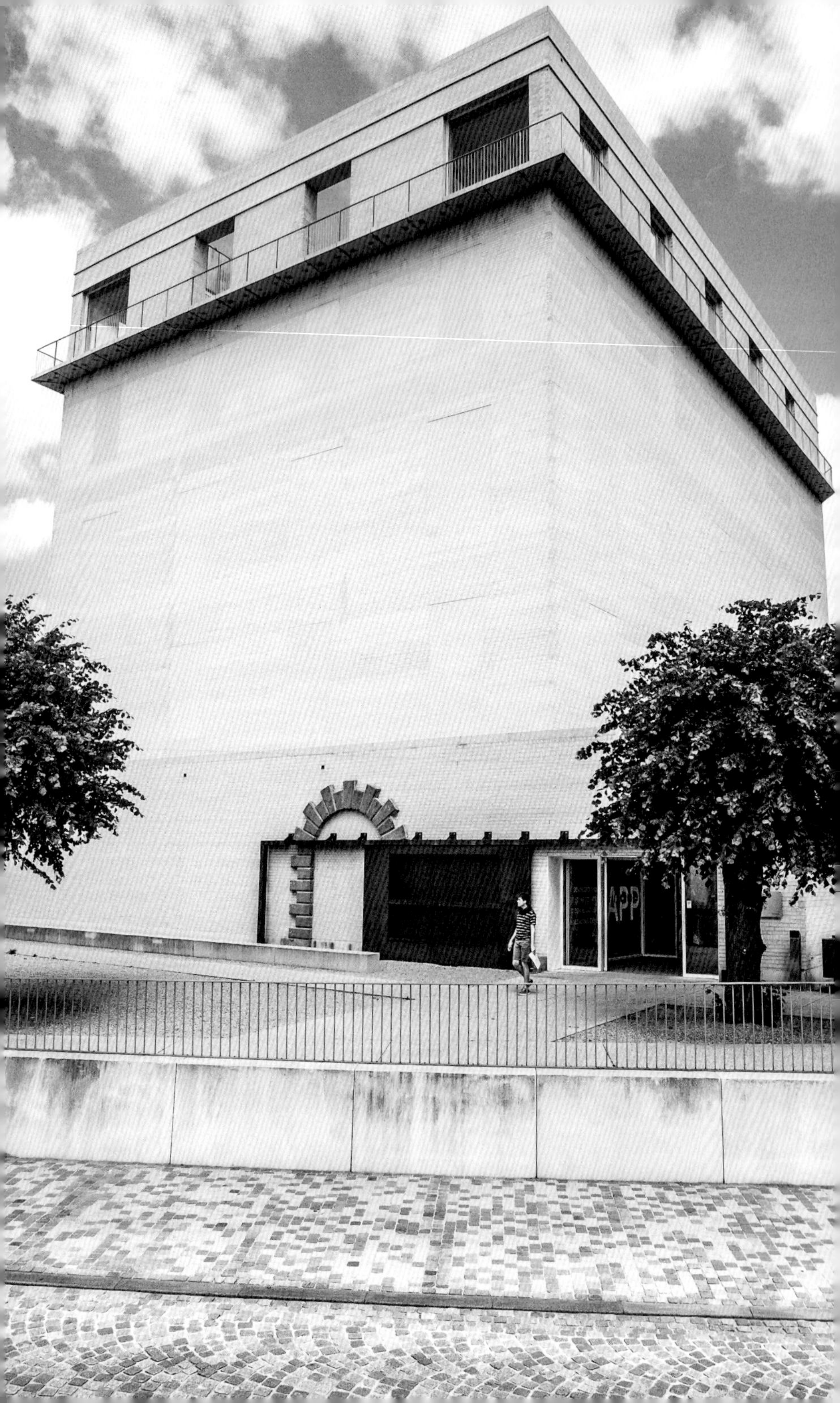

Kazerne Dossin

Empress Maria Theresa of Austria had the Belgian army barracks built in 1756. In 1936 the barracks were named after the commander of the seventh line regiment during the First World War: Lieutenant General Emile de Dossin de Saint Georges, who was from Liège. He was honored as a war hero because of the decisive role he had played in the Battle of the Yser.

A sinister new use was found for the building during the Second World War. The Nazis used it as a *Sammellager*, a strategic assembly camp from where Jews and Gypsies were deported to Auschwitz-Birkenau and several smaller camps. On May 30th 1948 a plaque was affixed to the façade of the barracks to commemorate those horrors and every year a ceremony is organized in memory of the victims.

In 2012 a museum of the same name opened alongside the former Kazerne Dossin. The new building was designed by the Belgian architect bOb Van Reeth. During the Biennial of the Moving Image, monsters and martyrs from the black pages of history wander here.

Sander Breure
& Witte van Hulzen

Sander Breure and Witte van Hulzen's double projection suggests we are seeing an image and its reverse, the counter-image. What the videos shown here reveal is a series of reversals and biting juxtapositions. The first screen displays images from a small and seemingly uninhabited island. The camera calmly observes the island's vegetation as if this discreet and undisturbed piece of land surrounded by a quiet sea could offer an idyllic existence. Only when we learn that this in fact is Utøya, the place of the politically motivated massacre committed by Anders Breivik in 2011, do the images acquire a menacing tone. On the now empty island, almost eighty young people were brutally killed in what was supposedly intended as a revenge for the flooding of Europe with migrants. In this context, the reverse side of the screen indeed offers a counter-image, as it shows a montage of diverse found-footage fragments on migration. Most images have a low resolution and are shaky or unfocused, indicating they were filmed with small mobile cameras. On one of the clips we see migrants smuggled in cargo vehicles. Next, an early twentieth-century ship arrives on what probably is Ellis Island near New York. In one of the most dramatic clips, a pontoon filled with African migrants approaches a sunny beach filled with bikini-clad and carefree tourists, only some of them slightly disturbed by the incongruous view. This disconcerting comparison between the Utøya case and the current migration crisis is given a yet more sardonic commentary in the montage of texts heard in the voice-over. The excerpts including quotations from Don Quixote or Herbert Marcuse point towards the perils of utopian thinking. As the poet Wisława Szymborska, also quoted in the voice-over, says, utopia is that ideal island where all knowledge is readily available and all problems are solved. But somehow it is empty, because all its inhabitants escaped into the sea. The reverse movement of migrants through the sea into Europe shows that what some people imagine as utopia is in fact its opposite.

– KRS

BIO   The Dutch artistic duo Sander Breure (°1985) and Witte van Hulzen (°1984) uses diverse media such as video, performance, photography, drawings, and installation. Families, migration, insignificant behaviour, the art world and its unwritten laws, the attack on Utøya: the various subjects are always translated into images, with specific attention to the human condition.

Their work is rooted in a romantic tradition. Due to the way in which they attempt, through the continual reuse of images, to investigate the essence of art and its relationship to our world, that tradition takes on new connotations. Central to their œuvre is the issue of where images originate, what they portray, and what they mean to us.

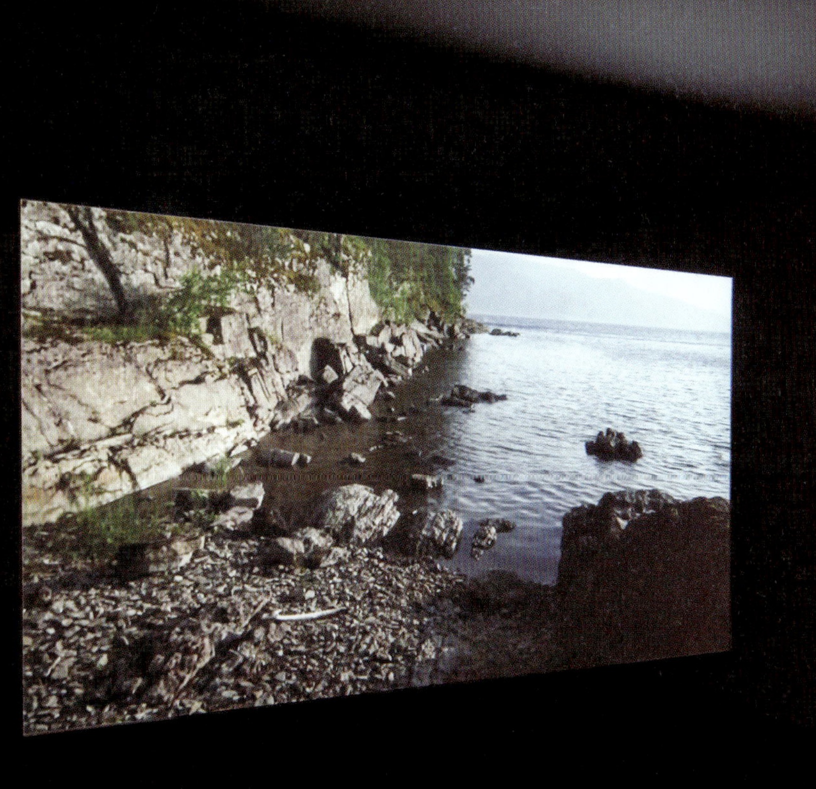

The Shores Of An Island I Only Skirted, 2012
video-installation, sound, 14′ 00″
Courtesy the artists / Supported by Mondriaan Fund,
Hollandse Maatjes and Embassy Koninkrijk der Nederlanden /
Courtesy tegenboschvanvreden Amsterdam

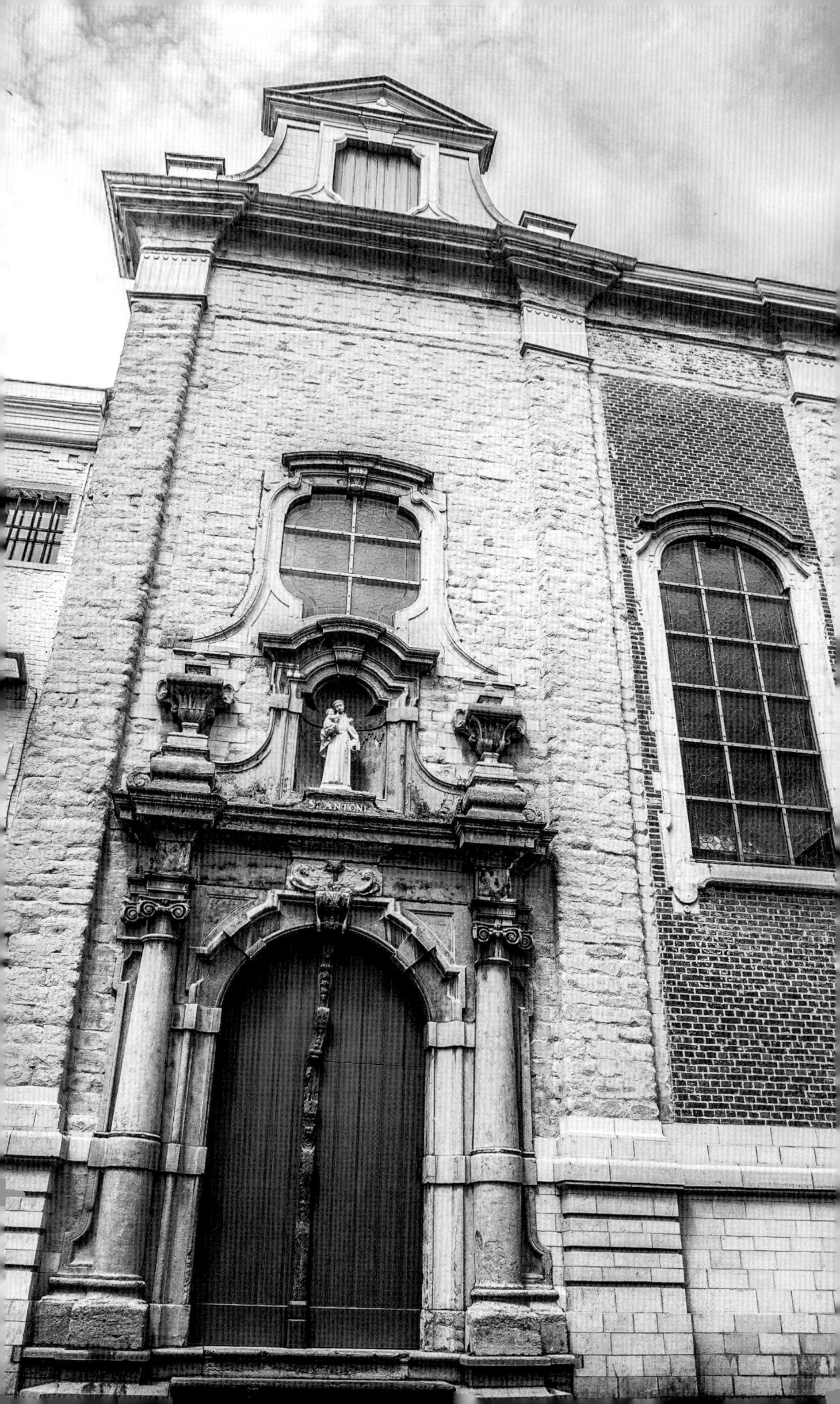
S. ANTONI

De Noker

CONTOUR 7 culminates at the carefully restored chapel and classic inner courtyard of de Noker. The fourteenth-century House of God of the Holy Trinity was known for the hospitality it extended to the sick and marginalized. The Alexian Brothers took over the building at the beginning of the seventeenth century and at the beginning of the eighteenth century, they the chapel and ambulatory as we know them today.

The scale and variation of the stuccowork on the late-baroque ceiling makes it unique in the Low Countries. At the beginning of the twentieth century the Franciscan nuns moved into the building. They did community work, providing children with an education and adults with training.

As the headquarters of the non-profit welfare organization Emmaüs, the site is still associated with care today. During the Biennale, the inner courtyard and chapel where the sick, plague-stricken and mentally ill once came to pray provides the setting for a high mass of contemporary video art.

Chiara Fumai

The characters appearing in Chiara Fumai's installation are all remarkable historical figures. Yet besides the fact that they all are women, they do not seem to have that much in common. They lived in geographically distant places and different historical circumstances. Among them are feminist activists, writers, terrorists, freaks, and mediums, such as Eusapia Palladino, Carla Lonzi, Zalumma Agra, Ulrike Meinhof, or Annie Jones. Female curiosities, one might think, gathered here in a chapel, with a mock-religious reverence as if the artist wanted to offer us new models to venerate. In many respects, the key figure in this eccentric company is Eusapia Palladino. This Italian peasant woman of the early twentieth century became well-known as a spiritualist medium possessed by mysterious powers. In the period of intense interest in occult knowledge, ranging from ghost séances to secret theosophical societies, Palladino attracted attention with her supernatural abilities, such as moving objects without physically touching them and making contact with spirits. Quite surprisingly, not only sensation-greedy aristocrats sought to participate in a séance with Palladino. Many of the greatest authorities in science, from psychologists to physicists, attempted to verify the medium's claims to mystic faculties. One of them was the French astronomer Camille Flammarion, whom Fumai imitates in the voiceover. Together with other scholars, he admitted he was not able to explain some of the observed anomalies when using the available scientific methods. At the same time, Palladino was repeatedly caught cheating by means of tricks and gimmicks. Was she truly remarkable, or simply an imposter? The ambiguity of that mysterious figure is its central attraction for Chiara Fumai. The artist also acts as if she were a medium, allowing her characters to speak through her body. At the same time, her masquerades are never entirely serious. Her eagerness to trick the viewer also allows her to create a necessary distance from which these strong but controversial female characters can be reflected upon from a fresh perspective.

– KRS

BIO The performative practice of Italian artist Chiara Fumai (°1978) belongs to the tradition of female psychics, who are "spoken by" different controversial entities, which the artist freely (mis)interprets and combines into new stories, questioning their symbolic meaning and representation in the mind of the viewer.

Fumai lives and works in Milan. Dealing with radical feminism, media culture, language, and repression, her light-esoteric and symbolic performances and visual art have garnered international acclaim.

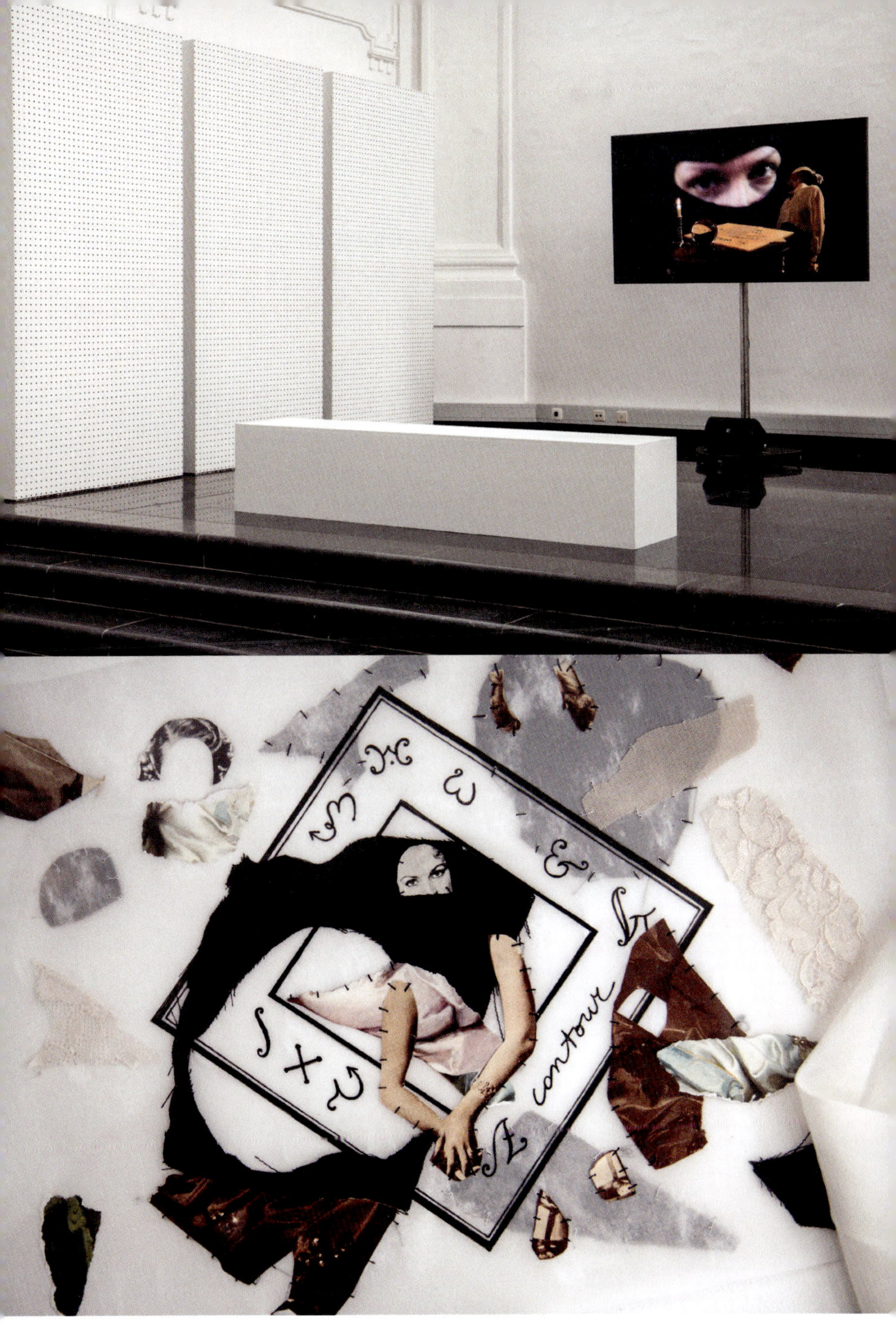

The Book Of Evil Spirits, 2015
ink and collage on paper, mixed media, video, 26′ 24″
Commissioned and co-produced by CONTOUR 7 / Supported by
A Palazzo Gallery, Brescia and Dena Foundation for Contemporary Art

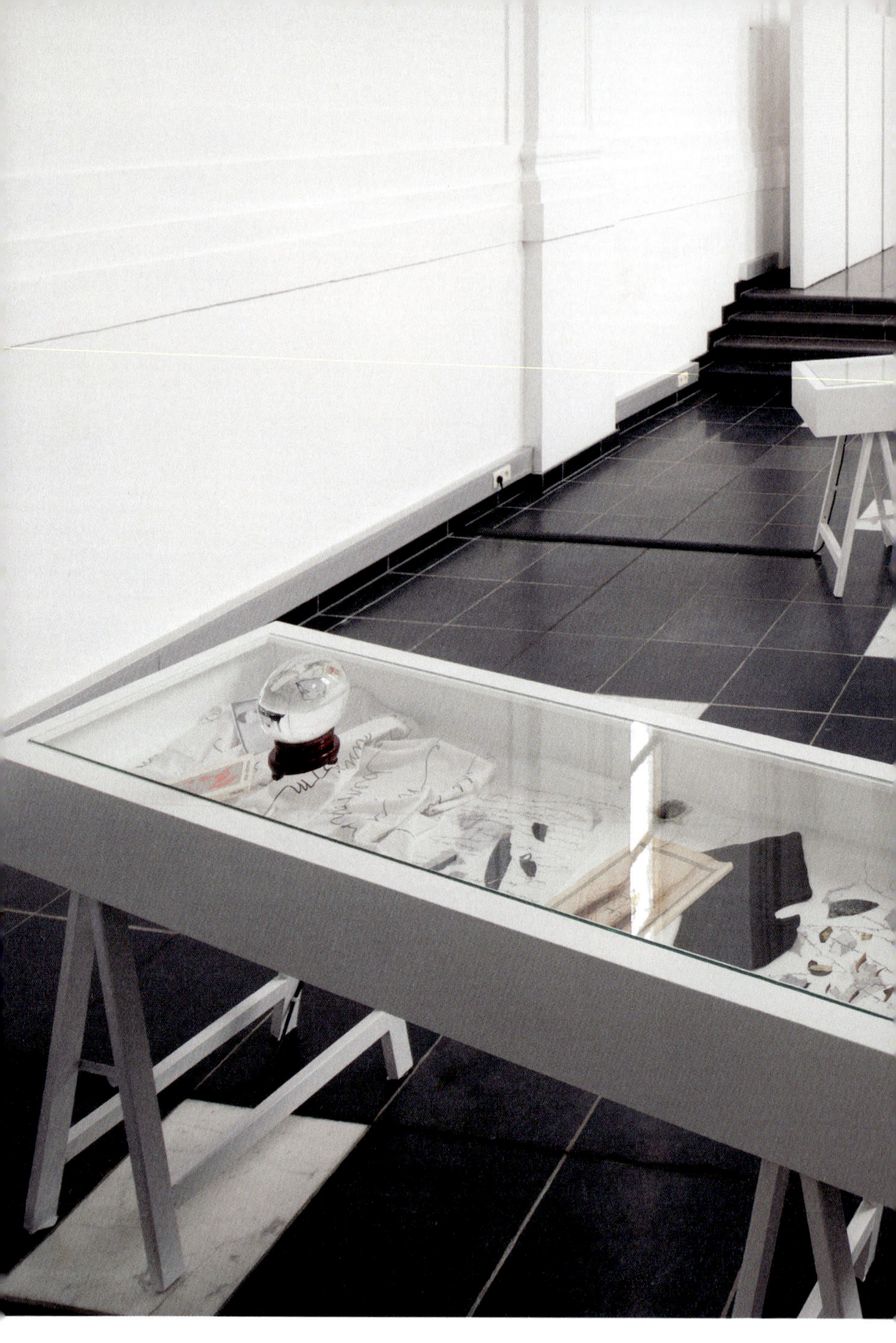

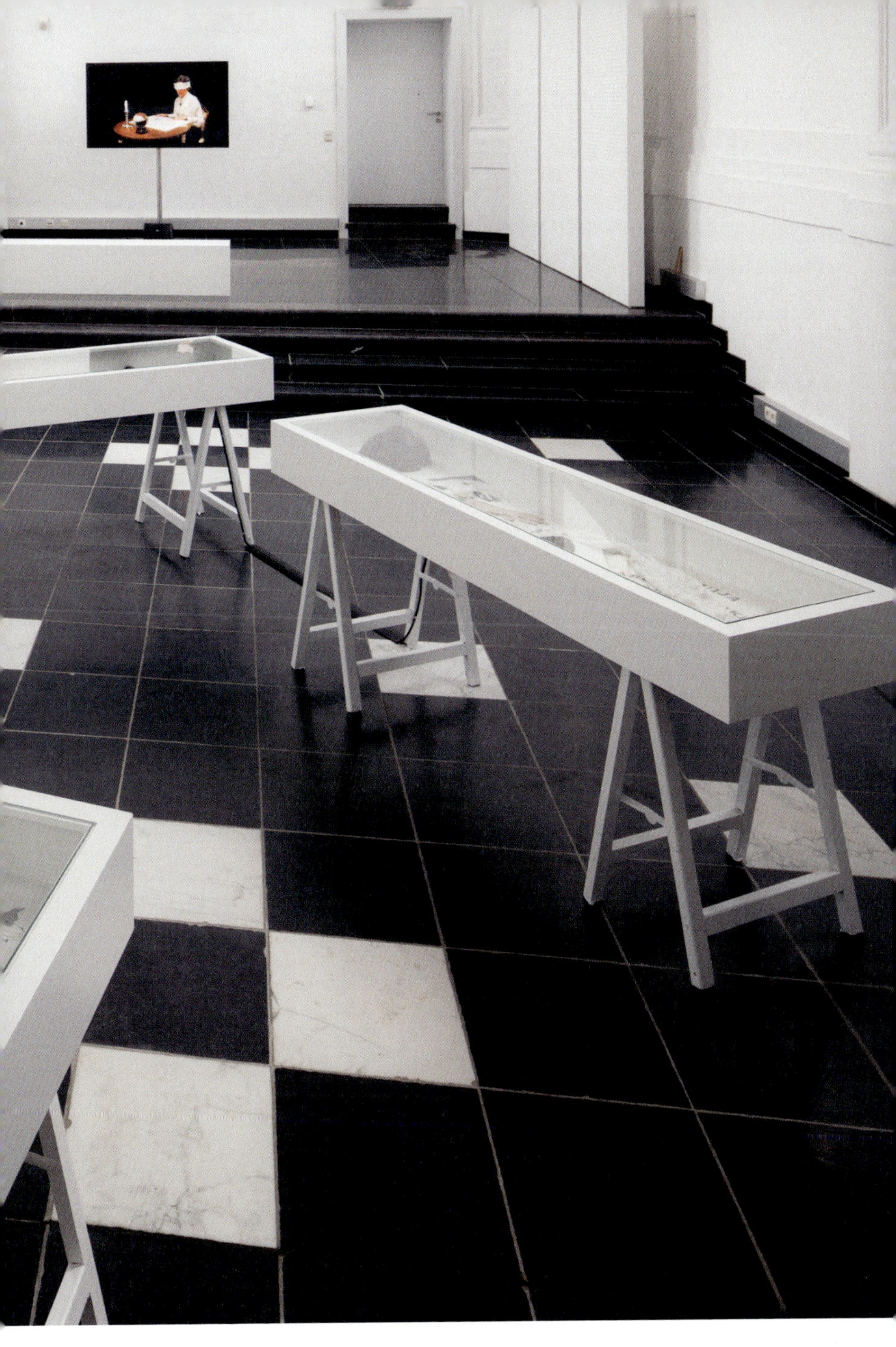

The Book Of Evil Spirits, 2015
ink and collage on paper, mixed media, video, 26' 24"
Commissioned and co-produced by CONTOUR 7 / Supported by
A Palazzo Gallery, Brescia and Dena Foundation for Contemporary Art

Angel Vergara

The work in situ by Angel Vergara connects different threads of the exhibition with its specific location. The artist chose the garden of the former monastery De Noker as both the backdrop and the very subject of his installation. The monastery belonged to the Alexian brothers, the congregation devoted to caring for the sick and the outcast. The geometric design of the small garden hidden in between the walls of the cloister inspired the artist to muse on the theme of the Enclosed Garden known from 16th century art. He also linked it to the idea of an artificial paradise. There is only one tree here, while the rest of the garden is organized in geometric, highly decorative forms. Such a space has many characteristics of a utopian island. It is secluded, inaccessible for outsiders, and structured in such a way as to keep the growth of plants under complete control. The presence of the singular tree calls to mind the biblical paradise, with its centrally located tree of knowledge. To taste from that tree is to know good and evil, which for the first inhabitants of the paradise turned out to have quite disastrous consequences. Knowledge appears to deliver an ambiguous advantage, bringing enlightenment but also a burden. Learning about good and evil gives the ability to act malevolently. It brings to light the monstrous element in human nature. The serene and harmoniously structured garden was meant to inspire pious meditation, but as we know, such contemplative atmosphere was also capable of unleashing monstrous visions. Similar ambiguity can be found in the sheer idea of the secluded garden. One can ask whether it is to protect or to imprison the people frequenting it. These places can be seen as sources of both delight and torture. Perhaps it is even so that monsters and saints are two aspects of the same, multifaceted human nature. The best example of it is Thomas More himself: sentenced and executed as a dangerous enemy of the Anglican Church, he became a Catholic saint several centuries later.

– KRS

BIO The work of Spanish artist Angel Vergara (°1958) is concerned with continued research into the power of the image. Through performances, videos, installations, and paintings, he tests the limits of art and reality. He questions the way the contemporary image shapes our own reality. Every work is an attempt to break through the image and to make its impact come to the surface, on an aesthetic as well as a sociocultural and political level.

Decontextualised images of reality are mediated by the artist and transformed into art. Vergara's work is the result of a constant dialogue between the artist, the ever transforming reality, and its image. He creates a kind of reality "in-between." In this process, viewers are encouraged to question their way of perceiving the everyday, and the way it is presented to them in an avalanche of images.

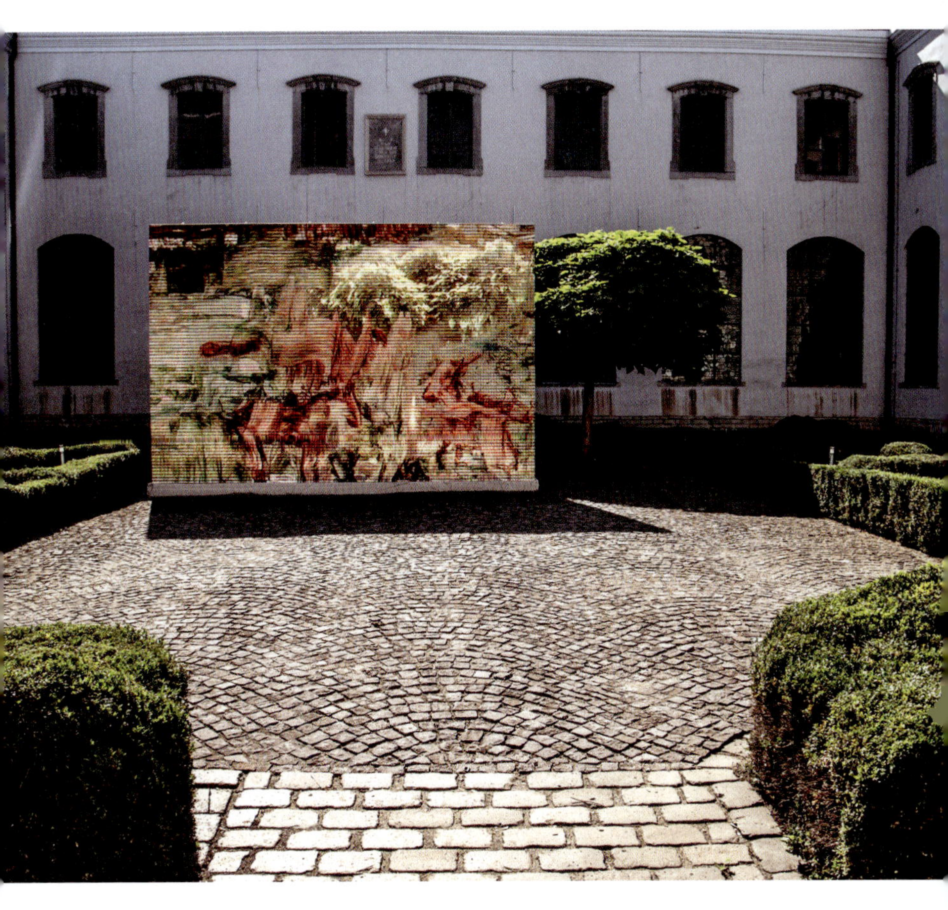

De Nekker Tree!, 2015
hd video installation, multi-channel sound, 13′ 11″
Commissioned and co-produced by CONTOUR 7

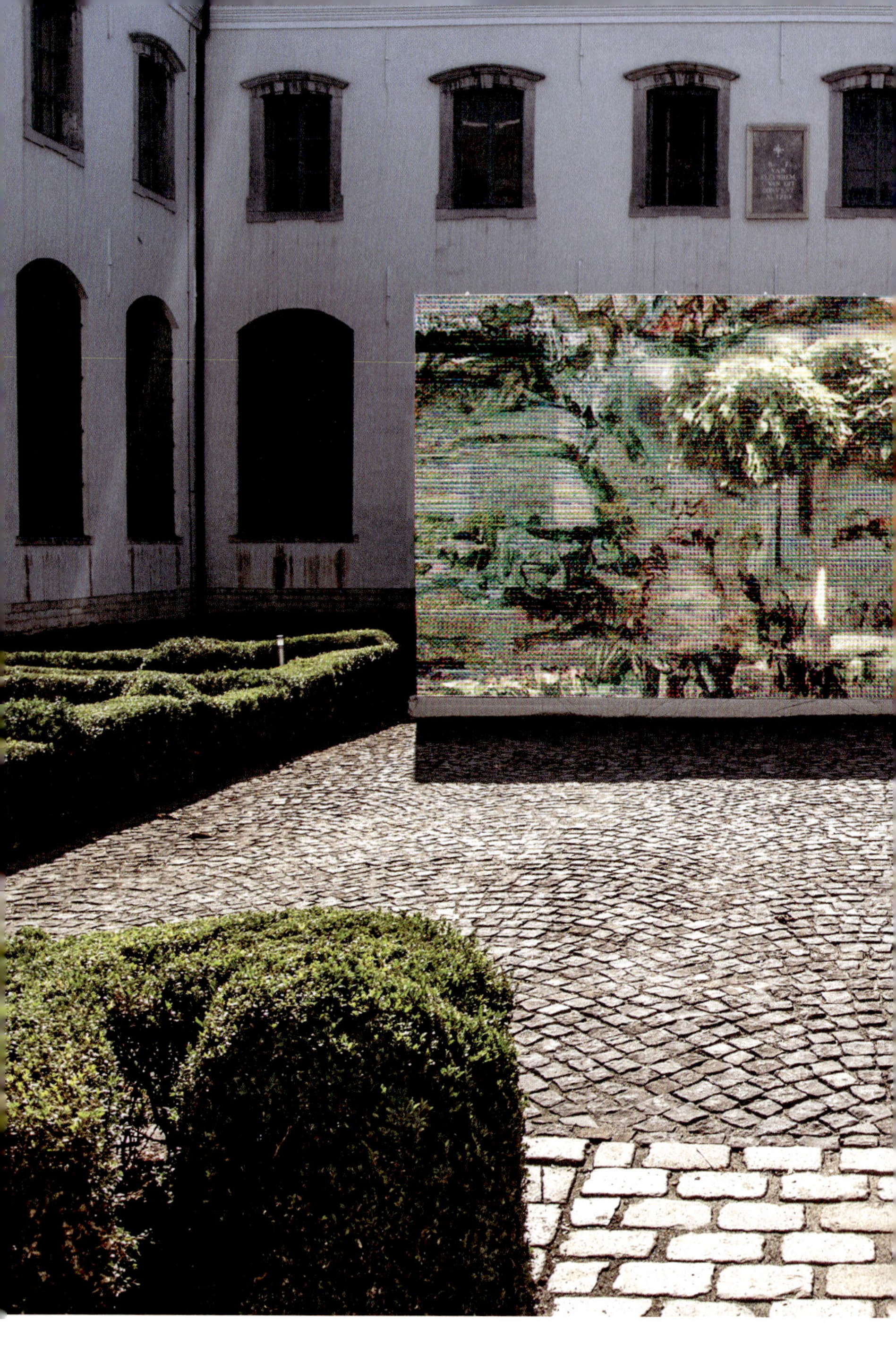

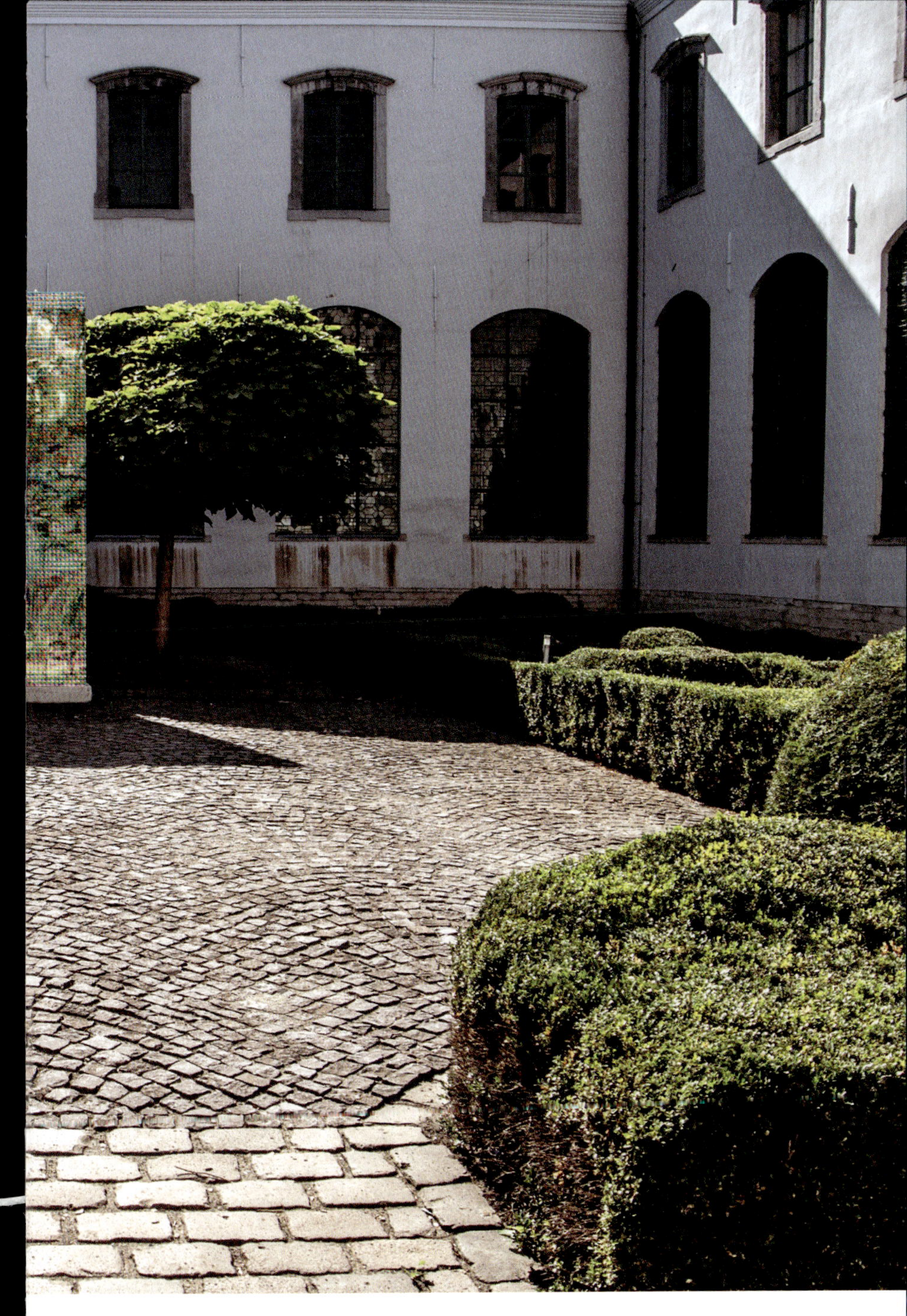

De Nekker Tree!, 2015
hd video installation, multi-channel sound, 13′ 11″
Commissioned and co-produced by CONTOUR 7